WHAT HAS NO PLACE, REMAINS

The Challenges for Indigenous Religious Freedom in Canada Today

The desire to erase the religions of Indigenous Peoples is an ideological fixture of the colonial project that marked the first century of Canada's nationhood. While the ban on certain Indigenous religious practices was lifted after the Second World War, it was not until 1982 that Canada recognized Aboriginal rights, constitutionally protecting the diverse cultures of Indigenous Peoples. As former prime minister Stephen Harper stated in Canada's apology for Indian residential schools, the desire to destroy Indigenous cultures, including religions, has no place in Canada today. And yet Indigenous religions continue to remain under threat.

Framed through a postcolonial lens, *What Has No Place, Remains* analyses state actions, responses, and decisions on matters of Indigenous religious freedom. The book is particularly concerned with legal cases, such as *Ktunaxa Nation v. British Columbia* (2017), but also draws on political negotiations, such as those at Voisey's Bay, and standoffs, such as the one at Gustafsen Lake, to generate a more comprehensive picture of the challenges for Indigenous religious freedom beyond Canada's courts. With particular attention to cosmologically significant space, this book provides the first comprehensive assessment of the conceptual, cultural, political, social, and legal reasons why religious freedom for Indigenous Peoples is currently an impossibility in Canada.

NICHOLAS SHRUBSOLE is a lecturer in the Department of Philosophy at the University of Central Florida.

WHAT HAS NO PLACE, REMAINS

The Challenges for Indigenous Religious Freedom in Canada Today

Nicholas Shrubsole

UNIVERSITY OF TORONTO PRESS
Toronto Buffalo London

© University of Toronto Press 2019
Toronto Buffalo London
utorontopress.com
Printed and bound by CPI Group (UK) Ltd, Croydon, CR0 4YY

ISBN 978-1-4875-0470-0 (cloth)   ISBN 978-1-4875-2344-2 (paper)

♾ Printed on acid-free, 100% post-consumer recycled paper
with vegetable-based inks.

Library and Archives Canada Cataloguing in Publication

Title: What has no place, remains: the challenges for Indigenous religious
    freedom in Canada today / Nicholas Shrubsole.
Names: Shrubsole, Nicholas, 1981– author.
Description: Includes bibliographical references and index.
Identifiers: Canadiana 20190090960 | ISBN 9781487523442 (paper) |
    ISBN 9781487504700 (cloth)
Subjects: LCSH: Freedom of religion – Canada. | LCSH: Indians of North
    America – Canada – Religion. | LCSH: Indians of North America –
    Legal status, laws, etc. – Canada.
Classification: LCC KE4430 S57 2019 | LCC KF4483.C52 S57 2019 kfmod |
    DDC 342.7108/52—dc23

This book has been published with the help of a grant from the Federation
for the Humanities and Social Sciences, through the Awards to Scholarly
Publications Program, using funds provided by the Social Sciences and
Humanities Research Council of Canada.

University of Toronto Press acknowledges the financial assistance to its
publishing program of the Canada Council for the Arts and the Ontario Arts
Council, an agency of the Government of Ontario.

Canada Council **Conseil des Arts**
for the Arts **du Canada**

ONTARIO ARTS COUNCIL
CONSEIL DES ARTS DE L'ONTARIO
an Ontario government agency
un organisme du gouvernement de l'Ontario

Funded by the   Financé par le
Government   gouvernement
of Canada   du Canada

Contents

Preface

This book is a contemporary exploration of the many interrelated challenges that Indigenous Peoples face with respect to religious freedom in Canada. This is not an ethnographic examination of Indigenous religions, an analysis of the content of the many diverse and diachronic traditions within the colonially determined borders of Canada, or a detailed documentation of the historical mistreatment of Indigenous religions at the command of the Canadian state. It is a study of the state itself and how the present continues to be informed by the past. During the final stages of writing this book, the Supreme Court issued its ruling in *Ktunaxa Nation v. British Columbia,* the first case of Indigenous religious freedom to be considered under the modern constitutional framework. The court's decision is both a clear and troubling reminder of the real and present threat to Indigenous religions in Canada and a sober affirmation of the need to answer the following: *Why, in Canada today, is the realization of Indigenous religious freedom so challenging?*

This book is intentionally generalist in its approach. I am guided by the words of Lakota scholar Vine Deloria Jr (1933–2005), who wrote, "The age of the specialist is over, and the generalist must consume an increasing amount of material in order to make sense of the world."[1] For Deloria, the disciplinary boundaries which define modern academia do not capture the complex interconnectedness of our world, fragmenting something that is not, in nature, distilled into such bits and pieces. On this, the book draws on material from religious studies, Indigenous studies, cultural theory, legal studies, political philosophy, and the interdisciplinary literature that already ebbs and flows across such tenuously constructed boundaries. Yet the book is still guided by my own positionality. I am a scholar-ally working within the interdisciplinary fields of religious studies and Indigenous studies, which help to map the course through this material.

This book brings to light an even deeper understanding of the challenge of Indigenous religious freedom in Canada through an assessment of the conceptual, institutional, metaphysical, and social factors that actually impact Indigenous Peoples today. For this reason, the book is anchored by real (rather than hypothetical) cases related to Indigenous religious freedom. The book is organized as a series of overlapping conceptual frames through which the challenge of Indigenous religious freedom, I hope, is called into focus, like peering through lenses in an optometrist's refractor.

I am an ally and I offer this work in solidarity; I am not an Indigenous person. I have sought to locate my work among Indigenous voices, weaving Indigenous thought throughout this book in the scholarship referenced as well as the public records reviewed. Indigenous scholars will hopefully have more to say on the method, evidence, and argument I offer throughout this book and I look forward to that dialogue. For this reason, I hope this book is both a contribution to existing discourse and a point of departure for new avenues of enquiry.

This book is first and foremost about Indigenous religious freedom in Canada. In a conscious attempt to remain focused, this book does not engage in comparative work with cases in other countries. Certainly, scholars working on Indigenous religious freedom outside of Canada may find this study elucidating and even meaningful in their own jurisdictional locales, but I make no explicit suggestions that any generalities can be distilled and transported elsewhere. Broader themes undoubtedly resonate across borders – identifiable in the scholarship of, for example, Kristen Carpenter, Greg Johnson, and Tisa Wenger – but a comparative assessment of Canada with, say, the United States is beyond the scope of this book.[2] My concern here is the complex and real problems faced by Indigenous Peoples in a country that supports multicultural policies and constitutionally protected Aboriginal rights. This context has refined the analytical pursuit that follows in a particular way. For example, it would be difficult to apply the lessons of communicative democracy to Indigenous-state relations where no consultation doctrine exists (or is upheld).[3] Nevertheless, I hope that those outside of Canada gain a clearer picture of the complexity of Indigenous religious freedom in this country, including both its uniquely Canadian and its shared challenges. This book will also resonate in broader discussions of religious freedom in Canada – such as those offered by Lori Beaman, Benjamin Berger, and Richard Moon, among others – but the intention is not to offer any explicit statements beyond the scope of Indigenous religious freedom, though the book is firmly embedded within that broader, ongoing dialogue.

Additionally, my task is not to construct a new theory of the short, albeit extensive, history of Aboriginal rights or Charter rights in Canadian jurisprudence. To provide interpretations of the law in order to construct the meaning and nature of Aboriginal rights or the fundamental freedom of conscience and religion would be an extensive endeavour that would draw focus from the central task of this work. Legal scholars, in particular, will notice that I tend to conduct analysis of legal interpretations rather than the law itself when the scope widens to include the entire framework in question, relying on the work of scholars such as Brian Slattery and Dwight Newman, to name just two.

On a more specific note, this book is limited to explorations of what I would awkwardly classify in Western religious categories as cosmologically significant space. Vine Deloria Jr elaborates on what I hope to communicate through this construct in his essay "Reflection and Revelation: Knowing Land, Places, and Ourselves." He writes, "The most important aspect of sacred places, and in particular the holy places of which we have knowledge, is that they mark the location and circumstances of an event in which the holy became an objective fact of existence."[4] I use "space" rather than land to denote an extension beyond the physical materials of a living Earth to include knowledge, ceremony, and other living creatures that reside in that space. Deloria explains that "some places were perceived by Indians as sacred because they were inhabited by certain kinds of birds and animals."[5] He continues, "The sacred place and the myriad forms of life which inhabit the land require specific forms of communication and interaction. These forms are the particular ceremonies which are performed at the sacred places."[6] At other times, Deloria suggests, that the knowledge of these spaces may be restricted to only one or two people in a community and the locations may be a source of knowledge but only returned to in the case of crisis.[7] I use the phrase "cosmologically significant" to emphasize that the space is not just an outgrowth of belief but something that may be the origin of knowledge and belief, temporally, relationally, and spiritually orienting a community.

I touch on the specific matter of ceremonial space, but land that is "used" in some manner often finds protection while spaces significant to a community in a more abstract manner do not. For example, the Poplar Point Ojibway First Nation were granted protection of a burial site near Namewaminikan River outside of Thunder Bay, Ontario, but they were not afforded the protection of the river itself, which was to be dammed for a hydroelectric project. For the Ojibway, the river acts as a spiritual pathway for those buried nearby. Thus, the river and the burial site were inextricably connected, but the river was not considered the same way the burial site was, and it was dammed.[8] There are, of course, many other subjects that could be explored in an investigation of Indigenous religious freedom in Canada. The withholding of ancestors and religious objects in both private and public collections is a critical issue of Indigenous religious freedom, but it is beyond the scope of this book.[9] Another important avenue of enquiry is the protection of Indigenous religious practices in Canadian prisons, which also lies beyond the scope of this book.[10] This is not to say that cultural artefacts and religion in prison are not connected to the land, which lies at the centre of the pages that follow. To do so would be to distil Indigenous religions into a series of disconnected bits and pieces. In this respect, I hope that this book is read in dialogue with other explorations of Indigenous religious freedom in Canada.

I considered including many explicitly prescriptive assertions throughout this text. Admittedly, a criticism of some of my favourite postcolonial works is that their analytical deconstruction leaves the reader with nothing but a quagmire of what appear to be incommensurable issues. I conclude the book with reference to the final report of the Truth and Reconciliation Commission (TRC) to address pathways forward, but I decided that bringing focus to the issues was of central importance, hence the analytical approach. As a non-Indigenous person, I also feel that any prescriptive work I offer cannot and should not be offered independently but rather in solidarity. Prescriptive responses to the issues raised in this book will best be addressed through dialogue, guided and decided by Indigenous Peoples. Thus, for example, I do not weigh in on prevailing discussions of whether to discard frameworks such as "religion" or "religious freedom," or whether Indigenous Peoples should turn to international bodies and dismiss domestic mechanisms as irreconcilably incapable. Additionally, readers will notice that many tensions are exposed but left unresolved in the conclusion of this book. Such tensions include those between liberty and equality, tradition and innovation, the local and the global, Indigenous sovereignty and Crown sovereignty, and the Charter of Rights and Freedoms and Aboriginal rights, to name but a few. The decision to leave these tensions exposed and unresolved is intentional and speaks to the analytical frame of the book.

In its final report, the TRC wrote, "The urgent need for reconciliation runs deep in Canada. Expanding public dialogue and action on reconciliation beyond residential schools will be critical in the coming years."[11] While this book is written for an academic audience, I hope that it does its part to meet the call of the TRC by expanding the dialogue to include Indigenous religious freedom.

A Comment on Terminology

My decision to employ two constructs – namely, "Indigenous Peoples" and "religion" – requires some attention before we begin. While my decision to use the category of "Indigenous Peoples" throughout this book – rather than the constitutional category of "Aboriginal Peoples" or the legal category of "Indian" (also enshrined in the Constitution) – likely requires no explanation, a comment on some complications around the term are necessary. The use of a singular, homogeneous label can have serious ramifications. The adoption of singularities can obscure and even eradicate the diversity of the many Original Peoples of Turtle Island that now fall under its banner. Recognizing Indigenous world views means recognizing the myriad of world views that exist from community to community. This is not to say that world views between communities are necessarily incommensurable, just that sameness should not be the starting point.

Reflecting on a study of Lakota/Dakota metaphysics from an Ojibwa perspective, Dennis H. MacPherson and J. Douglas Rabb assert, "We should not be looking for networks of inferential associations between Lakota and Ojibwa concepts. Any such inferential associations between Lakota and Ojibwa concepts would likely be imposed by the investigator."[1] MacPherson and Rabb complicate this position by acknowledging that Indigenous Peoples did not exist in isolation but, rather, in relationship with other communities. These relationships sometimes involved the movement of peoples along with their specific cultures.[2] Thus, MacPherson and

Rabb call attention to both the diversity and interconnectedness of communities of Indigenous Peoples.

This reality of diversity and movement can pose problems when considered through the homogenizing lens of colonialism. A problem arises when difficult differences are dismissed and favourable world views are held as normative. This is certainly true with Gustafsen Lake – a case that occupies an entire chapter of this book – but it is also evident in other cases such as *Cameron v. Ministry of Energy and Mines*, where multiple communities held vastly different views on the drilling site in question. It is clear that the state often views difference with suspicion, privileging perspectives most compatible with the state position.

The claim that there is diversity among Indigenous Peoples, even at times within a community, is far from controversial in Indigenous studies and the subject-field of religious studies, despite noticeable complications in the courts. However, the claim that Indigenous Peoples hold something in common from community to community may be met with greater scepticism for good reason. Assertions of universalisms across all Indigenous Peoples risk homogenization. On this, I turn to Lakota philosopher Vine Deloria Jr, Apache philosopher Viola Cordova, and Anishinaabe political philosopher Dale Turner, all of whom contend that there is an underlying world view discernible among Indigenous Peoples.[3] These Indigenous philosophers do not discount the unique cultural traditions of their own communities and others; rather, they speak to underlying general distinctions that separate Indigenous metaphysics from European perspectives. For example, one of the most critical distinctions identified by Deloria, Cordoba, and Turner is the land-person relationship. This distinction is affirmed in the Report of the Royal Commission on Aboriginal Peoples. The Commission writes, "To non-Aboriginal people and governments, the many millions of unfarmed, undeveloped hectares of Canada were 'Crown land,' public land – their land. To Aboriginal people, land belonged only to the Creator, but by virtue of their role as stewards, it was theirs to care for, to use – and to share if they chose."[4] In this sense, there is something that is shared across all Indigenous Peoples – distinct from European heritage – that provides a common feature of distinct cultural perspectives.

We should not think of the differences and commonalities between different communities under the banner of "Indigenous" as mutually exclusive locales of identity and world view. Just as culture was transmitted between communities historically, as noted by MacPherson and Rabb, the same sorts of transmissions take place on the global level today. Those who have embraced the more global identity of "Indigenous" have been influential in and influenced by that collective identity. This relationship between the local and the global, and how it is negotiated, is a resonating theme throughout Greg Johnson and Siv Ellen Kraft's edited volume, *Handbook of Indigenous Religion(s)*. Johnson and Kraft write, "Indigeneity is a discursive and performative repertoire that has myriad authors (indigenous and not), stratum upon stratum of multiple-source sediment, unpredictable sympathisers and antagonists, uneven histories, and starkly consequential if wildly diverse legal ramifications."[5] Johnson and Kraft explain that some communities may "draw upon and enhance their ... identities when translating their core values and traits for indigenous others in global forums; the common ground they find in doing so is then articulated back into the local spaces from which it emerged."[6] At no point do I intend on marginalizing or dismissing the unique traditions of each community identified in this book. At the same time, I acknowledge that the relationship between the cultures of communities, internally and externally at local and global levels, is complex.

There has been a tendency to use the word "spirituality" when referring to Indigenous religious traditions. There is good reason for this, as the category of "religion" has been used as a tool of colonialism and oppression. Sociologically, there is no consensus on how these terms ought to be defined. It would appear that spirituality denotes a more personal and experiential phenomenon, whereas religion refers to institutions with formalized rituals and dogma.[7] If this is how "religion" is understood, then it is inappropriate for Indigenous spiritual traditions.[8] Many practitioners, including Splitting the Sky – interviewed for this book – reject the term "religion" in favour of spirituality. Complicating matters further is that spirituality, generally, may also be inadequate. In their literature review on resilience and Indigenous spiritualities, Joan Fleming and Robert Ledogar write, "Spirituality is closely bound up with culture and ways of living in Indigenous communities and requires a more holistic or comprehensive ... approach."[9] Stepping beyond the spiritual-religious dichotomy, matters are complicated even further when we acknowledge that many Indigenous language systems do not possess adequate or equivalent terms for what "religion" has come to represent.[10]

The distinction between "Indigenous religion" and "Indigenous spirituality" is important for practitioners and for scholars, but it is of less consequence here.[11] Canada's courts are not concerned with the distinctions between these two constructs. The decision in *Syndicat Northcrest v. Amselem* very clearly defines religion in terms removed from institutional orthodoxy, which is often associated with "religion."[12] Anishinaabe legal scholar John Borrows succinctly addresses this complication in the context of the law. He writes, "Most Anishinabek spiritual expression differs substantially from what many people regard as religious ... Fortunately, definitions of the religious nature of Anishinabek spiritual beliefs may not prove fatal to their claims." He continues, "The Charter's standard for finding that a belief is religious is a 'nexus' with the divine or spiritual. This requirement is fortunately judged by subjective standards, meaning that a person's own declarations are seemingly sufficient to meet this test."[13] In the most recent decision before the Supreme Court of Canada, the Ktunaxa Nation employed the term "spiritual." The court agree to use the term, though the court noted it still constituted a religion in the context of the law.[14] Therefore, I employ the term "Indigenous religions" throughout this book with the recognition that beyond the law, the conversation is mired in complexity.

Readers will notice that I do tend to conflate the terms "religion" and "culture" in the pages that follow. Certainly religion and culture are intimately tied together, and the idea that religion can be distilled and separated from politics, economy, law, and even culture is part of the processes of the secular state that seeks to categorize and differentiate different aspects of human existence.[15] Lori Beaman reminds us that "religion is separated out [from culture] as an analytical and lived category both in law and in public discourse at certain times and for certain purposes" and it is important to understand why such distinctions are made.[16] For example, Beaman explains that Sunday closing laws may be viewed as cultural rather than religious and therefore protected.[17] As for minority cultures, Beaman contends that "a *hijab* can ... be imagined as culturally specific (but not 'ours') and therefore not *really* religion and, consequently, not eligible for protection under religious freedom provisions."[18] Michael McNally points to the dangers of translating religion into culture in legal frameworks, claiming such activities help to "re-inscribe and maybe even extend the reductive logic of the Enlightenment even as it seems to move beyond the religious/secular divide."[19] While a more detailed investigation of the discourse surrounding the relationship between religion and culture is beyond the scope of this book, it is important to maintain an awareness of such tensions. As I will demonstrate, the courts understand Indigenous culture and religion to be bound together under section 35(1) cultural rights. For this reason, I tend to move between the two terms freely with an awareness of the complexity of the relationship between these concepts.

Abbreviations

AFN	Assembly of First Nations
AIM	American Indian Movement
APC	armoured personnel carrier
BCCA	British Columbia Court of Appeals
BCSC	British Columbia Supreme Court
BCTC	British Columbia Treaty Commission
CBC	Canadian Broadcasting Corporation
EIS	Environmental Impact Statement
EMRIP	Expert Mechanism on the Rights of Indigenous Peoples
ERT	Emergency Response Team
FPIC	free, prior, and informed consent
HBC	Hudson's Bay Company
HRC	Human Rights Committee
HTG	Hul'qumi'num Treaty Group
IACHR	Inter-American Commission of Human Rights
ICCPR	International Covenant on Civil and Political Rights
ICECR	International Covenant on Economic, Social, and Cultural Rights
ILO	International Labour Organization
KKTC	Ktunaxa/Kinbasket Tribal Council
LIA	Labrador Inuit Association
MEM	Ministry of Energy and Mines
MOU	memorandum of understanding
NGO	nongovernmental organization

OAS	Organization of American States
PFII	Permanent Forum on Indigenous Issues
RCAP	Royal Commission on Aboriginal Peoples
RCMP	Royal Canadian Mounted Police
RFRA	Religious Freedom Restoration Act
SCC	Supreme Court of Canada
TRC	Truth and Reconciliation Commission
TSSMC	Twin Sisters Management Committee
UN	United Nations
UNDRIP	United Nations Declaration on the Rights of Indigenous Peoples
UDHR	Universal Declaration of Human Rights
VBNC	Voisey's Bay Nickel Company
WCIP	World Conference on Indigenous Peoples
WGIP	Working Group on Indigenous Populations

WHAT HAS NO PLACE, REMAINS

The Challenges for Indigenous Religious Freedom in Canada Today

Introduction

While the ideological foundations of European colonialism that treated European culture as superior and all Indigenous cultures as inferior can be traced back to some of the earliest encounters between Europeans and Indigenous Peoples on Turtle Island, it was in the latter portion of the nineteenth century and throughout the twentieth century when that ideology manifested most prominently in Canadian law and policy. A central fixture of the perceived superiority of Euro-Canadian civilization was religion – or, more specifically, Christianity. While elements of Indigenous religions were formally banned, Indigenous children were forcibly removed from their homes and sent to Indian residential schools, state-sponsored, church-operated boarding schools.[1] The express intent of these policies, among others, was to eradicate Indigenous cultures and replace them with what colonizers deemed to be more "civilized." The message was clear: Indigenous cultures had no place in the newly formed Canada.

Despite damage to and loss of some aspects of Indigenous cultures through punishment, seizure, displacement, and forced removal, ingenuity and resilience on the part of Indigenous Peoples themselves and the adaptive, fluid, diachronic nature of Indigenous religions meant that regardless of governmental desires, the diverse cultures of Indigenous Peoples remained.

The twentieth century saw a series of Indigenous-led pursuits to dismantle aggressive, assimilationist policies of the Canadian government. Significant changes began to take place in Canada following the Second World War. Inspired by activists such as Cree politician James Gladstone and the international embrace of human rights standards, the government slowly began to reform its policies towards Indigenous Peoples. In 1960, the granting of Indigenous suffrage provided Indigenous Peoples with a means to affect, at least in principle, the government that had sought to control their lives through the imposition of Euro-Canadian institutions, legislation, and law. Until this point, Canada withheld the basic political rights afforded to Canadian citizens from Indigenous Peoples, encouraging, and at times forcing, "enfranchisement" – that is, to give up their special rights and association as Indigenous Peoples – if they wished to participate at the political level.

In the pursuit of a more just society, the Liberal government of Pierre Trudeau attempted to take the next step towards rectifying the mistakes of the past with the *Government Statement on Indian Policy* in 1969. The document, popularly called the "White Paper," sought to dissolve the legislative distinctions that, they felt, had led to the oppression and marginalization of Indigenous Peoples in Canada. Supported by classical liberal ideals, the White Paper understood justice through equal treatment. The proposal would have dispossessed Indigenous Peoples of the few cultural protections they were afforded. Most importantly, the proposal would have ended the reservation system. While small, the land base was and continues to be integral for the maintenance and continuation of Indigenous cultural practices.

The Indigenous response was overwhelming. In *The Unjust Society*, Cree legal and political scholar Harold Cardinal criticized Trudeau's Liberal government for continuing to ignore the existence of Indigenous rights. He was particularly critical of the paternalism apparent in government decisions that did not include Indigenous perspectives or input. He writes, "We will not trust the government with our futures any longer. Now they must listen to and learn from us."[2] He argues that the direction of the Liberal government would only send Indigenous Peoples into "despair, hostility, [and] destruction."[3] The Indian Chiefs of Alberta expressed similar concerns in their response to the White Paper, "Citizens Plus." They argued that the current policy offered "despair instead of hope." They expressed particular concern over the lack of consultation made with Indigenous Peoples in the creation of the policy.[4] Borrowing their title from the 1966 Hawthorn Report, the Alberta Chiefs produced a counter proposal defending the protection of special rights for Indigenous Peoples.[5] Seemingly to the surprise of the federal government, Indigenous Peoples and their cultures were still here and still unwilling to be assimilated into Euro-Canadian society.

Noticeable changes in Indigenous-state relations began to take place over the course of the 1970s, culminating in the affirmation and recognition of Aboriginal and treaty rights in the Constitution Act of 1982. Notably, Aboriginal title was recognized in *Calder et al. v. Attorney General of British Columbia*, and treaty negotiations recommenced after a more than fifty-year absence.[6] Eventually, domestic and international campaigns helped to embed Aboriginal rights in the Constitution.[7] Importantly, the language of section 35 did not create Aboriginal rights but "recognized" and "affirmed" them. These rights include several different categories of rights, including cultural rights.[8]

Through the 1980s and 1990s, the government continued to move towards a more inclusive, less patriarchal relationship with Indigenous Peoples. These included the removal of enfranchisement legislation in 1985 and a report from the Royal Commission on Aboriginal Peoples (RCAP) in 1996, which recommended a nation-to-nation Indigenous-state relationship. While the policy suggestions and future direction of Indigenous-state relations articulated by the RCAP has had virtually no impact on policy or procedure, the report is a comprehensive examination of Indigenous issues, cooperatively authored by Indigenous and non-Indigenous Peoples.

While there have been several other seemingly forward movements on the part of the Canadian government when it comes to its historical treatment of Indigenous Peoples – including the duty to consult and accommodate and the adoption of the United Nations Declaration on the Rights of Indigenous Peoples (UNDRIP) – the most publicized action was that of an official apology for Indian residential schools and a subsequent Truth and Reconciliation Commission (TRC) created to collect and document the experiences of those most impacted by the residential schools system. In his widely cited apology, Conservative prime minister Stephen Harper stated the following:

> For more than a century, Indian Residential Schools separated over 150,000 Aboriginal children from their families and communities. In the 1870s, the federal government, partly in order to meet its obligation to educate Aboriginal children, began to play a role in the development and administration of these schools. Two primary objectives of the Residential Schools system were to remove and isolate children from the influence of their homes, families, traditions and cultures, and to assimilate them into the dominant culture. These objectives were based on the assumption Aboriginal cultures and spiritual beliefs were inferior and unequal. Indeed, some sought, as it was infamously said, "to kill the Indian in the child." Today, we recognize that this policy of assimilation was wrong, has caused great harm, and has no place in our country.[9]

This apology marks an important historical shift in Canada's position towards Indigenous Peoples. Whereas Indigenous traditions were once unwelcome in Canada, now intolerance towards Indigenous cultures is said to have no place. Yet the contemporary record indicates that Indigenous religions remain under threat in Canada. This book follows in the wake of the Supreme Court decision in *Ktunaxa Nation v. British Columbia*, the first case of Indigenous religious freedom to come before Canada's highest court under the modern constitutional order. In the case, the Ktunaxa claimed that any movement of the Earth in the construction of a year-round ski resort in Qat'muk would threaten the presence of the Grizzly Bear Spirit. The threat to the Grizzly Bear Spirit also meant a threat to the existence and vitality of Ktunaxa religion. The Supreme Court denied the Ktunaxa appeal for reasons that I will discuss at length in the opening chapters of this book. This recent case affirmed a reality of which Indigenous Peoples are all too aware. The evidence that follows raises a difficult question: Is it the destruction of Indigenous cultures or Indigenous cultures themselves that have no place in Canada?

In the pages to come I argue that Indigenous religious freedom is currently an impossibility in contemporary Canada, where the mechanisms of the colonial project continue to manifest. Assumptions, institutions, and systems persist that exclude Indigenous perspectives and mask culturally specific ideas regarding religion generally and Indigenous religions specifically. Legally, politically, and socially, these assumptions, institutions, and systems continue the colonial project of the marginalization, forced reshaping, and erasure of Indigenous cultures and ways of life.

Indigenous religions tend to be misunderstood, often historicized and homogenized, ignoring the contemporary, lived, fluid, revelatory, and adaptive nature of those diverse traditions. This misunderstanding is complicated by the tendency of the courts to protect a superficial breadth of religious freedom rather than any measure of depth, while requiring Indigenous Peoples to conform to certain conditions in public discussions of their religions if they desire any measure of protection for their cosmologically significant spaces, most of which fall on Crown-occupied land. Despite the Charter right to religious freedom, Aboriginal rights – including the duty to consult and accommodate – and an official commitment to an emerging global Indigenous rights framework, Canada continues to suggest to Indigenous Peoples that their dynamic traditional cultures have no place in the colonial Canadian state.

In the wake of the recent Supreme Court decision, some readers may be tempted to call an end to the possibility of Indigenous religious freedom in Canada altogether, but let me be clear about the arguments that follow. The claim here is *not* that Indigenous religious freedom is an impossibility but rather that it is *currently* an impossibility. To make the claim that it is definitively impossible would be predictive in nature. It would also assume that concepts, cultures, laws, legal orders, institutions, and knowledge and the people – and generations of people – responsible for them are static. It should be clear that this is not the case thus far, but it will become more evident in the pages that follow. Therefore, the arguments here pertain to the serious issues obstructing Indigenous religious freedom in Canada today. How and if these matters may be addressed in the years to come are inquiries that stretch beyond the scope of this book.

Before we return to the *Ktunaxa Nation* case and the many avenues of investigation cited above, we must first sketch the pervasive colonial ideology that lies at the foundations of the Indigenous-state relationship. We will then turn to eight interrelated challenges for religious freedom that coalesce in the undercurrents of the chapters that follow.

Colonialism as a Pervasive Ideology

The desire to change or destroy Indigenous cultures is a central fixture of the colonial ideology that led to the occupation of Indigenous territories and the subjugation of Indigenous Peoples. A portion of my argument in this book is that the continuing threat to Indigenous religions is evidence of the continuity of this pervasive colonial ideology. While many readers of this book will undoubtedly know what is meant by colonialism, it is important, nevertheless, to offer a brief comment on what this ideology entails within the Canadian context. Two features of colonialism are imperative to understand. First, it is an ideology of power and dominance that manifests institutionally, politically, legally, socially, and culturally. It is an ideology of superiority in that those who carry colonialism with them assume their superiority over those whom they encounter in the act of colonization. Second, colonialism cannot be undone or overcome as long as colonial powers and institutions persist in those social, legal, and cultural spaces where they initially presumed dominance and superiority. In this sense, colonialism becomes internalized. Canada is not a postcolonial state. Canada is a colonial state. This is not simply a recognition that Canada is dominated by European institutions and descendants of Europeans existing on the traditional lands of Indigenous Peoples. While this is true, colonialism is a persisting ideology that dismisses Indigenous cultures as inferior and, more insidiously, seeks to eradicate and replace those very cultures. We do not mean to retrace the historical narrative of colonization here, but it may be helpful to review an example to demonstrate how colonialism is rooted in a perception of cultural superiority that continues to manifest in (maybe not so) subtle ways today. Given the centrality of land in this book, it is appropriate to draw our example from the European perception of land and the justification for the occupation of Turtle Island.

The seventeenth-century resurgence of natural law theory among European political philosophers greatly complicated the Indigenous-settler relationship. The idea that there were observable truths in the world that extended beyond physics to human morality, ethics, and civility helped to mask culturally specific ideas as universal norms applicable to all peoples, everywhere. In his *Second Treatise on Civil Government* (1689), English philosopher and politician John Locke, like philosophers of property since Plato, asserted that all humans initially held land in common. Echoing other colonial voices, Locke refers to Genesis 1:28 where God instructs humankind to "subdue" (or labour upon) the earth, resulting in ownership (dominion).[10] According to Locke, God gave the world to the industrious.[11] Locke, like Aristotle and Thomas Aquinas before him, contends that the appropriation of land provides an opportunity to be good.[12] He writes, "He that incloses land, and has a greater plenty of the conveniencies of life from ten acres, than he could have from an hundred left to nature, may truly be said to give ninety acres to mankind: for his labour now supplies him with provisions out of ten acres, which were but the product of an hundred lying in common."[13] Land must be cultivated and not simply appropriated. Locke maintained that the spoiling of natural things was a violation of the natural law. Individuals could not appropriate more land and produce more conveniences than they could possibly use unless their intention was to maintain the land and distribute that common stock for the benefit of all. Following the Aristotelian tradition, Locke believed that private property provided people with the opportunity to achieve a more advanced ethical standing, meaning that the English way of engaging with the land was not only a mark of civility but also a mark of moral superiority.

Locke contrasts English people with his perception of Indigenous Peoples to demonstrate how one may claim ownership over land. He begins his chapter "Of Property" by citing the application of labour in the hunting of animals by Indigenous Peoples. Locke contends that Indigenous Peoples have the right to private property of moveable objects because of the application of labour to the objects (i.e., pursuing and killing an animal). However, when it comes to immovable objects such as land, Locke criticizes the rational and moral character of Indigenous Peoples. He writes,

> Several nations of the Americans are of this, who are rich in land, and poor in all the comforts of life; whom nature having furnished as liberally as any other people, with the materials of plenty, i.e. a fruitful soil, apt to produce in abundance, what might serve for food, raiment, and delight; yet for want of improving it by labour, have not one hundredth part of the conveniencies we enjoy: and a king of a large and fruitful territory there, feeds, lodges, and is clad worse than a day-labourer in England.[14]

In this sense, a specific relationship with the land and human progress are integrally connected. Locke, among other proponents of North American colonization in the seventeenth century, appealed to the argument that the land was vacuum domicilium, or empty space.[15] The idea that the land was nobody's (terra nullius) laid the foundations for the support of the Doctrine of Discovery, which provided justification for the European seizure of Indigenous lands.[16]

As we know, colonialism is not merely a subject of history but a contemporary reality. Locke's contributions to the modern Western discourse on property help to illuminate the culture of law and its power to impact the people under its rule. In this context, property entails a divide between public and private space. According to Benjamin Berger, participation in such a legal tradition of property entails the internalization of "a particular range of power relations and distinctive ways of imagining the subject's relationship to the world and to other subjects."[17] In his essay "Indigenous Peoples Struggles for and of Freedom," James Tully addresses the subject of what it means to speak of colonialism as internalized.[18] Internal colonialism refers to the historical processes by which structures of domination have been implemented and maintained without the consent of Indigenous Peoples. Tully explains that these systems become normalized, seeking to both "incorporate" and "subordinate" Indigenous Peoples.[19] It is not necessarily malicious, nor is it necessarily intentional. Nevertheless, internalized colonialism carries with it the presumption of cultural superiority. And its manifestations may implicitly function to carry out the colonial project of the eradication of those cultures deemed inferior.

Canada's legal culture presupposes a particular kind of land-person relationship. There are certain protections, such as Aboriginal title, that could be powerful mechanisms for the protection of cosmologically significant space, if such frameworks considered Indigenous perspectives on the land-person relationship. Instead, Indigenous Peoples are asked to conform to a particular kind of relationship with the land that necessarily requires the internalization of a perspective of domination over the Earth. Though it was first defined in *Delgamuukw v. British Columbia*, Chief Justice Beverley McLachlin affirmed Canada's commitment to its own legal culture in *Tsilhqot'in Nation v. British Columbia*. The chief justice clarified that Aboriginal title requires "sufficient," continuous, and "exclusive historic" occupation of a territory.[20] On the matter of sufficiency, McLachlin wrote, "Occupation sufficient to ground Aboriginal title is not confined to specific sites of settlement but extends to tracts of land that were regularly used for hunting, fishing or otherwise exploiting resources and over which the group exercised effective control at the time of assertion of European sovereignty."[21] This is markedly different from a spiritual relationship of land demanding responsibilities to a living Earth, as articulated in the RCAP Report and, more recently, by the Ktunaxa Nation.[22] With respect to his own community, John Borrows explains, "It might be difficult to establish these facts if certain pieces of land cannot be occupied in accordance with Anishinaabe law because the Earth is living. It seems to be logically inconsistent to use evidence of non-occupation as proof of occupation for Aboriginal title."[23] Therefore, a philosophical divide between public and private space, along with a particular set of power relations, continues to manifest in Aboriginal title. This, in turn, marginalizes Indigenous perspectives and leaves cosmologically significant spaces under threat. This legal culture is an example of internalized colonialism.

As we move through the arguments of this book, it should become clear that Indigenous cultures and, in particular, their perspectives on land continue to be excluded from the protections of the state in a way that not only renders them vulnerable but also pressures them to assimilate. Internal colonialism is embodied within the naturalized systems that regulate Canadian life – including the Constitution and its Charter of Rights and Freedoms – and it lies at the heart of many of the challenges for religious freedom outlined below.

Eight Challenges for Religious Freedom

This section does not provide an exhaustive list of the many challenges for religious freedom, as there are undoubtedly many more than those listed here. Instead, the intention here is to introduce readers to key challenges for religious freedom, applicable for the arguments that follow. The first seven challenges are broadly framed and speak to subjects that could extend beyond Indigenous religious freedom and the jurisdictional bounds of Canada. These interrelated challenges include (1) law's cultural form, (2) the incommensurability of choices or options, (3) cultural incommensurability, (4) inclusion and religious freedom, (5) diversity and religious freedom, (6) the impact of religious heritage, and (7) the homogenizing discourse of equality. While I am attentive to the particular issues faced by Indigenous Peoples in Canada in each challenge, it is the eighth challenge – assertions of Crown sovereignty – that is exclusive to Indigenous Peoples and inextricably tied to the colonial ideology introduced above.

Challenge #1: Law's Cultural Form

One of the greatest challenges for religious freedom is the misconception that law is somehow neutral, devoid of its own cultural contingencies and prejudices. In *Law's Religion: Religious Difference and the Claims of Constitutionalism*, Benjamin L. Berger explains, "This positioning of law as a structure above and apart from the particularly and contingently cultural is essential to prevailing public stories about the interaction of law and religion."[24] This "conventional story," as Berger terms it, is one that remains a standard of law schools and legal scholarship in both Canada and the United States. This "conventional story" privileges either law as a fixed set of conceptual frameworks to be utilized rather than questioned or law as theoretical ideals. In both cases, Berger suggests that "lived realities, the experience of power, and law's role in both" is noticeably absent.[25] He suggests that "culture" ought to be the phenomenological starting place in understanding law. Berger writes, "The constitutional rule of law is an engaged and forceful actor within the domain of culture, which is traditionally cast as the object of law's concern in models of multiculturalism, interculturalism, or secular legalism."[26] He explains that we must "knock law from its managerial or curatorial perch, from where it administers and assesses cultural claims, and to understand it, instead, as itself a cultural form – that is, an interpretive horizon composed of sets of commitments, practices, and categories of thought, that both frames experience and is experienced as such."[27] While those working in Indigenous studies and postcolonial studies will know the general thrust of Berger's argument well, it is a crucial observation to remember throughout this book. Whether by judge, police officer, or government minister, the law is typically understood as a neutral arbiter of difference. It is far from neutral. As noted above, one of the arguments presented throughout this book is that Canadian law, including the Charter and Aboriginal rights, functions as a mechanism of colonialism, an ideology rooted in the idea of cultural superiority.

In addition to being rooted in a particular culture, the imagined location of law as a universal standard apart from culture posits its canon in a position of power that also shapes the cultures it claims to mediate. On the matter of religious freedom, Elizabeth Shakman Hurd explains, "The state's job is to create the conditions for the emergence and flourishing of rational, tolerant, believing or non-believing consumers of free religion under law."[28] She continues,

"Particular inhabitations of what the authorities denominate as free, orthodox, and unthreatening religions are elevated and enabled while other ways of relating to community, place, and tradition are rendered unintelligible or even threatening."[29] Benjamin Berger said it most succinctly when he described law as "epistemologically colonial."[30] From a sociological perspective, I call this the conditions of public religion and I discuss them at length in chapter 2. For now, it is important to recognize that law is cultural in origin and its privileged location affords it the opportunity to shape the cultures of others.

Challenge #2: The Incommensurability of Choices or Options

A second challenge for religious freedom is the problem of incommensurability and the law. In the introduction to a special edition of the *University of Pennsylvania Law Review* on law and incommensurability, Matthew Adler defines the incommensurability of options or choices as follows: "(1) the incomparability of options or choices, such that no numerical ranking of the options in the order of their comparative worth is possible; (2) the failure of a particular kind of scale, such as a monetary scale or a consequentialist scale, to track the comparative worth of options; and (3) the fact that a scaling procedure (either a particular scaling procedure or any scaling procedure at all) is not the best procedure by which to choose among options."[31] In other words, this challenge calls into question the mechanisms by which vastly different, competing claims are reconciled, such as those between religious freedom and economic development. I return to the tensions between liberty and equality and Charter rights and Aboriginal rights in chapter 3, but it is helpful to briefly introduce the manner by which courts seek to scale and address potentially incommensurable claims. Under the Charter, the *Oakes* test requires that any state infringement of a right must be both minimal and proportional.[32] Under the Aboriginal rights framework, *R. v. Sparrow* outlines similar mechanisms by which competing state interest may be balanced with existing Aboriginal rights.[33] The inadequacy of these mechanisms and the misperception of commensurability of options is an important challenge for religious freedom to which I return throughout this book.

Challenge #3: Cultural Incommensurability

As noted, the law is not a neutral arbiter of competing claims but rather a culturally locatable order carried out by culturally positioned people. This leads us to a third challenge for religious freedom: cultural incommensurability between the law and claimants. How can a legal order create a reasonable and just scale to measure competing claims if the courts themselves are located within the cultural framework of one of those claims and unwilling to recognize their own cultural location?

Postcolonial scholar Talal Asad reminds us that the right to speak is contingent upon the right to be heard.[34] In fact, Harold Cardinal opens his book, *The Unjust Society*, with a call to non-Indigenous society: "We want to be heard as reasonable, thinking people, able to identify with our own problems and to present rational solutions. We want to be treated as human beings with the dignity and equality we feel is our right."[35] Arguably, the embedding of Aboriginal rights in the Constitution and an official consultation doctrine indicate that Canada is listening to Indigenous Peoples, at least to some degree. Whether Indigenous Peoples are being understood is an entirely different matter.

In her posthumous work *How It Is*, Apache philosopher Viola Cordova explains the challenge of cultural incommensurability. Drawing on the works of philosopher Ludwig Wittgenstein and linguist Benjamin Whorf and her own experiences, Cordova questions the universalist perception that all cultural elements have similar or identical forms in another culture. Cordova writes, "What ... symbols mean is often very different in each culture. We should be prepared to ask of seemingly similar symbols: 'This is what this means in my culture. What does it mean to you?' And we should question why we cling to the notion that there must be a commonality of concepts."[36] For Cordova, diversity and not uniformity is the lesson from nature, and this observation should "extend to how we organize and explain our diverse experiences."[37]

Cordova contends that anyone who speaks two or more languages is aware that certain concepts, words, and nuances cannot always be translated. The belief that everything is translatable can be detrimental. She writes,

> An attempt to understand the matrix of another society is complicated by the fact that we try to fit the strange ideas of a "strange people" into our own frame of reference without realizing that no such fit exists. Another complication is an attempt to bring to the "other" concepts from within our own context. In the first case we see the other's actions and say "that is just like this ..." In the second case we set out to see what the other thinks about a specific concept from within our own cultural context. In both cases one looks for similarities and ends by ignoring crucial differences that, despite apparent similarity, ensure continued lack of communication.[38]

For Cordova, misconceptions such as these can be particularly damaging for subjugated communities whose world views (or matrixes) are constantly under attack.[39]

Drawing on the work of Whorf, Cordova argues that one must understand the structures of a language and not just the language itself to gain access to the other's matrix. Even then, one must recognize that words, concepts, and phrases may be incommensurable. She draws on a conversation she had with a Shoshone speaker, whom she asked about translating the word "God." Cordova notes that as far as she knew there was no translation or any equivalents in "North American Indigenous languages." The speaker recounted that while her community uses the known term "God," the Shoshone word does not translate into English and it denotes more "the source (or force) of all things" rather than the idea of "God."[40] Concerns regarding the incommensurability of concepts is something with which Indigenous Peoples are all too familiar. In 2010, the Ktunaxa Nation issued a declaration affirming and explaining their important connection with Qat'muk, their threatened cosmologically significant space. In the

Qat'muk Declaration, the Ktunaxa remind readers "that the Ktunaxa language does not translate well into other languages and consequently our spiritual relationship with Qat'muk may not be fully understood by others."[41]

Drawing from Wittgenstein and departing from Whorf, Cordova asserts that language is an important element of one's matrix, but it is not its entirety. If that were the case, one could simply access a culture by learning a language. While learning a language is an important step in the direction of recognizing difference, it does not necessarily follow that someone who is fluent in a language is also fluent in a culture. After all, a child can learn the ways of existing in the world before they learn their language.[42] For Cordova, especially where there are competing world views, the home offers an important refuge for children to have their world view reinforced through speech, activities, and interactions with others who occupy that same matrix.[43] Cordova's lesson is not that cross-cultural communication and understanding cannot take place but that understanding begins with the recognition that the other is another and "not simply a distortion of oneself."[44]

What complicates matters here is the subject of power. The colonial state, with self-appointed sovereignty over the traditional lands of Indigenous Peoples, is the arbiter of Indigenous religions and their traditional territories. The colonial ideology that persists around the subject of religious freedom dictates that Indigenous Peoples communicate their traditions and their significances in a publicly intelligible way. That way happens to be in the language of the colonizer. Those claims and concerns are then more often than not voiced from the community to an outsider. The reception of that information is premised upon the idea that it can in fact be understood in a way that is discernable in the culture and language of the colonizer. This is how a sacred region of southeastern British Columbia can suddenly find its equivalent in a Catholic high school in Quebec, or how low attendance at a sacred mountain (equated to a church) can confound courts.[45] Unfortunately, Indigenous Peoples are often forced to express coherency with the dominant culture regardless of the incommensurability problem.

Challenges #4 and #5: Inclusion, Diversity, and Religious Freedom

It should become clear at this point how difficult it is to differentiate between the various challenges for religious freedom raised in this chapter. Here we turn to two further challenges for the realization of religious freedom that simply cannot be distilled and disconnected from each other: the challenge posed by the reality of lived, negotiated, and contested religions, and the question of what counts as worthy of protection under the banner of religious freedom. To introduce these matters, we turn to Winnifred Fallers Sullivan's seminal work, *The Impossibility of Religious Freedom*.

In her book, Sullivan contends that any attempt to protect religious freedom requires the establishment of parameters that define legal religion from outlaw religion, which means "what counts as religion for the purposes of law."[46] In a legal context, such action requires that a judge (or judges) navigate a religion to ascertain if not what counts as religion then what counts as legally protected religion. Judges will often hear expert testimony of both insiders and outsiders in their judgment, but the presiding judges themselves will also bring their own preconceptions of what constitutes religion to their decision.[47] When these elements collide, as they do in contemporary religious freedom claims, the protection of religion is, according to Sullivan, impossible.

Sullivan's analysis focuses on a case in Boca Raton, Florida, where a variety of religious items were removed by the city from a public, interfaith cemetery. Religious studies scholars, including Sullivan, were called during the trial to discuss whether the various religious items that had been removed were central to the religious traditions of those impacted by the city action and, therefore, worthy of protection under the Florida Religious Freedom Restoration Act (RFRA). The city contended that the placement of religious objects on the public property was an eyesore, violating decorum laws of one of the richest pockets in the United States, and an obstruction for maintaining the property. The plaintiffs, from Jewish, Catholic, and evangelical Protestant backgrounds, claimed that the items were placed at the graves for themselves and their loved ones buried in the plots. Following the testimony of the plaintiffs, two "insiders" testified on the plaintiffs' behalf, coming from orthodox Jewish and Eastern orthodox Christian backgrounds. The court then heard from two well-known religious studies experts, Nathan Katz and Daniel Pals, representing the city of Boca Raton. The case concluded with Sullivan, testifying as an expert in American religion, on behalf of the plaintiffs.

Both Katz and Pals contended that the practices and material features of the religion expressed by the plaintiffs was not central nor uniform to the tradition from which they claim to be connected. Instead, Katz and Pals contended, respectively, that these practices and material items ought to be considered "little tradition" (as opposed to "high tradition") and not "integral and essential to religious tradition."[48] Katz and Pals functioned as a rebuttal to the insider and practitioner claims that the removal of the objects was a substantial burden on their freedom of religion, as it obstructed a central component of their lived religion. In response, Sullivan contended that "in the American context it was inappropriate to set up a hierarchy of religious practices because there are no established or even well-recognized religious authorities in the United States for the courts to look to for criteria in determining where to place certain religious practices in such a hierarchy."[49]

Ultimately, the decision came down to Judge Ryskamp. Sullivan observes that the judge often discounted expert testimony on Christianity, considering himself to already be a sort of expert, being a Christian himself. Ultimately, Ryskamp concluded, "These views aren't central, they are not mandatory, and they are peripheral or marginal ... I would conclude on the basis of the facts based upon the testimony of all the witnesses and following the expert witnesses, that it does not provide a substantial burden."[50]

In *Werner v. Boca Raton*, Sullivan recognized that the vast diversity of lived religious experience posed a serious impediment to religious freedom for the judge, who sought to view religion through the lens of institutional hierarchies. Judge Ryskamp concluded that certain aspects of the plaintiffs' religion were not worthy of protection under the Florida RFRA. Sullivan expresses that the act of ranking aspects of religion into central and peripheral is a means by which courts effectively tell plaintiffs that they do not understand their own religion "or were not faithful adherents of that religion."[51] In this sense, the courts become religious experts responsible for assessing diverse theological perspectives and determining what is and what is not important and, therefore, what is worthy of inclusion under the protection of religious freedom.

There are important differences between the US and Canadian legal contexts, but the general themes raised by Sullivan resonate throughout this book. On the matter of diversity, the Supreme Court in *Syndicat Northcrest v. Amselem* explicitly disconnected religious freedom claims from institutional authority and common historical practices.[52] Whenever possible, Canada's courts have sought to avoid internal discussions of theological authenticity, evidenced in such cases as *Lakeside Colony of Hutterian Brethren v. Hofer, Bruker v. Marcovitz,* and *Bentley v. Anglican Synod of the Diocese of New Westminster.*[53] These cases address internal matters of theology and religious law, but the courts were careful to rule on only matters of public interest, such as property rights and contract law. That being said, it does not mean that diversity within religious communities does not confound the Canadian state in a myriad of ways, as we will see in chapter 4. More importantly, the *Amselem* decision only applies to Charter cases. Under the Aboriginal rights framework, the court, in *R. v. Van der Peet,* stipulated that historical authenticity is a requirement for protection under section 35(1) of the Constitution, drawing the challenge of diversity and religious freedom squarely into focus.[54]

On the matter of inclusion, Canada operates on the "more than trivial or insubstantial" benchmark rather than the much more onerous standard of the US "substantial burden" clause.[55] In the United States, "substantial burden" places the onus on the plaintiff to prove that a government action will impact their religion in both a substantial and burdensome manner.[56] On this, the discourse on a religious freedom claim is heavily focused (at least to begin) on the internal workings of the religion itself. In Canada, the first benchmark is quite easily met, quickly turning the attention of the court to whether the infringement is justified. At this point the court turns to the *Oakes* test (or in the context of Aboriginal rights, the stipulations laid out in *Sparrow*).[57] This returns us to the issue of the incommensurability of options. If the court declares that a particular state action only minimally infringes the religion of a claimant who says otherwise, then they are suggesting that the plaintiff does not necessarily understand their own religion. Thus, Canada's courts still weigh in on theological matters – deciding what is and what is not included under the protection of religious freedom – but they do so relationally in the desire to balance competing interests.[58]

Challenge #6: The Impact of Religious Heritage

The sixth challenge relates to the ways in which the religious heritage (or foundations) of a country may impact religious freedom claims. Lori Beaman calls attention to this very subject in her article, "Aboriginal Spirituality and the Legal Construction of Freedom of Religion."[59] Before reflecting on the general thrust of Beaman's argument, I would like to draw attention away from any fixation on the fact that Canada does not possess an official separation of church and state. Canada is a historically Christian state with no official non-establishment clause. It is, of course, appropriate to ask whether this poses a challenge for Indigenous religious freedom. We do not have to look too far or deep into Canadian history or law to recognize that non-establishment is not a principle supported in Canada. Section 93 of the Constitution Act of 1867, which brought Canada together as a country, stipulates certain rights and privileges for Catholic and Protestant schooling that is reaffirmed in section 29 of the Charter.[60] To change such a practice would require an amendment to the 1867 founding document.[61] Compounding matters further, for some, is that the preamble of the Charter, adopted in 1982, reads, "Whereas Canada is founded upon principles that recognize the supremacy of God and the rule of law."[62] However, this should not be read as an impediment to religious freedom as a matter of course.

Section 2(a) of that Charter protects the "right to freedom of conscience and religion."[63] The right, like all rights offered in the Charter, is protected by section 1, which claims that any violations of rights such as those of conscience and religion must be "demonstrably justified in a free and democratic society."[64] From a theoretical perspective, Veit Bader, in *Secularism or Democracy*, contends that we do not need a strict separation of church and state if the basic features of a liberal democracy are protected. In fact, Bader argues for liberal policies of religious freedom by a relationally neutral state (as opposed to a neutral state) that seeks even-handedness as a conception of justice. According to Bader, this counters both positions of conservative assimilationism with a strict separation of religion from the state and religious corporatism, which is characterized by rigid polarization.[65] The point here is that strict separation can lead to a false sense of state neutrality, while a state committed to liberal democratic principles should have no problem protecting religious freedom regardless of any relationship between church and state. In other words, free exercise and non-establishment are not necessarily tied together.

So what is the challenge with respect to the Christian heritage of Canada? In her article, Beaman suggests that the problem is the manner by which the standards of freedom of religion are framed through the Christian tradition, rather than any issues related to establishment and non-establishment.[66] Therefore, the challenge posed by the Christian heritage of Canada is rooted in the historical development of church-state relations, the expectations of religions in the public sphere, and some preconceptions around what constitutes "religion," discussed in greater depth in the opening three chapters of this book.

Challenge #7: The Homogenizing Discourse of Equality

As I noted at the outset of this chapter, the White Paper liberalism of equal treatment for all under the law was uniformly rejected by Indigenous Peoples. Calls for equal treatment raise the question of who defines, authors, and enacts such a treatment, especially when we acknowledge law's own cultural location. This is one of the reasons why Aboriginal rights were embedded in the Constitution: to guarantee special rights for Indigenous Peoples that recognized and affirmed the pre-existence of their peoples, cultures, and institutions prior to the colonial occupation of Turtle Island. This is what the 1966 Hawthorn Report called "Citizens Plus."[67] These rights are captured in section 35 of the Constitution. This, in a sense, raises Indigenous Peoples to a similar constitutional level as Protestants and Catholics in a sort of multiple establishment model, not unlike those of northern Europe.[68] In his assessment of Aboriginal rights, legal scholar Brian Slattery explains that Aboriginal rights trace their lineage back to the time of assertions of Crown sovereignty. All Aboriginal Peoples possess generic rights and their related intermediary rights.[69] In turn, specific rights stem from generic and intermediary rights and offer rights unique to each community. These generic rights have come to include Aboriginal title, cultural integrity, self-government, honourable treatment from the Crown, and ancestral territory. An example of an intermediary right would be the right to religion, though the specific contours of that right would be unique for each community.[70] So why does the homogenizing discourse of equality continue to pose a challenge for Indigenous religious freedom?

Not all Indigenous Peoples are granted Aboriginal rights, and Aboriginal rights are not applicable in all circumstances. In these cases – as discussed in chapters 3, 4, and 5 – Indigenous Peoples are excised from any sort of establishment section 35 may have granted. As the Ktunaxa Nation came to realize in their journey through Canada's courts, the special rights of Indigenous Peoples are not applicable in the case of Charter rights, relegating Indigenous Peoples to the homogenizing discourse of equality that Aboriginal rights sought to overcome.[71] In another case, the Kelly Lake Cree Nation were informed that the state had no obligation to consult with them over drilling operations in their traditional territory because they were not recognized as a rights-bearing Aboriginal group.[72] Additionally, Aboriginal rights are defined as a set of group rights that cannot be applied to any single individual, as articulated in *R. v. Sundown*.[73] Therefore, some Indigenous Peoples may find themselves excluded from the protections of Aboriginal rights for a variety of reasons, rendering them subject to the discourse of equality amplified by law's cultural form, cultural incommensurability, and the Christian heritage of Canada.

Challenge #8: Crown Sovereignty

It is impossible to address challenges of Indigenous religious freedom without addressing the subject of sovereignty. In fact, I have
already raised the subject in several challenges discussed above,
and we will return to it again in more depth in chapters 5 and 6.
The challenge here lies in Indigenous Peoples' lack of control and
decision-making power on their traditional territories – to which
Indigenous religions are intimately tied – and is compounded by
the seven other challenges already discussed. The RCAP Report
reminds us of the following: "Most Aboriginal people retain an
intensely spiritual connection to the land of their ancestors – one
that involves both continuity and stewardship. It is hardly surprising, then, that the most intense conflicts between Aboriginal and
non-Aboriginal people centre on the use and control of land."[74]
Complicating matters is the fact that Indigenous Peoples control
only a small fraction of the land mass, which means that many
Indigenous Peoples' traditional territories fall under the control of
the Canadian state.[75] This means that Indigenous Peoples are rarely
fighting solely for religious freedom but for religion itself. Impedi-
ments to self-determination and self-development, related to the
lack of decision-making and control Indigenous Peoples have over
their lands and communities, manifest as serious challenges in the
pursuit of Indigenous religious freedom. This is a subject to which
the TRC, in its final report, was acutely aware.

Mapping the Argument

What follows is an assessment of the real threat to the existence of
Indigenous religions, the failure of existing mechanisms to protect
those religions, and the pervasive institutionalized ideology that
facilitates such a lack of protection. While this book largely draws
upon cases that have come before the courts, we have to remember
that when Indigenous Peoples enter a courtroom, they do so not
as their first choice but as their last, as the final report of the TRC
reminds us.[76] The book begins in the legal sphere, moving through

discussions of the conceptual framework of religious freedom in Canada's courts, the conditions and expectations of public religion in a secular state, and the competing constitutional frameworks of Indigenous religious freedom found in sections 2(a) and 35(1). We will then turn our attention to the state's challenges when it comes to the diverse, diachronic, and revelatory nature of Indigenous religions. We conclude with an examination of the limitations of the constitutionally protected consultation doctrine and the potential for international mechanisms of redress.

Chapter 1 explores the ways in which the court's evolving treatment of Indigenous religions and religious freedom continues to pose a serious threat to Indigenous religions. While the courts seem more willing to accept a wide breadth of features of Indigenous religions, they have made it abundantly clear that any such protections are superficial – meaning, conceptual integrity and the objects of belief are not protected under the Charter right to religious freedom. The court's unwillingness to protect any measure of depth is particularly problematic for Indigenous religions where the protection of land without the protection of the significance of that land could result in the erasure of traditions.

Chapter 2 explores the secular expectations of religious actors who enter the public sphere to engage in dialogue on matters of public interest. Religious perspectives are welcome in public dialogue but under the conditions that their arguments are intelligible beyond their faith tradition and open to the politics of compromise and negotiation. In the context of secularization theory, this process is called deprivatization. The problem for Indigenous Peoples is that most of their cosmologically significant spaces are considered Crown or public land, which means the object of public debate is, for Indigenous Peoples, their religions. In this respect, Indigenous Peoples have little to no choice in entering the public sphere if they desire any semblance of protection for their cosmologically significant spaces. In doing so, Indigenous Peoples are subject to the conditions of public religion, rendering their religions themselves subject to the politics of compromise and negotiation.

Under both section 2(a), the right to freedom of conscience and religion, and section 35(1), Aboriginal rights, the expectations of public religion manifest in many of the same ways, but the theoretical underpinnings and limitations of each framework are markedly different. Chapter 3 explores why both frameworks have been relatively unsuccessful for Indigenous religious freedom claims. On the one hand, Aboriginal rights, theoretically, are located within intersocietal law, conscious of the colonial history of Canada, and founded upon the desire to reconcile Crown sovereignty with the pre-existence of Indigenous Peoples – including their cultures and institutions – on the same territory. At the same time, Aboriginal rights are historically restricted to cultural practices that predate assertions of Crown sovereignty, excising revelatory and new manifestations of Indigenous religions from section 35(1). On the other hand, the Charter right to freedom of conscience and religion is more than capable of addressing the diachronic and revelatory nature of Indigenous religions, but it ignores Canada's colonial history and the cultural bias of, to return to Berger, its own "curatorial perch."[77] Read together these frameworks might be useful, as each seems to pick up where the other leaves off, but the court reminds us that those frameworks are not complementary – a realization affirmed in *Ktunaxa Nation v. British Columbia*.

Chapter 4 examines the subject of diversity in greater depth, exploring how the Canadian state tends to perceive and interact with Indigenous religions, particularly when it comes to matters of contestation over authority, authenticity, and interpretation. The complex, contested, diverse, contemporary, diachronic, and revelatory characteristics of Indigenous religions pose a significant problem for the Canadian state, which tends to think of Indigenous religions as homogeneous, historically fixed traditions. Complicating matters further is the state's tendency to interact only with those Indigenous Peoples who, in Mohawk scholar Taiaiake Alfred's view, help to legitimate the bureaucratic systems of the assimilationist agenda.[78] As an example, the chapter focuses on the manifestation of a politically charged intertribal Sun Dance in the interior of British Columbia in 1995, which did not have the support of the elected Secwepemc (Shuswap) leadership on whose traditional territories the Sun Dance took place. At Gustafsen Lake, the religious motivations and commitments of many of the Ts'peten

Defenders were quickly forgotten. Local media and elected leadership called into question the authenticity and sincerity of the Sun
Dancers. Eventually, tensions at the Sun Dance site grew, leading
to an armed standoff between the Ts'peten Defenders and the state.
The police cut off communication between the Sun Dancers and the
media and proceeded unsuccessfully to resolve the matter through
elected local and national Indigenous leadership, whose authority
the defenders rejected. After some time, police turned to the list of
mediators offered by the Sun Dance leader, returning the Medicine
Man of the ceremony back to Gustafsen Lake, at which point the
standoff ended. Gustafsen Lake is a reminder of the potential danger of the marginalization and dismissal of Indigenous religions
in all their complexities. The Ts'peten Defenders were treated as
criminals and, as such, their cries of cultural genocide and violations of their religious freedom went largely unheard. This is not
the case for all Indigenous Peoples.

For those communities who are officially recognized, section
35(1) demands the state consult and accommodate with Indigenous Peoples on all activities that may impact existing or potential
Aboriginal rights. Chapter 5 examines the consultation doctrine
in greater depth. The doctrine marks an important step towards
enacting justice based on the inclusion of Indigenous voices
and perspectives in decision-making processes. Here I turn to
the theoretical lens of communicative democracy to identify the
ways in which the consultation doctrine embraces principles of
self-determination and self-development. The theory also helps
us to identify the limits of the doctrine, especially in the state's
unwillingness to address its own position of domination in the
Indigenous-state relationship. The chapter concludes with an
examination of the Voisey's Bay negotiation in Labrador, which
demonstrates a relatively successful application of communicative
democratic principles, providing some precedent for a just relationship. However, as the Ktunaxa Nation were reminded in their
recent Supreme Court decision, consultation is a guarantee of process and not outcome.[79]

A portion of the argument raised in chapter 5 is that the principle of
self-determination so crucial to communicative democratic theory

must be understood as relational autonomy and non-domination.[80] According to this theory, the state ought to be a regulatory-neutral nucleus that holds the power to implement decisions generated by the deliberation of diverse peoples in the public sphere (that is, the periphery). In a situation where the state is an interested party, it moves from the nucleus to the periphery and, at that point, a third party is needed to provide the necessary regulatory body to avoid the domination of one group over another – since one group would be both an interested party and the regulator. In the case of Indigenous-state relations, this draws our attention to the viability of international mechanisms for redress. Chapter 6 explores the potential for international mechanisms such as the UNDRIP for addressing Indigenous religious freedom claims. UNDRIP, among other mechanisms, is relatively new, though the short history of the impact of both binding and non-binding mechanisms on Canadian policy is promising, if limited.

We conclude with consideration of the final report of the TRC, drawing connections between the specific arguments and theoretical undercurrents of the book and the broader project of reconciliation. In the attempt to mark some potential pathways forward, the chapter focuses on the interconnected themes of education, the self-determination of Indigenous Peoples, and a renewed Indigenous-state relationship.

chapter one

The Depth of Religious Freedom

"Religion" is a four-dimensional concept. In conversations on religion and law, we sometimes get bogged down in the subject of breadth – what is included and excluded from the category. Mapping the length and width, so to speak, are the most tangible dimensions of religion and, consequently, the most superficial. What is often left unspoken is the third dimension of depth and the fourth dimension of time, though the challenge of diversity has drawn most people – including the courts – to recognize this fourth axis. The fact is, if we fail to recognize any one of these four dimensions, we risk failure in understanding this important category of human identity and existence. This leads us to an important question: How do Canada's courts understand "religion"?

In the public, there is a vibrant discourse on religion, informed by prevailing sentiments subject to relationships of power and helping to reshape that discourse through historical, cognitive, and social processes in an increasingly global and (post-)secular world. Discourse on religion has extended far beyond its Christian origins, gaining traction among non-Christian communities as a powerful construct of asserting identity and securing legal protection.

Complicating the use of "religion" as a means of securing legal protection is that law, as culturally located, is impacted by such discourses shaped by and helping to shape the construction of "religion." Therefore, the law – and those involved with it – participates in public discourse, sometimes even engaging with academia, from the self-assigned position of neutrality and universality. In this sense, the law often conceives itself much like classical scholars of religion, as observing other cultures from above. But the law is not just another voice in the discourse on "religion." It holds a position of authority in matters of religious freedom.

Academics have come to realize that the preferential status of the outsider has been overstated in the history of the discipline, where early interest in religion was merely the application of one's own cultural construction of religion onto the other. For example, early Christian missionaries used to identify aspects of other religions that looked like Christianity, discarding that which did not fit as magic or superstition, without understanding that what they were willing to accept was conceptually different and carried distinct meanings in the cultures they encountered. In a sense, these early inclusions under the banner of "religion" were both narrow and superficial. In contemporary academia, scholars often adopt a stipulative definition that acts to pragmatically narrow of the scope of the focus of enquiry without committing to immovable parameters that may impede the study of dynamic, lived traditions. This allows the scholar to conduct their analysis of the contents, depths, and developments of religion without concern that their parameters may be too narrow.

In *Jack and Charlie v. The Queen* – the first case of Indigenous religious freedom to come before Canada's highest court – the Supreme Court of Canada (SCC) offered a narrow reading of "religion" somewhat consistent with the historical treatment of Indigenous religions. In 1985, the SCC decided that something Coast Salish peoples said was part of their religion was in fact not part of their religion. I use the qualifier "somewhat," as the court rejected aspects of the ceremony but not the religion in its entirety. This is an important step forward from the first half of the century, when Indigenous Peoples were described as having no "fixed and clear belief in religion." Nevertheless, "religion" was read narrowly.

More recent cases of Indigenous religious freedom demonstrate an important shift in the court's understanding of "religion" that moves towards some self-awareness of the importance of a stipulative understanding of religion, flexible enough to include diverse and fluid forms of religion. In broadening its scope, the courts have come to recognize religion as a stipulative and constructed category that may change and adapt over time. Though courts have demonstrated a willingness to increase the scope of what is included under "religion" in Canada's courts, they have made it clear that they are unwilling to protect any measure of depth. In this sense, the colonial mistreatment and misrecognition of Indigenous religions continues, albeit in a different way.

The outright rejection and denial of Indigenous religions in the most overt period of Canadian assimilationist policies continues to implicitly manifest in the legal protection of religious freedom in Canada's courts. The courts appear willing to include a wide breadth under the banner of religion, but protection is superficial. This failure is detrimental for the religious freedom of all Canadians but threatens the existence only of Indigenous religions today.

The Concept of Religion

We use religion in many different ways. The concept is inextricably tied to both power and culture. In his important chapter "Religion, Religions, Religious," Jonathon Z. Smith points to the pragmatic, functional, and academic nature of the concept of "religion." Religion is not a tangible object that exists outside the mind of the observer but rather an abstract category used to classify certain human phenomenon. This is not to say that, for example, Roman Catholicism or Pure Land Buddhism do not exist in some tangible form but rather that the term "religion," which we would commonly use to describe both Christianity and Buddhism, speaks to pragmatic sets of generalities instead of fixed elements of a singular, universal phenomenon. In other words, religion exists as a system of classification and not a tangible object of study. However, this is not necessarily how religion has been conceptualized historically.

Smith makes several assertions about the expansion of the term "religion" from the sixteenth century onward. These assertions include the claims that religion is a foreign term imposed by outsiders on native communities, that "religion is believed to be a ubiquitous human phenomenon," and that the characteristics of the category are those natural to the observer.[1] While the concept of religion has expanded and even contracted at times, Smith explains that these concerns continue to impede upon our ability to understand religion today. Ultimately, Smith warns students of religious studies not to abandon the concept but to understand it for what it is, "a disciplinary horizon" that ought to guide our research, not dictate it.[2]

The etymological origin of the term "religion" is unknown, but for Smith, this is of little concern given the fluctuating meaning of the term depending on the context of the observer using it. It is in the sixteenth century, with the advent of the exploration of "new" worlds, that the term expands to include non-Christian communities. It begins with observations of what appear similar to monastic orders and practices evident in, for example, the writings of Spanish conquistador Hernán Cortés. Smith points to the manifestation of ritual as the benchmark for religion later in the same century. On this, Smith writes, "The myths and beliefs of other folk could simply be recorded as 'antiquities,' to use the term employed by [Christopher] Columbus. They raised no particular issues for thought."[3] Observers focused on similarities and discounted that which did not resemble their own Christian tradition, in an unconscious desire to view Indigenous religions as a mere historicized distortion of themselves.

By the eighteenth century, the influence of the Protestant Reformation, particularly thinkers such as John Calvin and Ulrich Zwingli, resulted in a more faith-based, interiorized conception of religion. Smith explains that concepts such as "reverence," "adorn," and "worship" were stripped of their ritual connotations, focusing more on one's state of mind.[4] This shift to a discussion of faith gave rise to discussions of truth, especially with growing Protestant divisions and awareness of non-Christian religions. Smith writes, "It is the question of the plural religions (both Christian and non-Christian) that forced a new interest in the singular, generic *religion*."[5] An emphasis on the singularity of "religion" led to discussions of natural religion, where similarities were stressed and differences historically located, the product of either "progressive or degenerative processes."[6]

By the late eighteenth century, there was an influx of information, including ethnographic accounts from missionaries and other colonial agents and an increased fluency in foreign languages, which led many to seek out methods of categorizing the newly acquired knowledge. By this point, scholars of "religion" recognized the difference between questions of origin and questions of truth, which had conflated early inquiries into natural religion, but this anthropological shift did not mean that cultural biases of the observer had been excised. The comparative approach to religion continued to focus on similarities, categories rooted in a Protestant Christian perspective of their own context. Adopting taxonomies to classify religions, scholars moved the study of religion into the realm of science. However, despite the various systems of categorization employed, Smith contends, it "is dualistic and can be reduced ... to 'theirs' and 'ours.'"[7] The common differentiation from the seventeenth through the nineteenth century came in the form of the Abrahamic religions (Judaism, Christianity, and Islam) set against the category of idolatry, which included Asian and Indigenous religions.

In the nineteenth century, there was an epistemological shift towards supernatural and naturalistic religions, which raised Christianity, Buddhism, and Islam to the rank of rational and universal traditions, while relegating all other traditions, including Judaism, to lower levels of development. Smith explains, "Often mistermed evolutionary, these theories conceded no historical dimensions to those being classified but rather froze each ethnic unit at a particular 'stage of development' of the totality of human religious thought and activity."[8] It was Cornelius Petrus Tiele, in Smith's view, who embodied the most enduring taxonomy of "world" or "universal" religions. In 1885, Tiele wrote,

> Modern history of religions is chiefly the history of Buddhism, Christianity and Islam, and of their wrestling with the ancient faiths and primitive modes of worship, which slowly fade away before their encroachments, and which, where they still survive in some parts of the world and do not reform themselves after the model of the superior religion, draw nearer and nearer to extinction.[9]

Commenting on Tiele, Smith notes that "from the point of view of power," Indigenous religions and all minor religions "are invisible."[10]

In his book *From Primitive to Indigenous*, historian James Cox explains that there were two common trends at work in the interest in Indigenous religions. The first, a pro-Christian enquiry, sought to establish the Christian faith at the apex of human development. The second, a more secular approach, sought to trace the origin of religion back to superstition, which observers believed was still readily discernable within the communities of Indigenous Peoples throughout the world. Cox argues that both approaches operated on many of the same assumptions "which later became embedded as cardinal principles in academic programmes in Indigenous religions."[11]

The establishment of particular parameters around the definition of religion were very much connected with the colonial projects of the latter half of the past millennium. This may be an obvious assertion in the twenty-first century, but it is a point that warrants emphasis. In *Genealogies of Religion*, Talal Asad contends that the activity of studying non-Western religions within academia played an important role in the subsuming project of modernity. In Asad's view, anthropology is involved in "definitions of the West while Western projects are transforming the (preliterate, pre-capitalist, premodern) peoples that ethnographers claim to represent."[12] For Asad, "religion" has played an important role in Western projects, and academia, particularly anthropology, has been part of those processes. Asad argues, "There cannot be a universal definition of religion, not only because its constituent elements and relationships are historically specific, but because that definition is itself the historical product of discursive processes."[13] To argue that "religion" is something discernable from, say, politics or science, "invites us to define religion (like any essence) as a transhistorical or transcultural phenomenon."[14] In turn, religion is distinguished from politics, among other spheres, separating it from the domain of power – a product of a Protestant Christian historical narrative.[15]

Asad, like Smith, points to the changing definition of religion around the time of the Protestant Reformation, drawing attention to the shifting boundary between the religious and the secular as the authority to define what constituted religion shifted from the papacy to belief and conscience.[16] "This emphasis on belief," Asad argues, "meant that henceforth religion could be conceived as a set of propositions to which believers gave assent, and which could therefore be judged and compared as between different religions and as against natural science."[17]

In the final pages of "Religion, Religions, Religious," Smith contends that certain presumptions that remain rooted in the historical lineage of the complicated construct continue to influence the study of religion. Ultimately, he reminds readers that they need to define the parameters of their field, just as a linguist must define language. Conceptually, the history of the subject-field suggest that these parameters are four-dimensional. The historical treatment of Indigenous religions in academia is marked by exclusions of content, meaning, and development.

Of course, scholars do not operate in a realm outside of the world in which they live, helping to shape and being shaped by broader discourses on religion. "Religion" is, for many individuals and communities, a first-order category that holds immense value. When someone expresses the sentiment "This is my religion," they are not suggesting that the thing to which they refer is a pragmatic theoretical construct that includes the many things that academics have come to classify as "religion." Instead, individuals and communities use the term in a very specific sense that refers to particular communicable aspects, feelings, moods, and motivations, among other things. In contrast to academic discussions of religion that seek to develop a mode (or modes) of classification, public discourse on "religion" contributes to an ever expanding (and contracting) understanding of the concept outside of the academy.[18]

With the prevailing myth of law's neutral, universal character behind us, its cultural colouring means that law's religion is also subject to the ebbs and flows of ongoing discourses around "religion." Importantly, the reality of law's powerful position to protect (or not protect) religions demands that some peoples may need to transform (to borrow from Asad) or reform (to borrow from Tiele) to law's religion or potentially face demise. In the past, of course, this meant that Indigenous Peoples needed to conform to a Christian conception of religion in order to find protection, as described by Tisa Wenger in *We Have a Religion* – a powerful and complicated act of agency in a "culture of survival."[19] The issues before us are what kind of religion Indigenous Peoples have encountered in Canada and how it has changed over time.

The Exclusion of Indigenous Religions

Talal Asad notes that religion in the colonial period became "abstracted and universalized."[20] It was intimately tied to a landscape of both power and knowledge.[21] This connection between power, knowledge, and the concept of "religion" is evident in Canadian history. The task in this section is not to recount the historical treatment of Indigenous religions in Canada. With that said, a portion of my argument is that there is a continuity in the mistreatment of Indigenous religions today. For this reason, I want to highlight a couple of clear examples of the kind of mistreatment, or denial, of Indigenous religions that represents the colonial heritage of Canada's past. I restrict my examination to a couple of examples from the Indian Act, which offers some of the most appropriate examples of Canada's historical exclusion of Indigenous religions.

The Indian Act was established in 1876. It was a consolidation of existing legislation on the management of Indigenous Peoples and the lands reserved for them. The consolidation brought together legislation that sought to eradicate Indigenous status and land title through a process of enfranchisement. In addition to enfranchisement, the Indian Act sought to regulate all facets of Indigenous life on reserves, including governance, education, economy, and religion. The most obvious affront to the protection and continuance of Indigenous religions was the ban on religious practices imposed from 1894 to 1951.[22] An 1895 amendment elaborated on the ban:

> Every Indian or other person who engages in, or assists in celebrating or
> encourages either directly or indirectly another to celebrate, any Indian
> festival, dance or other ceremony of which the giving away or paying or
> giving back of money, goods or articles of any sort forms a part ... and
> every Indian or other person who engages or assists in any celebration

or dance of which the wounding or mutilation of the dead or living body of any human being or animal forms a part or is a feature, is guilty of an indictable offence and is liable to imprisonment.[23]

This ban applied to several important rituals among the diverse Indigenous Peoples within the borders of Canada, including the Sun Dance and the Potlatch. This, of course, did not mean that all Indigenous religious ceremonies ceased. Many communities defied the law, while others altered their practices to hide their religions.[24] The implementation of the ban coincided with mandatory schooling for children under the age of eighteen at church-run, residential schools.[25] While Indigenous religions were being marginalized, the state promoted Christianity as the proper religion.[26]

Maybe the most telling piece of legislation with regard to the definition of religion is found in the legislation on the testimony of non-Christian Indigenous Peoples. The clause, in place from 1876 to 1951, described "non-Christian Indians" as "destitute of the knowledge of God and of any fixed and clear belief in religion or in a future state of rewards and punishments."[27] Here, the legislation affirms Canada's adoption of a particular understanding of religion that, in this period, is explicitly associated with Christianity. Thus, the colonial ideology excluded Indigenous religions from the state conception of religion, just as early scholars did in their analyses.

From Issues of Breadth to Issues of Depth

With the important exception of the continuation of mandatory attendance at residential schools, explicit denials of Indigenous religions did not survive the major revision to the Indian Act in 1951. Over the decades, growing attention to human rights and, more specifically, Indigenous rights, domestically and internationally, established a context where the outright denial of Indigenous religions, synonymous with the first half of the twentieth century, would be a mark of Canada's past rather than its present. In 1985, the SCC had its first opportunity to define the extent to which Indigenous religions might be recognized in the modern constitutional era. In this period, the court made it clear that the recognition of Indigenous religions came with significant limitations in both breadth and related depth.

Though *Jack and Charlie v. The Queen* was decided after the patriation of the Constitution, the Charter right to freedom of conscience and religion did not technically apply since the criminal case under consideration was from 1979. Nevertheless, the SCC took the opportunity to comment on religious freedom in a manner discernable in the Charter framework. In the case, Anderson Jack and George Louie Charlie, Coast Salish Peoples of the Tsartlip First Nation in Saanich, British Columbia, shot and killed a deer out of hunting season and off reserve lands while collecting deer meat for a religious ritual. This violated the Wildlife Act of 1966. The court reported, "The deer, they contend ... was killed in preparation for a religious ceremony, in which the meat thereof would be burned to satisfy the requirements of an ancestor by means of a sort of reverse transubstantiation."[28] Anthropologist Barbara Lane, in support of the appellants' claims, explained that Coast Salish peoples' beliefs include the understanding that deceased relatives stay in close proximity to their community, having many of the same needs as living members. Lane also made the point that Coast Salish beliefs are very different from those familiar with a Judeo-Christian religious world view.[29] The two men killed the deer for Elizabeth Jack, who explained that she was visited by her deceased grandfather, who had asked for raw meat to be burned for him.[30] The sincerity of the ritual for the appellants, Elizabeth Jack, and the Tsartlip elders was unquestioned by the court.

The court summarized the appellants' claim in three statements. First, the appellants believed they should be exempt from the Wildlife Act in this case because it was a violation of their religious freedom. Second, the act's violation of Indigenous religious freedom infringes upon the very identity of Indigenous Peoples and, therefore, it should not apply to them. Finally, the appellants broadened their second concern, stipulating that hunting was an integral part of Indigenous cultures and should, therefore, not be subject to the act.

In the criminal trial, the judge determined that the act did not violate Jack and Charlie's religious freedom. The presiding judge wrote, "If Indians wish to exercise their historic religious practices there are ways within the bounds of the provincial statute in which to exercise those religious practices. They can, for example, retain a supply of deer meat in storage for such purposes."[31] The SCC declared this a "crucial finding."[32] In the SCC decision, Justice Jean Beetz stipulated that the appellants did not adequately address the central concerns brought forth by the Crown. The first was the question of whether the hunting for sustenance of the dead was distinguishable from hunting for sustenance of the living. Since protection for sustenance was clearly not permitted under the act, why would hunting for the sustenance of the deceased be any different? Respectfully, Justice Beetz rejected a dissenting opinion in the British Columbia Court of Appeals (BCCA), where Justice H.E. Hutcheon asserted that the hunt was part of a religious ritual. For Beetz, the deer was killed "in preparation" for a religious ceremony, not as part of a religious ceremony.[33] Beetz further stipulated that if Mr Jack had killed two deer at the same time, there could be no distinction made between the use of one or the other. The second claim by the Crown was that motive was not applicable in a legal ruling of the violation of a particular law, on which the court also agreed.[34] In this respect, neither the significance of the act of hunting nor the physical act of the hunt was included under the banner of religious freedom.

In her assessment of *Jack and Charlie*, Lori Beaman argues that "religious beliefs, religious organizations, and religious practices are framed according to Christian standards."[35] In the *Jack and Charlie* case, Beaman suggests, "the court effectively distills the ritual into bits and privileges," distinguishing what constituted religion and what did not. This, in Beaman's view, is part of a larger hegemonic process that narrows the definition of religion to a form conducive to mainstream Christianity. In the dismissal of the content of Indigenous religions, the courts also ignore important aspects of depth. John Borrows and Len Rotman explain how the SCC misunderstood several dimensions of Coast Salish religion:

The event's narrow construction overlooks community participation that would accompany the preparation and dressing of a newly killed deer. The Court did not account for the people lifting the deer from the truck, taking it in the house or shed, skinning it, sitting around the table working at it, and discussing their routines and relationships in very specific ways ... Finally, the Court did not mention how the use of fresh deer meat for the ceremony would draw the community together in a way that retrieving frozen deer meat from a freezer never would. The immediacy of life and death would not be as culturally poignant if frozen deer meat were used.[36]

In other words, the court understood religion in the *Jack and Charlie* case in a far narrower sense than the appellants conceptualized their own religion. The decision ignores important features of the breadth and depth of religion as articulated by the claimants. The exclusion of content (i.e., the length and width) of Coast Salish religion also resulted in the exclusion of the meaning and significance of that content.

The SCC had a second opportunity to comment on Indigenous religious freedom in 2017 in *Ktunaxa Nation v. British Columbia*. As we should expect, the court's treatment of Indigenous religions had changed over thirty-two years. The courts have expanded the framework of religious freedom to include a wider breadth of content. This fact is most evident in the definition of religion offered in *Syndicat Northcrest v. Amselem*. In 2004, Justice Frank Iacobucci explained,

Defined broadly, religion typically involves a particular and comprehensive system of faith and worship. Religion also tends to involve the belief in a divine, superhuman or controlling power. In essence, religion is about freely and deeply held personal convictions or beliefs connected to an individual's spiritual faith and integrally linked to one's self-definition and spiritual fulfilment, the practices of which allow individuals to foster a connection with the divine or with the subject or object of that spiritual faith.[37]

There are, of course, limitations with this definition, to which I return in chapter 3, but the stipulative and conditional definition offered here is noteworthy. This is, in many ways, an indication of the court's awareness of the function of their understanding of religion as a second-order mode of classification. While we cannot know for sure, it would be difficult to imagine that the act of hunting excluded from the construction of religion in *Jack and Charlie* would have met the same fate in a post-*Amselem* legal culture. Of course, widening the scope of religious freedom does not necessarily correlate with an expansion of its depth. In other words, while the act of hunting may find protection under Iacobucci's definition, it is no guarantee that the cultural poignancy of the use of fresh meat over frozen meat would be protected.

Before the SCC heard *Ktunaxa Nation v. British Columbia*, the case first moved through the provincial courts. For its part, the British Columbia Supreme Court (BCSC) set its precedent on Indigenous religious freedom in 1998. Despite being six years before *Syndicat Northcrest v. Amselem*, this early BCSC decision embodied, to some degree, the spirit of Iacobucci's construction of religion. *Cameron v. Ministry of Energy and Mines* marks an important shift away from issues of breadth to expose the more complicated subject of depth, which has serious implications for Indigenous religious freedom.

In 1991, Mount Monteith and Beattie Peaks in north-eastern British Columbia, also known as the Twin Sisters, became the site of a proposed drilling project. The region is home to several communities of Indigenous Peoples, including the West Moberly First Nations and Halfway River First Nation, direct descendants of the Deneza, who have called the region home since time immemorial. The Saulteau arrived in the nineteenth century and are descendants of the Cree and Deneza. Finally, the Kelly Lake Cree Nation also identify with Deneza heritage. In addition to sharing some of the same cultural roots and living in the same region, intermarriage has also brought many of these communities together over generations. For this reason, there are commonalities among the groups and important differences as well. For example, all communities share a prophecy of the significance of the region. The court paraphrased a hereditary chief of the West Moberly First Nations who explained the Deneza were "to be stewards of the two mountains that sit together as a place of spiritual refuge."[38] The Saulteau, who migrated from Manitoba toward the end of the nineteenth century, did so in accordance with a more recent prophecy based on visions from a spiritual leader, who saw the region as a sanctuary for his people.[39] The court was not too concerned with differences in the significance of the space, stipulating "what is significant is that each aboriginal group has a history of spiritual reverence towards the area known as the Twin Sisters mountains and the surrounding area, however, the confines of that might be defined."[40]

With proposed drilling operations in the Twin Sisters area, the province and the drilling company entered into conversation with Indigenous Peoples who would be impacted by the resource project. The West Moberly and Halfway River First Nations were satisfied with the agreement to provide protection at the peaks of the mountains, while drilling operations would be allowed to commence lower on the mountainside and at the base. The Saulteau First Nations and Kelly Lake Cree Nation were opposed to this decision, which they felt violated their right to religious freedom. In particular, the claimants argued that their exercise of stewardship over the area was an exercise of their freedom of religion.[41] Justice James Taylor of the BCSC accepted that there was a "territorial aspect to the [Kelly Lake Cree's] religious practices that involves the Twin Sisters mountains even though there is no actual use in current or recent history of this area for such purposes."[42] Taylor was sceptical about how coercive the project might be when, in the court's opinion, "it is not that ... anyone can be said to have actually gone there on any consistent basis, as might one visit a temple, shrine or church."[43] Here Justice Taylor demonstrates his assumption of commensurability between the cosmologically significant space of the Saulteau and Kelly Lake Cree and the more familiar locales of temples, shrines, and churches. Importantly, this scepticism did not lead the court to exclude such practices, as was the case in *Jack and Charlie*. Instead, Taylor makes an important conceptual shift from rulings on breadth to rulings on depth. Justice Taylor asserted the following:

> I conclude that s. 2(a) does not protect a concept of stewardship of a place of worship under the protection of religious freedom. I also find that even if I were incorrect in that conclusion, the adherence of the

decision-makers to the ... recommendations within the protected area in fact protects an area for both alpine and sub-alpine activities upon which there can be an absolute stewardship and within areas I and II a lesser form of stewardship.[44]

While not satisfied with the intrusion into the area generally, the Kelly Lake Cree Nation do not point to any actual deprivation or incursion of the right to religious freedom as a consequence but rather it is the defilement of a concept that is paramount. Thus, I conclude that there is no contemplated activity that inhibits or coerces the right to exercise religious beliefs or practices either on an actual usage basis or in an intellectual sense in this area as viewed by those who regard themselves as stewards of it.[45]

Taylor's concern is not with the content of the Saulteau and Kelly Lake Cree religions but rather with the court's inability and unwillingness to protect "defilement of a concept." Importantly, he clarifies that he may in fact be wrong on the matter that stewardship is not included under section 2(a), a deliberate attempt to sidestep an explicitly exclusionary position. In this respect, the land and the idea of stewardship can find protection under section 2(a), but the conceptual integrity of the land and the depth and meaning of stewardship responsibilities will not.

Sixteen years later, the Ktunaxa Nation met a similar decision in the BCSC. In the *Ktunaxa Nation* case, a proposed ski resort was to be built on Qat'muk, the home of the Grizzly Bear Spirit. In the *Qat'muk Declaration* and adjoining Stewardship Principles, the Ktunaxa Nation explained the significance of the space and their responsibilities to the area. A portion of the *Qat'muk Declaration* reads,

We, the Ktunaxa, have lived in our territory since time immemorial and have a deep spiritual connection to the animal world and, in particular, to the grizzly bear. Qat'muk is a very special place where *Kławła Tukłułak?is*, the Grizzly Bear Spirit, was born, goes to heal itself, and returns to the spirit world. The Grizzly Bear Spirit is an important source of guidance, strength, protection and spirituality for the Ktunaxa ... The Ktunaxa have a stewardship obligation and duty to the Grizzly Bear Spirit and Qat'muk.[46]

Desiring to make several features of their religion abundantly clear, the Ktunaxa Nation offered several affirmations. The *Declaration* continues, the Ktunaxa Nation

> Affirms that having been created in interdependence with the land, its living things, and the spirit world, the Ktunaxa possess and are entitled to enjoy our inherent and pre-existing sovereignty over our land and our lives thereon; ...
>
> Affirms that the Creator gave the Ktunaxa covenants, one of which is to protect, honour, and celebrate what the Creator has given us;
>
> Reaffirms that our Law, *?aknumuꞔtiꞭit*, requires the protection of our sacred places for ourselves, our children, and our grandchildren; ...
>
> Reaffirms that we are of one heart and one mind to protect Qat'muk from desecration;
>
> Insists that we will strengthen and revitalize the Ktunaxa Nation through our spiritual connection to Qat'muk.[47]

In the Stewardship Principles, the Ktunaxa affirm that they are "part of the land" and it is their responsibility to protect it.[48] They continue, "The Ktunaxa phrase that captures the interconnectedness and the stewardship concepts applicable to land management is *YaqaꞭ HankatiꞭiꞭki na ?amak*. This phrase translates to 'our people care for the land, the land cares for our people.' It is about our relationship with the land."[49] Much like in the case of the Saulteau and Kelly Lake Cree, the Ktunaxa Nation only use a small portion of Qat'muk for religious ceremonies. The significance of the space lies in its importance for Ktunaxa identity and existence.

The Ktunaxa sought a complete halt to the recreation development project. The major turning point came in 2009 when a Ktunaxa knowledge keeper expressed that there was no middle ground for negotiation.[50] Siding with the province, BCSC justice John Savage concluded, "In my opinion, constitutional protection of freedom of religion does not extend to restricting the otherwise lawful use of land, on the basis that such action would result in a loss of meaning to religious practices carried out elsewhere."[51] Here, the court is willing to accept the fact that Qat'muk is an important feature of Ktunaxa religion, but they are unwilling to protect "loss of meaning" from an "otherwise lawful use of land." Despite its paramount importance, let us put aside the latter statement, as it is a subject of the coming chapters.

When the Ktunaxa Nation brought their case before the BCCA, they sought to have their claims re-examined based on the assertion that the BCSC had erred in its approach to the subject of religious freedom. Justice Richard Goepel writes,

> It is not the role of s. 2(a) of the Charter to engage in a purely conceptual and academic inquiry regarding the hypothetical scope of the freedom of religion. Rather, the courts focus on the more narrow and practical inquiry: whether a particular state action (or a series of state actions) amount to an impermissible interference with the asserted s. 2(a) right based on the *effects* of state interference on religious practices or beliefs. In this case, the material effect on the asserted s. 2(a) right is, ultimately, the loss of meaning produced by the alleged desecration of a sacred site.[52]

In addition to supporting the BCSC decision, the BCCA offered an important point of clarification regarding the court's limited commitment to religious freedom. By the court's own admission, the scope of section 2(a) has been narrowed, but not in terms of breadth. The real narrowing of religious freedom here takes place in depth. Qat'muk, at least in part, found protection under section 2(a), but the conceptual significance of the space and its broader holistic connection to Ktunaxa identity, well-being, and world view did not. The court has effectively reduced religious freedom to the most superficial and overt aspects of religion, without concern for the integrity, significance, and meaning of those features.

On 2 November 2017, the SCC issued its first ruling on Indigenous religious freedom under the modern constitutional framework, providing troubling clarifications to which I will return throughout this book. On the breadth and depth of religious freedom, the SCC commentary is revealing. In the majority reasoning,

Chief Justice McLachlin clarified that religious freedom is limited to belief and the manifestation of belief.[53] McLachlin explained, "This case is not concerned with either the freedom to hold a religious belief or to manifest that belief. The claim is rather that s. 2(a) of the Charter protects the presence of Grizzly Bear Spirit in Qat'muk. This is a novel claim and invites this Court to extend s. 2(a) beyond the scope recognized in our law."[54] McLachlin rejected the invitation, concluding "the state's duty under s. 2(a) is not to protect the object of beliefs, such as Grizzly Bear Spirit."[55] In a clear demonstration of the shallow nature of religious freedom, the chief justice misunderstood the important connection between belief and the object of belief for the Ktunaxa. Even if we restrict freedom of religion to McLachlin's limitations, the Ktunaxa freedom to believe and manifest belief is seriously threatened by Glacier Resort's year-round ski resort. The presence of *K̓awla Tukⱡukʔis* is directly tied to the integrity of Qat'muk. In turn, the beliefs and rituals of the Ktunaxa related to the Grizzly Bear Spirit are tied to the land itself. Therefore, Ktunaxa belief is tied to the conditions of the presence of the Grizzly Bear Spirit. In effect, the chief justice offered an explicit affirmation of the court's inability to protect the depth of religion. As noted at the outset of this chapter, the failure to understand any dimension of religion is a failure to understand religion altogether. It follows that the failure to protect any dimension of religion is a failure to protect religion.

This shallow reading of religious freedom is something of which Justices Michael Moldaver and Suzanne Côté were aware in their minority reasoning, despite supporting the rejection of the Ktunaxa claim. Moldaver writes,

> In my respectful view, where state conduct renders a person's sincerely held religious beliefs devoid of all religious significance, this infringes a person's right to religious freedom. Religious beliefs have spiritual significance for the believer. When this significance is taken away by state action, the person can no longer act in accordance with his or her religious beliefs, constituting an infringement of s. 2(a). That is exactly what happened in this case. The Minister's decision to approve the ski resort will render all of the Ktunaxa's religious beliefs related to

Grizzly Bear Spirit devoid of any spiritual significance. Accordingly, the Ktunaxa will be unable to perform songs, rituals or ceremonies in recognition of Grizzly Bear Spirit in a manner that has any religious significance for them.[56]

Appropriately, Moldaver concludes, "With respect, my colleagues' approach amounts to protecting empty gestures and hollow rituals, rather than guarding against state conduct that interferes with 'profoundly personal beliefs,' the true purpose of s. 2(a)'s protection."[57] Moldaver and Côté still upheld the decision based on a balancing test (to which I return in the coming chapter), but their insight here is an important indication of the ongoing discourse around religion and religious freedom in the courts.

Conclusion

A major impediment for Indigenous religious freedom is not the failure to include the "length and width" (or content) of cosmologically significant space as "religion," but rather the failure to protect its meaningfulness and conceptual importance. This is not to suggest that the breadth of religious freedom is no longer an issue for Indigenous religions. I have no intention of drawing focus away from the argument that is often raised about the limits of religious freedom, namely that the right is culturally constructed to prioritize belief and significantly limit other manifestations of religion.[58] The decisions in *Cameron* and *Ktunaxa Nation* are firmly rooted within the construct of belief, even if that belief is inextricably connected to land. My argument is that even if religious freedom is restricted to "freedom of thought," as articulated by Webb Keane[59] – and discussed in far more depth in chapter 3 – it is even further limited by the shallowness of the protections offered. Certainly, exclusions of "loss of meaning," "defilement of a concept," and "objects of belief" would affect even mainstream Protestant Christians.

This shallow reading of religious freedom creates the possibility for the destruction of Indigenous religions when we acknowledge the integral location of land in those traditions. In their alternative reasons in the SCC decision in *Ktunaxa Nation*, Moldaver and Côté were particularly attuned to the impact of a superficial reading of religious freedom on Indigenous religions. Moldaver writes,

> This approach ... risks excluding Indigenous religious freedom claims involving land from the scope of s. 2(a) protection. As indicated, there is an inextricable link between spirituality and land in Indigenous religious traditions. In this context, state action that impacts land can sever the spiritual connection to the divine, rendering Indigenous beliefs and practices devoid of their spiritual significance. My colleagues have not taken this unique and central feature of Indigenous religion into account. Their approach therefore risks foreclosing the protections of s. 2(a) of the Charter to substantial elements of Indigenous religious traditions.[60]

There are issues in the Moldaver and Côté decision that I will return to in the concluding pages of the next chapter, but this aspect of their decision is worthy of some praise. While the chief justice, writing for the majority, did not agree with Moldaver and Côté, it indicates that the court's conception of religion may continue to evolve.

After all, the court's understanding of religion is complex and malleable. It is not the same as when Canada viewed Indigenous Peoples as possessing no religion, nor is it limited by the theological assumptions latent in the *Jack and Charlie* decision. The courts, in many respects, have come to recognize the second-order nature of their employment of the concept of "religion." At the same time, the courts advance a certain type of freedom that is restricted to the most superficial and observable facets of religion – law's cultural commitment to its own, dynamic first-order construction. The contradiction is best summarized in the assertion of Justice Goepel that the court is not interested in the "conceptual and hypothetical scope" of religious freedom but the "practical and narrow" question of whether infringement can be justified. What the court fails to realize is that a true assessment of what they desire necessarily requires what they seek to avoid.

It is not that Canada is unwilling to recognize land within Indigenous religions; it is just that the conceptual integrity and meaning of that land are not protected. When Indigenous Peoples lose a land-based religious freedom claim in court, they may not be able to return to the source of that religion, the subject of legal judgment. Complicating matters further, Indigenous Peoples are often forced to enter the public sphere with their religions and conform to certain conditions that open their cosmologically significant spaces to the politics of negotiation, compromise, and demise.

chapter two

Secularization, Dispossession, and Forced Deprivatization

With growing social, economic, and military expansion into the traditional territories of Indigenous Peoples, many communities have entered the public arena in order to seek protection for the cosmologically significant spaces they hold sacred.[1] In this process, the Canadian state expects Indigenous Peoples to enter the public forum in the same manner as all other religious groups in a modern secular liberal state: as one group with one perspective among other groups with equally relevant perspectives. The premise is that religious communities can enter the public sphere in order to provide input on morally relevant public issues rather than to assert control over them. The conditions of modern, liberal, democratic public religion create an environment where conflicts are open to negotiation and compromise.

The requirement of Indigenous Peoples to enter the public forum in accordance with these conditions poses a significant problem. The expectation of the community as contributor rather than authority over the space opens sites to the politics of negotiation and compromise with competing public and private interests. Given the intimate connection between land and religion for many Indigenous communities, Indigenous Peoples are, in many ways, publicly negotiating their religions. The division or desecration of cosmologically significant space may compromise or even destroy the religion of a particular community. Put simply, for some Indigenous Peoples, sacred space is non-negotiable.

With recognition of the limited amount of traditional territory controlled by Indigenous Peoples, public dialogue on matters of religion are often not entered into voluntarily. Rather, historical processes force Indigenous Peoples to enter their religions into the public arena. As such, in a liberal democratic society, these religious practitioners must then meet the conditions of public religion. The demands of these conditions of compromise and negotiation in the context of what I call "forced deprivatization" seriously threaten Indigenous religions today.

Secularization and the Conditions of Public Religion

Traditionally, secularization refers to the broad historical socio-structural processes of the differentiation, decline, and privatization of religion. Differentiation is the process by which secular spheres such as politics, economics, and science separate from the religious sphere. Decline refers to the diminished and diminishing significance of religious beliefs, practices, and institutions. Privatization refers to the confinement of religion to its own sphere apart from the other "spheres," such as economy and state. Until the mid-twentieth century, scholars largely accepted secularization theory despite the fact that academia had offered little empirical evidence to support its fundamental claims. Even among the fathers of the sociology of religion (i.e., Max Weber and Émile Durkheim), the undisputed assumption was that religion would decline and disappear as the world became more modernized.[2]

It was not until the 1960s that secularization began to receive critical attention from scholars. This involved distinguishing between what David Martin calls the "viable core" and "doubtful peripheries" of secularization theory.[3] More specifically, this critical analysis involved distinguishing between the empirical evidence and anticipated outcomes of secularization.[4] Thomas Luckmann was among the first to address critically the validity of the theory by challenging the notion of the decline of religious mentalities. Luckmann writes that secularization "in its early phases was not a process in which traditional sacred values simply faded away. It was a process in which autonomous institutional 'ideologies' replaced, within their own domain, an overarching and transcendent universe of norms."[5] In response to the evident growth and expansion of religion following the Second World War, scholars called the religious decline theory into serious question. The subsequent emergence of overtly public forms of religion in the 1970s such as the Islamic Revolution in Iran and the rise of the religious Right in the United States further weakened secularization theory by calling privatization into question.[6]

Despite the fact that one can empirically dismiss the classical theory of secularization, scholars such as Bryan Wilson and Karel Dobbelaere continue to assert the usefulness of the paradigm. Others such as David Martin, Mark Chaves, and Steve Bruce have sought to revise the theory in response to the criticisms that have led so many to abandon it.[7]

Sociologist José Casanova offers the most comprehensive revision of secularization theory in his seminal work *Public Religions in the Modern World*. According to Casanova, differentiation remains the central defensible core of secularization theory. Even critics of the theory have accepted differentiation as a fixture of the modern (Western) world.[8] Along with Luckmann, Casanova dismisses religious decline as an empirically unsupportable theory. Where Casanova distinguishes himself from other theorists is with his revision of the privatization thesis. He draws a connection between privatization and differentiation by identifying certain conditions of public religion that allow religions to undergo a process of deprivatization (i.e., to re-enter the public sphere to some degree). Secularization theory continues to be a relevant and important theory because the conditions of modern public religion directly relate to the historical processes of differentiation that dictate contemporary social-spatial structuring. Religious communities and their beliefs can enter public arenas (such as politics and economics), but they must do so in accordance with certain conditions if they wish to find any success. In order to understand why these conditions exist and why they are required, it is important to chart the historical processes of differentiation.

Casanova identifies four historical developments that collectively contributed to the emancipation of the secular spheres from the control of the Church, which, in other words, contribute to the process of differentiation. These instigators of differentiation are the Protestant Reformation, the rise of the modern state, the onset of modern capitalism, and the scientific revolution. Religious diversity, modern state policies of religious toleration, a growing interest in the economy as an end in itself, and the discovery of new epistemological avenues of enquiry raised a multitude of different and sometimes competing world views to an equal place in the secular sphere. Religion, as one of these perspectives, became its own specialized sphere distinct from that of economy and state.[9]

Despite this social-spatial restructuring, Casanova contends that the theory of privatization becomes problematic when one understands it as a normative theory of how religion "ought to behave in the modern world."[10] The privatization of religion is an integral facet of Western modernity. This is evident in the constitutional protection of the right to conscience and religion, which infers a right to freedom from both government and ecclesiastical control, and in the processes of differentiation that have constructed a "private sphere" separate from that of economy, science, and state. In the modern world, this private sphere has gradually come to house religion, but religious actors are not necessarily restricted to that social-spatial locale. They may choose to leave the private sphere to participate in public discourse.

Deprivatization refers to "the process whereby a religion abandons its assigned place in the private sphere and enters the undifferentiated public sphere of civil society to take part in the ongoing process of contestation, discursive legitimation, and redrawing of the boundaries."[11] Casanova addresses the important but limited role religions can play in the modern world. He argues that religion can enter the public arena but cannot exert any authority over it.[12] Religious communities must meet certain conditions in order to facilitate religion's entry into the public sphere. First, religious communities must accept their position as an equal participant as they engage with others in the public sphere. Second, they must recognize the legitimacy and autonomy of the state. This includes respecting others' freedom of conscience and right to privacy. Finally, they must engage in a reasonable and logical discourse and refrain from assertive claims of truth and belief. Once participating parties meet these conditions, conflicts encountered in the public sphere are open to the politics of negotiation and compromise.[13]

Religious communities cannot enter the public sphere without adhering to these conditions if they hope to achieve any success. This means that these communities will have to accept their location in the modern world and abandon fundamentalism – that is, rigidly held beliefs unreceptive to compromise. Casanova explains the implications of this discursive model of public engagement:

> Those who accept the rules of engagement in the public sphere and begin to argue with their neighbors will have to abandon their fundamentalism, at least procedurally. Their claims that their normative wares are the only genuine ones or are more valuable than those of their denominational competitors will be exposed to open appraisal, to the typical plausibility tests, and to the bargaining adjustments regnant in an open pluralist market of ideas ... Those who prefer not to compromise their ideas or to expose their fundamentals to public [discursive] validation and to a probable "plausibility crisis," will most likely abandon the public square and return to their isolated hamlets, where they can protect the worth of their sectarian wares uncontested.[14]

In short, religious communities who wish to enter the public arena to debate issues from their specialized position in the private sphere must do so in conformity with the conditions resulting from the process of differentiation.

Casanova's theory is not without its critics. Talal Asad is concerned about the potential of a particular religion to assume control through deprivatization and questions the perceived neutrality of the public sphere. Asad writes, "If the legitimate role for deprivatized religion is carried out effectively ... the allegedly viable part of the secularization thesis ... [is] undermined."[15] Secularization is not simply a mask for Christianity. Asad's point is that certain religions who have adapted to the new *type* of religion that accompany secularization may be able to manipulate the public sphere in a way that renders the differentiation thesis unsupportable. Casanova responds by asserting that secularization is a useful analytical category for understanding the "transformation of modern European societies" and "the historical transformation of all world religions under conditions of modern structural differentiation."[16] He continues, "All world religions are challenged to respond to the global expansion of modernity by reformulating their traditions in an attempt to fashion their own versions of modernity."[17] Therefore, if religion is to successfully engage the public sphere, it must meet the required conditions of public religion. In turn, all religions must project the universalized components of freedom of conscience and religion, which they legitimate through teaching and doctrine.[18] For Casanova, deprivatization confirms rather than dismisses differentiation and privatization.

With respect to the neutrality of the public sphere, Asad criticizes Casanova for not addressing how the religious and secular spheres interconnect. Although Casanova contends that his view of the public sphere is fluid and not as fixed as Asad makes it out to be, he does not fully address Asad's criticism that "the public sphere is *necessarily* (not just contingently) articulated by power ... The dependence of some on the goodwill of others."[19] Instead, Casanova reasserts that the public sphere is a "discursive or agonic space" where issues of "power and the power to set the terms of the debate" can be negotiated.[20] Asad reminds Casanova that public spheres are not inherently neutral spaces in which such discourses take place. The legal apparatus of the state is responsible for deciding what falls under the protection of religious freedom and where religion ought to be properly located in modern societies. Asad maintains that the right to speak is contingent upon being heard. An uneven balance of power in the public sphere may privilege some groups over others.[21]

In 2008, Casanova revisited *Public Religions*. He admits that his theory had a number of shortcomings, including its "Western-centrism."[22] He explains that while we must acknowledge the Christian roots of "the secular" in modern Western countries, "the secular" may manifest in non-European communities, but this does not mean that European forms of modernity *act upon* them. He writes,

> All traditions and civilizations are radically transformed in the process of modernization, but they also have the possibility of shaping in partic-ular ways the institutionalization of modern "religious" and "secular" traits. Traditions are forced to respond and adjust to modern conditions, but in the process of reformulating their traditions for modern contexts, they also help to shape the particular forms of "religious" and "secular" modernity.[23]

Casanova appropriately reiterates that it is important to note the origins of specific manifestations of secularization, but Indigenous Peoples emerge only in his discussion of global and transnational communities and not in, I think, the more appropriate discus-sion of the development of a functionally differentiated society. He writes, the call for the protection of Indigenous cultural rights "could easily be turned into a general principle of the reciprocal rights and duties of all peoples of the world to respect each other's traditions and cultures, constituting the basis of what could be called an emerging global denominationalism."[24] If religion is an inherently private endeavour, then this may be an ideal sufficient to foster religious freedom. However, Indigenous Peoples have not been afforded the historical luxury of negotiating a divide between the religious and the secular, if such a divide exists. Additionally, if land is at the centre of one's religion and land is public, then religion is far from a private matter.

In sum, structural differentiation raised a variety of religious and non-religious world views to a legitimate position in European modernity. In this modernity, ultimate authority in the public sphere rests in the state, and it has relegated religion to its own specialized space in the private sphere. If religions hope to affect matters of public interest, they must do so in accordance with con-ditions of compromise, negotiation, and discursive legitimation. Asad's challenges point to two questions regarding deprivatiza-tion important to current debates regarding the protection of Indigenous religions in Canada: What type of religion is allowed into the public sphere and who holds the power to make decisions regarding the exercise of religion in the public arena?

Here, we see an implicit manifestation of Christianity, but that is not to say that non-Christian communities cannot conform to such standards if they wish to effect change in the public sphere. In this sense, deprivatization is a choice. However, the intimate connection between Indigenous religions and land poses yet another unique problem in this contemporary secular religious landscape. Indigenous Peoples cannot return to their "isolated hamlets," nor can they choose to disengage from public discourse given the centrality of (what are deemed) public lands for Indigenous religions. Indigenous Peoples are forced to participate in deprivatization as a consequence of differentiation and dispossession. In turn, deprivatization mandates a certain type of religion open to compromise and negotiation.

The Location of Religion in Canada

Secularization theory provides a theoretical foundation for understanding the differentiation of modern societies and the privatization of religion. However, as demonstrated by contemporary scholars of secularization theory, secularization is altered by specific historical contingencies.[25] David Martin argues that secularization in Canada developed along a variety of different paths due to the "two, or possibly three," founding cultures of the nation.[26]

As noted in the introduction, the close connection between church and state in Canadian history is not a new observation. In the century prior to Confederation, some degree of acceptance and tolerance characterized English Protestant and French Roman Catholic relations. Following the defeat of the French in 1775, the English (i.e., Anglican, Presbyterian, and, later, Methodist) rulers established exceptions for the French colony allowing Roman Catholics to serve in the government. Continuing tensions between mainstream religious communities would lead to further accommodations regarding separate schooling in the colonies.[27] This early relationship laid the foundations for negotiation and compromise among some religious communities in the public sphere.

The few years prior to Confederation, and, arguably, the first century of Canadian statehood, indicate that the state accepted and tolerated only mainstream Christian communities, a sort of "shadow establishment."[28] However, early economic relationships with Indigenous Peoples demonstrate that the state was willing to put religion aside for the sake of the growing colonial economy. Historian J.R. Miller demonstrates that Indigenous Peoples and state officials participated in traditional Indigenous ceremonies to commence early treaty negotiations.[29] As early as the seventeenth century, prospects for economic prosperity brought with them some form of tolerance of religious pluralism outside of Christianity in the public arena.

In English-speaking Canada, debates regarding the relationship between church and state began as early as the mid-eighteenth century. The Clear Grit party (later to become the Liberal Party of Canada) was particularly concerned with the state-sanctioned financial support received by churches. It was also concerned with state-sponsored religious education and the one-seventh of Crown lands set aside for the de facto established Anglican Church in Canada West (Ontario). In 1854, despite opposition from French colonists in Canada East who felt religion was under attack, the colonial government redistributed the so-called clergy reserves. Historian John Moir argues that the Clergy Reserve Act (1854) sought to "remove all semblance of connection between Church and State."[30] With the liquidation of the clergy reserves died any possibility that Canadian society would be united by a single church. After Confederation, the process of differentiation accelerated, especially with the growth of the state and the market society, which created powerful social institutions that could compete with the churches. Moreover, this growth created spheres of activity (political society and economic society) in which Christianity played only a minor role.[31]

In Quebec, Roman Catholicism remained an important facet of public and social institutions until the 1960s. The Second Vatican Council (1962–5) dramatically altered the Catholic relationship with modern states. The ultramontane emphasis on the Church as the ultimate authority in the world weakened with the acknowl-edgment of the temporal authority of modern liberal states and the universal acceptance of religious freedom.[32] Martin argues that as key distinctions separating Catholics in Quebec from others in Canada deteriorated, other markers of distinction also began to collapse and a differentiated Quebec emerged.[33]

The unofficial acceptance of Indigenous religious traditions from early European settlers quickly changed as their political and economic significance declined. Although a level of differen-tiation seems to have taken place by the time of Confederation, the experience of Indigenous Peoples shows that the close connec-tion between church and state did not subside until well after the Second World War. As noted earlier, the state placed churches in charge of mandatory, federally funded residential schools, which served as the gatekeepers to Euro-Canadian social and political life. Additionally, the state banned Indigenous religious practices for over half of a century.

Following the Second World War, Canada, like many countries in the world, adopted fundamental human rights that enabled dif-ferentiation and the privatization of religion.[34] In 1960, section 1 of the Canadian Bill of Rights declared that "there have existed and shall continue to exist without discrimination by reason of race, national origin, colour, religion or sex" certain "human rights and fundamental freedoms." These rights and freedoms included equality under the law and, under subsection c, "the freedom of religion." This adoption correlates with a variety of social mark-ers that reflect the fading shadow establishment of early Canada. Peter Beyer identifies six such markers, including declines in mem-bership for mainstream Christian churches, increased acceptance of individual authority rather than expert authority, increased institutional pluralism, and greater religious diversity (related to the opening of Canada's borders).[35]

In support of the Charter right to freedom of conscience and reli-gion, the courts have sought to neither infringe on the private rights of citizens to engage in their religion nor to allow overt discrimina-tory actions against religion in the public arena without measures of discursive legitimation, compromise, and accommodation.[36] In the first section 2(a) case before the SCC in *R. v. Big M Drug Mart Ltd*, the court determined that the laws prohibiting businesses from operating on Sundays were unconstitutional. At the heart of this case was the title of the legislation in question, the "Lord's Day Act," which had clear religious overtones. The court determined that the legislation "creates a climate hostile to, and gives the appearance of discrimination against, non-Christian Canadians."[37] Similar decisions were made on matters of religious education in schools and prayers at city council meetings.[38] The decisions made by the SCC emancipate, to some degree, political and economic spheres from Christian hegemony and provide the opportunity for equality under the law for minority religious communities.

R. v. Edwards Books and Art Ltd provides an interesting clarification, which dealt with Sunday closing laws just as *Big M* had done sixteen months earlier. The result was noticeably different. What is noteworthy is the manner by which the court justified infringement. They had no doubt that forcing larger businesses to close on Sundays impacted Jewish and Seventh-Day Adventists who close on Saturdays for religious observance. But the law did allow an exemption for smaller businesses. For the court, provinces had the right to enforce a "pause day" for the benefit of all citizens. Chief Justice Brian Dickson found the following: "I am ... unable to extract ... any legal principle dictating that pause day legislation is inherently legislation in respect of 'public morals.' Nor, incidentally, can I extract a rule of law that a province's selection of Sunday as a common pause day must inevitably be held to be a colourable attempt to enforce majoritarian religious beliefs."[39] Dickson concluded, "The infringement is not disproportionate to the legislative objectives. A serious effort has been made to accommodate the freedom of religion of Saturday observers, in so far as that is possible without undue damage to the scope and quality of the pause day objective."[40]

The major difference between *Big M* and *Edwards Books* is that the former dealt with a law protecting the Christian day of worship while the latter dealt with a law of general applicability regarding a day of rest for all Ontarians. The difference is in how the laws were framed. For those who support a day designated for family and leisure, "pause day" legislation is coherent in a non-religious setting regardless of the day chosen. More importantly, for the court, the accommodation included in the law was deemed sufficient despite the fact that the law would still burden some members of the province. The decision reflects a desire for compromise and discursive legitimation in a diverse society. At the same time, it reflects how majoritarian religion, reframed as culture, can still come to dominate the public sphere.[41]

The other condition raised by Casanova is that of negotiation. We can see this clearly in *Amselem*, where the court ruled on a Quebec case between Jewish tenants of a condominium complex and property management. In short, management raised issues of safety and decorum when Jewish residents expressed a desire to build *succahs* on their shared balconies in which they would reside for a period of eight days. The appellants had agreed to leave access to fire escapes free and even build the *succahs* in a way that blended in with the condominium exterior. Proportionally there was no concern with upholding the plaintiffs' case, especially since they had offered accommodations for management. If there had been safety concerns the SCC concluded that the decision may have been different.[42]

Therefore, Canada is differentiated despite having no establishment clause and a history of Christian-state historical relations. It would be inappropriate to suggest that the borders between differentiated spheres are necessarily rigid. Rather, boundaries are fluid and porous, as noted by both Asad and Casanova. *Big M* suggests that there are discursive limits to the manipulation of non-religious spheres by religious actors no matter their population size, while *Edwards Books* and *Amselem* remind us that compromise, negotiation, and discursive legitimation are required in matters related to religion and state action and law, which could benefit both majoritarian and minority religions.

The Dispossession of Indigenous Lands

With the exception of much of British Columbia, modern-day Canada consists of several major and many smaller treaties with Indigenous Peoples. These treaties, going back to the *Royal*

Proclamation of 1763 – a proclamation protected under section 25(a) in the Charter – assumed Crown sovereignty while offering protection for Indigenous territories.[43] This assumption of Crown sovereignty remains a staple of constitutional law. In fact, the existence of Aboriginal title was not acknowledged until the *Calder* case in 1973.[44] For the time being, I simply want to state a simple but important fact: while treaties of peace and friendship marked the early years of treaty-making in Canada, treaties in the nineteenth century and first part of the twentieth century (while treaty negotiations were still taking place) were entered into by the state for socio-economic development at the expense of Indigenous Peoples who, at a transitional period following the decline of the bison, the end of the War of 1812, and expanding European settlement, were forced into requiring some transitional support in certain regions. The reserves set aside for Indigenous Peoples were often neither the size nor the locations that they desired. To complicate matters even further, the interpretation of treaties is a contested subject.

The treaties of commerce and alliance that characterized early relations between Indigenous Peoples and European settlers in the first two centuries of contact were not unlike the treaties which Indigenous Peoples had with each other since before the arrival of Europeans. Due to the specific geographical location, expertise, and needs of the nations of Turtle Island, trade was essential for sustaining life and culture, and peace was essential for the maintenance of trade. Once the state and Indigenous Peoples established these relationships (best understood as kinship), they were maintained through ceremonies that involved pipe smoking, gift giving, and feasts. Treaty signatories typically repeated these ceremonies regularly to re-establish the compact. Friendship and cohabitation characterized these early commercial relationships. Hudson's Bay Company (HBC) representatives would participate in ritual smoking and gift giving with Indigenous Peoples in the spirit of the pre-contact North American compacts. French, English, and Dutch settlers would adopt this kinship model in the northeast in the early period of colonization. These settlers understood quite quickly, as Indigenous Peoples had always known, that peace and trade were synonymous.[45]

Following economic and peace treaties, the *Royal Proclamation of 1763* marked the second phase in treaty-making in Canada: territorial treaties. To avoid mistreating Indigenous Peoples and their lands, the British government made provisions in the *Royal Proclamation* concerning the sovereignty of the Crown, the sale and purchase of Indigenous territories, and the rights of Indigenous Peoples to those territories. The *Royal Proclamation* established the framework for treaty-making in Canada that remains today: treaties would have to be between the Crown and Indigenous Peoples, negotiations would have to be public, and the state had to inform other Indigenous Peoples of the proceedings.[46]

Large territorial treaties began to emerge following the influx of British Loyalists after the American Revolution (1775–83). One of the most notable characteristics of these early settlement treaties was that the state acquired land along waterfronts "for the simple reason that rivers and lakes were the highways on which people travelled in these regions."[47] Some communities realized that the acquisition of waterfront property and assurances under the *Royal Proclamation* of fishing rights were not sufficient to protect the fishing rights of Indigenous Peoples. In the Head of the Lake Treaty (1805), the Mississauga demanded and received access to the waterfront. Many of the early settlement treaties continued the protocols of pre-contact compacts.[48]

Following the War of 1812, peace between the United States and Britain resulted in a significant rise in the number of immigrants settling in British North America. In 1812 in Upper Canada, Indigenous populations had dwindled to 10 per cent of the total population. Between 1821 and 1851, the number of British immigrants in North America tripled, further decreasing the Indigenous presence and increasing the settler need for land. By 1827, the state had acquired nearly all the arable land in southern Ontario for European settlement. Although Crown negotiations continued to maintain the protocols of Indigenous treaty-making, the tone of the treaties changed following the war and influx of immigrants. J.R. Miller notes that Indigenous Peoples quickly became "obstacles" for settlement as their military and economic value dissipated. Miller writes, "From the settler perspective, Indians were ceasing to be desirable partners and assuming the role of barriers to the winning of wealth."[49]

Many Indigenous Peoples understood that their relationship with the Crown was changing and either sought the protection of their fishing and hunting rights or lamented the irreversible effects of colonial expansion on their traditional ways of life. In the 1830s, the civilization policy of the British Empire began to take form, and Christianization and civilization took precedent over participating in Indigenous traditions of treaty-making. In 1836, Sir Francis Bond Head secured the last remaining arable land in southern Ontario from the Saugeen by promoting civilization and isolation, relocating the Saugeen away from the land they desired.[50]

As Canada entered Confederation in 1867 and acquired Rupert's Land from the HBC in 1870, the government began to secure the land of the many Plains and Woodlands Indigenous Peoples. The construction of a railway to the Pacific Ocean and the need to establish agricultural communities on the prairies made negotiations with Indigenous Peoples imperative. Unlike the communities in southern Ontario which were sceptical of the often-violated treaties with Europeans, Indigenous Peoples in the West were accustomed to dealing with fur traders who had upheld the protocols characteristic of Indigenous Peoples' legal traditions. Given the significant decline in buffalo herds by the late eighteenth century, Indigenous Peoples were both willing to accept and in need of transitional support.[51]

In the southern numbered treaties from 1871 to 1877, the government granted Indigenous Peoples far smaller portions of land than initially anticipated. For example, in Treaty 1, Indigenous representatives in the treaty area asked for nearly two-thirds of Manitoba but the government allotted only 160 acres to each family of five. In return, the state provided Indigenous Peoples with compensation, schools, continued hunting rights, and promises of instruction in farming. Miller notes that the "written text silently passed over a lengthy, sometimes acerbic, argument over the extent of reserve lands."[52] In Treaty 3 (1873), the government increased reserve lands to 640 acres (one square mile) per family of five, and the government redressed shortcomings of the first two numbered treaties through language that was more explicit. Treaty 3 provided written assurances of hunting rights and the supply of farming equipment (unlike in the first two treaties). There were some restrictions identified. The treaty reads,

> Her Majesty further agrees with Her said Indians that they, the said Indians, shall have right to pursue their avocations of hunting and fishing throughout the tract surrendered as hereinbefore described, subject to such regulations as may from time to time be made by Her Government of Her Dominion of Canada, and saving and excepting such tracts as may, from time to time, be required or taken up for settlement, mining, lumbering or other purposes by Her said Government of the Dominion of Canada, or by any of the subjects thereof duly authorized therefor [sic] by the said Government.[53]

These restrictions on hunting and the allotment of one square mile to each family of five would remain a constant throughout the first seven numbered treaties.[54]

The paternalism characteristic of the recent consolidation of official state policies towards Indigenous Peoples also characterized the remaining treaties before treaty-making virtually stopped from 1923 to 1975. Tensions grew as the Indigenous participants of the southern treaties realized that the government was not upholding its end of the compacts. For example, a signatory of Treaty No. 6, Cree Chief Ahtahkakoop voiced his concern that reserves were not located where he wished them to be. Despite these violations, northern communities sought treaties based on the evolving crises regarding the bison and the fur trade. The government was reluctant to negotiate with those Indigenous Peoples until it was understood that acquiring their land would contribute to the economic development of the north-west and the prosperity of Canada. In particular, the pro-business thrust of Wilfrid Laurier and the Liberal government supported a wider infrastructure in pursuit of Canada's abundant natural resources. These economic aspirations dictated the placement of reserves. For example, in Treaty 9 (1905) in northern Ontario, the government did not grant reserve land near rivers that had the potential to produce hydroelectric power. These treaties continued to preserve hunting and fishing rights in the same manner as earlier numbered treaties. Eventually, the prioritization of non-Indigenous economic interests in the land over Indigenous concerns characterized the half a century when the government stopped making treaties.[55]

Indigenous Peoples across Canada entered into what they believed were spiritual agreements with Euro-Canadians in good faith and, in many ways, out of necessity. Crown negotiators silently dismissed the amount of land they sought, and federal surveyors most often ignored the particular plots of land they desired. With the exception of the Arctic and British Columbia, Indigenous Peoples had, without much choice, relinquished control of their land to the Crown. Despite the spiritual components of early compacts and the religious language of Indigenous chiefs, use of the land to hunt and fish were the only rights afforded under these treaties. Well before Confederation, colonial authorities ignored the spiritual importance of the land and the complex Indigenous relationship to it.

Although a new and lengthy land claims negotiation process would begin in the 1970s, the Crown had already acquired most of the land in the provinces early into the twentieth century.[56] According to Indigenous and Northern Affairs Canada, as of 2014, Indigenous Peoples controlled approximately 35,548 square kilometres of Canadian soil. The vast majority of that land consists of reservations as opposed to comprehensive land agreements.[57] With Canada spanning close to 1 million square kilometres, this means that Indigenous Peoples occupy approximately 3.5 per cent of the Canadian land mass. Complicating matters even further is that these reservations were not always where communities desired them to be. Thus, the vast majority of cosmologically significant spaces for Indigenous Peoples now exists on what the Crown considers its land.

Aboriginal Rights, Compromise, and Disclosure

Indigenous Peoples occupy a special place within the Canadian state as national minorities with a special status popularly described as "citizens plus."[58] The "plus" refers to unique group rights outlined in section 35 of the Constitution Act. Generally speaking, Aboriginal rights traditionally referred to land usage rights, but the court has broadly interpreted the framework to include several generic rights.[59] Although much of Canada acquired most of its land from Indigenous Peoples through treaties, the government guaranteed Indigenous Peoples access to traditional lands as stipulated in the *Royal Proclamation* and affirmed in *St Catherine's Milling Company v. The Queen*.[60] The protection of and access to land and the use of resources on Crown lands for traditional ceremonial and food purposes indirectly provides a method by which Indigenous Peoples may protect cosmologically significant spaces. However, section 35(1) is not absolute. In *R. v. Sparrow*, the Supreme Court found that section 35(1) "does not promise immunity from government regulation in a society that, in the twentieth century, is increasingly more complex, interdependent and sophisticated, and where exhaustible resources need protection and management, it does hold the Crown to a substantive promise."[61] In other words, Aboriginal rights are subject to the politics of compromise, particularly with respect to the management of resources.

In a case regarding fishing regulations, a Musqueam man claimed that drift net regulations for commercial fishing violated his Aboriginal right to fish for ceremonial and food purposes. Chief Justice Dickson and Justice Gérard La Forest took the opportunity to outline how a claimant may argue that the state has infringed section 35(1) and, subsequently, how the state may justify such an infringement. In *Sparrow*, it was determined that the "onus of proving a *prima facie* infringement lies on the individual or group challenging the legislation."[62] The court also determined that the Crown has a duty to provide justification for any infringement and ensure that such infringements are limited and that guidelines are established (especially with respect to "the limited nature of the resource") to address the conflicting interests of others.[63] In a later decision in *Mitchell v. M.N.R.*, Chief Justice McLachlin clarified that Aboriginal rights cannot be framed in the negative, nor can they hold specific qualifications.[64] For example, a generic right of cultural integrity cannot be attached to a demand that the state cannot approve the development of a ski resort in a particular location.[65] Such a demand would leave no room for negotiation and compromise.

In *R. v. Van der Peet*, Chief Justice Antonio Lamer provided important clarification on the matter of public discourse and the limitations of Aboriginal rights. The decision reads, "In assessing a claim for the existence of an aboriginal right, a court must take into account the perspective of the aboriginal people claiming the right [but] ... that perspective must be framed in terms cognizable to the Canadian legal and constitutional structure."[66] In other words, the Supreme Court is willing to recognize the unique cultural traditions of Indigenous Peoples, but those cultures still need to be discernable in Canada's legal culture. This important decision acknowledges the reality of the cultural foundations of the law while, at the same time, asking Indigenous Peoples to frame their cultures – which are presumably outside of the majoritarian culture – in a manner cognizable to Canadian law (and, of course, the interpreters of that law). Together, the decisions in *Sparrow* and *Van der Peet* indirectly require the public disclosure and explanation of Indigenous religions as they relate to land and resources in order that the court may protect asserted Aboriginal rights. Aside from the more obvious issues of the problems rooted in cultural incommensurability, secrecy, which may be an integral component of a religion, is an extraordinarily difficult ethic to maintain when a group seeks protection in the public square.[67]

In his practical review of Indigenous strategies on matters of religious freedom in Canada's courts, lawyer Michael Lee Ross explains that one primary means by which Indigenous Peoples seek the protection of their off-reserve sacred sites is through a temporary legal halt to development known as an interlocutory injunction. In *MacMillan Bloedel Ltd v. Mullin*, the strategy was first employed.[68] Typically, the subject of Aboriginal title and rights satisfies the first question of pursuing an interlocutory injunction: whether the pursuit of the right is a fair one. The second question refers to the "balance of convenience."[69] In short, the court weighs the potential injury to either party against each other and makes a decision based on this test. In this particular case, Justice Peter Seaton determined that allowing MacMillan Bloedel to log the particular tract of land on Meares Island would be more devastating for the Nuu-Chah-Nulth than it would if logging stopped for a temporary period. The court explains that not only must the court take the material and legal repercussions into consideration but the cultural implications as well. Quoting a 1976 landmark legal ruling in Australia on customary rights and secrecy, Seaton asserts that "monetary damages cannot alleviate any wrong to the plaintiffs that may be established and perhaps, there can be no greater threat to any of us than a threat to one's family and social structure."[70] Although the case did not address Indigenous religions directly, the ruling in favour of the Nuu-Chah-Nulth provides the means by which Indigenous Peoples may protect certain facets of their traditions. Seaton, however, stipulated that the decision of the court spoke to the unique circumstances of the case. He added that in a different situation "the balance of convenience may be seen to have shifted to favour the industry."[71] Subsequent cases, where Indigenous appellants directly communicated religious significance to the court, help to demonstrate how Indigenous Peoples must make their religious traditions public to protect certain sites and that the court will inevitably subject such land to the politics of compromise with competing economic interests.

Two cases help exemplify these points: *Tlowitsis Nation v. MacMillan Bloedel Ltd* and *Siska Indian Band v. British Columbia*. In these cases the religious significance of the contested space was an important aspect in the arguments of both claimants and, in both cases, the balance of convenience was determined to favour the industry. In the first case, Justice D.B. MacKinnon wrote, the "major emphasis by the plaintiffs as to the irreparable harm was directed to this area encompassing holy grounds that have great importance to these Native nations as spiritual grounds. Counsel referred to it an analogous to a Christian church or a Garden of Eden."[72] MacKinnon dismissed (secular) environmental concerns that accompanied the claim since the logging company had sufficiently investigated the effects of logging on the coastal whale habitat. Left with only the claim to sacred space and a lack of physical evidence to support such a claim, the judge questioned why the sacredness of the site did not appear in preliminary discussions with MacMillan Bloedel or press releases in the period since the site was under contention. Upon dismissing the injunction, he expressed his concern not only for the losses to MacMillan Bloedel but also that "the potential loss of employment of this Province is ... a proper factor to consider in the balancing process."[73]

On appeal, the court dismissed the affidavits of two Indigenous Peoples who attempted to explain their reluctance to enter the subject of religion into the debate. The court explained, "May Smith and Simon Dick deposed that they attended residential Anglican schools many years ago and were punished if they spoke Kwakwala. For this and other reasons they had been afraid in the past to speak out about their religious beliefs and cultures." The court concluded, "In my opinion, those affidavits do not offer an explanation for the lateness of the applicants' raising a claim that their right to engage in spiritual practices in the Lower Tsitika Valley Watershed was endangered."[74] The Tlowitsis Nation's reluctance to enter the space's religious significance into public dialogue greatly affected the outcome of the case. In his analysis of the case, Ross hypothesizes, "If the Tlowitsis had asserted the valley's sacredness sooner, [the chamber judge] might have found, other things being equal, that it was sacred enough to qualify as sufficiently unique to tilt the balance of convenience."[75] In this sense, deprivatization is mandatory.

In the second case, the Siska First Nation claimed that if logging were to continue in the Siska Valley and Siska Creek area, "the Applicants will have lost their aboriginal rights to cedar and to certain sacred spiritual practices forever."[76] The Siska presented affidavits and academic reports regarding the cultural, spiritual, and economic importance of the space to the court to support the Siska claim that the contested space was of "exceptional spiritual and cultural significance."[77] In denying the injunction, Justice Jon Sigurdson pointed to many of the same economic reasons stated in the *Tlowitsis Nation* case and questioned the spiritual and cultural uniqueness of the space to be logged. The Siska First Nation claimed that since the area had not been subject to industry activity, it allowed them the opportunity to continue their spiritual and cultural practices in a natural setting. Sigurdson acknowledged this fact and the importance of the cultural and spiritual ceremonies when he affirmed that they could conduct them in many of the other pristine places that exist within their traditional territory.[78] The protection of an entire space is difficult to ascertain because the economic concerns of industry and state will inevitably dictate a compromise. In these cases deprivatization and the conditions of discursive legitimation and negotiation are, in a sense, mandatory if Indigenous Peoples hope to protect some semblances of their religions.

Cameron v. Ministry of Energy and Mines

Although the preferred means of protecting Indigenous religions is through section 35(1), Indigenous Peoples have brought section 2(a) claims before the court as well. As noted in the previous chapter, *Cameron v. Ministry of Energy and Mines* is the first of two cases before the BCSC where a Charter violation on the matter of Indigenous religious freedom is addressed.

In 1998, the Saulteau First Nations and the Kelly Lake Cree Nation sought a legal halt to oil drilling operations by Amoco (an American oil and chemical corporation) in a portion of territory that falls under Treaty 8 in north-eastern British Columbia. The claim was twofold: that the Crown had not satisfied its fiduciary duty to consult as established in *Sparrow* and elaborated upon in *Delgamuukw*, and that the drilling operation violated their right to freedom of conscience and religion guaranteed by the Charter. The reason why the court rejected both claims relates to the extensive negotiations that took place before the trial and the fairness of the agreement that negotiators reached during the consultation process. The Saulteau rejection of this compromise and the Kelly Lake Cree Nation's refusal to participate in the discussions did not stop Justice Taylor from ruling in favour of the compromise reached during the negotiations leading up to the trial.

As noted earlier, the area holds religious significance for four communities: the Saulteau, Kelly Lake Cree Nation, the West Moberly First Nations, and the Halfway River First Nation. Justice Taylor noted that the prophetic nature of the space for the

Indigenous Peoples in the region demonstrated a "significant spirituality" of the Twin Sisters.[79]

In 1991, Amoco sought a drilling licence for the Twin Sisters area, at which point "aboriginal interests were required to be considered."[80] In 1992, the Treaty 8 Tribal Association completed an ethno-historical report. The public report outlined the importance of the space to the Indigenous Peoples of the region and expressed the concerns of elders for any industrial development of the area. In the following year, interested parties met to discuss the report, and they formed a Co-Management Advisory Committee involving the Saulteau, West Moberly First Nations, Halfway River First Nation, the Ministry of Energy and Mines (MEM), and Amoco. The committee decided at this point that drilling could not commence in the Twin Sisters area without further discussion. Reports indicated that parties might be discussing the possibility of drilling in a less contentious area.[81] Between 1995 and 1997, negotiations continued between First Nations, MEM, and Amoco. Throughout this period, the Saulteau were unconvinced that the committee was adequately addressing their cultural interests.

In 1997, the Advisory Committee identified the Twin Sisters area as one of uniqueness for Aboriginal history, culture, and religion, subsequently forming the Twin Sisters Management Committee (TSSMC).[82] The TSSMC quickly arrived at a compromise among the interested parties that they felt would allow all interests to be reasonably satisfied. The report from the TSSMC divided the contested area into three zones: a protected space near the peaks of the mountain and two sub-levels lower on the mountain that allowed for varying degrees of industry operation.[83] The West Moberly and Halfway River First Nations signed the agreement in October 1997. The Saulteau did not sign the agreement. Over the course of 1997 and 1998, MEM attempted to contact the Saulteau regarding the drilling project, and the court interpreted the few responses of the Saulteau as a rejection of the project altogether. The court reported, "The [Saulteau] continued to press their fundamentally different approach ... one of adamant resistance to any development."[84]

The Kelly Lake Cree Nation were not involved in the Twin Sisters negotiations for unresolved political reasons stemming from their division from the Kelly Lake First Nation in 1996. Although the Crown did not recognize the state's obligation to consult the Kelly Lake Cree Nation – a subject to which I return in chapter 5 – Taylor asserted that even if there were a duty to consult the community, the fact that the Kelly Lake Cree Nation did not seek to participate in the discussions nullified any existing rights.[85] With respect to the Saulteau, it was clear to the court that consultation on the part of MEM and Amoco had taken place. Taylor notes that "consultation is a two way process."[86]

The Saulteau claimed that there was an error of fact regarding the size and scope of their sacred space. The judge quickly dismissed this point, writing, "A complete reading of the decision makes it abundantly clear to any right-minded person that [the MEM representative] was alive to the sacredness of a much broader area."[87] Moreover, Taylor asserted that the Saulteau's right to be heard had been satisfied and that it was apparent that MEM understood the importance and breadth of the space. The major issue for Taylor was not the MEM's duty to consult but rather the Saulteau's and Kelly Lake Cree Nation's willingness to participate.[88]

The only viable claim remaining for both the Saulteau and Kelly Lake Cree Nation was that the operation violated their section 2(a) right.[89] Taylor remarked, "Assertion of the freedom of religious practice is a discrete issue that relates to all Canadian citizens."[90] As noted in the previous chapter, Taylor concluded that the compromise allowed for "sub-alpine activities," a limited "absolute stewardship," and a "lesser form of stewardship," while allowing for drilling operations to occur.[91] Taylor concluded his judgment by returning to the issue of religious freedom. He stated,

The intellectual aspect of a concept of stewardship for times of need in refuge is not impugned and while in a perfect world as viewed by the [Saulteau], such drilling would never occur, the activity does not deny that concept. The provisions of a protected area provide a basis for that continued intellectual stewardship that is an aspect of the area's spirituality. While geographically constricted, it is not eliminated to the extent that there is limitation or coercion of the existence of the religious rights.[92]

Taylor was critical of the unwillingness of the Saulteau to compromise on the drilling activities in the consultation process, citing the idealist desire for a "perfect world" without drilling as untenable. He continued to criticize the Saulteau and Kelly Lake Cree Nation for making a claim that was not susceptible to compromise and negotiation. Taylor admits that there are geographical limitations but contends that the protected space still allows them to maintain their beliefs and practices. What is implied is that this decision allows for both socio-economic interests and religious concerns to be satisfied. The fact that the Saulteau clearly believed that the space was non-negotiable was an unacceptable position. The problem, of course, is that a retreat to their "isolated hamlets" to protect "the worth of their sectarian wares uncontested" is not an option for Indigenous Peoples. Their "wares" are the subject of debate. And yet, failure to engage in discursive processes in the public could mean the loss of cosmologically significant spaces and, in turn, religions themselves.

Conclusion

Processes of secularization defined a new type of religion based on the conditions of liberal democratic engagement. At the same time, the state has dispossessed Indigenous Peoples of most of their traditional territories. These two contexts culminate in forced deprivatization, offering Indigenous Peoples two options regarding their religions: disclose and explain or remain silent. In both cases, cosmologically significant spaces are subject to modification and destruction. The courts understand that land holds an important place within Indigenous religions. However, the "public" label assigned to the traditional territories of Indigenous Peoples alongside conditions of compromise and the understanding that economic and religious interests must be balanced make the protection of land – a central feature of Indigenous religions – difficult, if not impossible.

The Supreme Court decision in *Ktunaxa Nation v. British Columbia* is a troubling confirmation of the requirements of public religion imposed upon Indigenous Peoples under both sections 2(a) and 35(1). The Ktunaxa, like all communities discussed above, do not control Qat'muk, the home of the Grizzly Bear Spirit. It was in 2009, following nearly two decades of negotiations, when the Ktunaxa expressed their "no middle ground" position, indicating what the court would deem an absolutist position. The "no middle ground" position was viewed with scepticism by the BCSC, BCCA, and the SCC. I return to this case in greater depth in the next chapter, but given the recentness and significance of the SCC decision, it is important to highlight that the state continues to require Indigenous Peoples to adhere to the conditions of public religion whether or not they choose to do so. The SCC was explicit on matters of compromise and disclosure. Chief Justice McLachlin expressed the following:

> The claim now was not a claim to generalized spiritual values that could be accommodated by measures like land reserves, economic payments, and environmental protections. Instead, it was an absolute claim to a sacred site, which must be preserved and protected from permanent human habitation ... There was no way the proposed resort could be reconciled with this claim. The Minister made efforts to continue consultation, but, not surprisingly, they failed.[93]

Compromise is a requirement well known by the Saulteau and Kelly Lake Cree, and the Ktunaxa too were reprimanded for possessing an absolutist claim. McLachlin also clarified the requirement of disclosure, seeming to affirm the "late-2009" "no middle ground" position of the Ktunaxa as weak. As in *MacMillan Bloedel*, the SCC reminded the Ktunaxa that claimants need to be forthcoming with their information, stating, "Claims should be identified early in the process and defined as clearly as possible. In most cases, this will lead to agreement and reconciliation."[94] Disclosure and compromise remain standards of the conditions of public religion.

In chapter 1, I expressed a great deal of praise for the minority reasoning of Justices Moldaver and Côté in their identification of the superficiality of religious freedom, as reasoned by the majority in the *Ktunaxa Nation* case. Despite a keen awareness of the importance of land for Indigenous religious freedom, Moldaver and Côté read the Ktunaxa section 2(a) claim through the lens of the conditions of public religion and, in turn, the homogenizing discourse of equality, discounting the colonial legacy of dispossession. Moldaver writes,

> Granting the Ktunaxa a power to veto development over the land would effectively give the Ktunaxa a significant property interest in Qat'muk – namely, a power to exclude others from constructing permanent structures on over fifty square kilometres of public land. This right of exclusion is not a minimal or negligible restraint on public ownership. It gives the Ktunaxa the power to exclude others from developing land that the public in fact owns. The public in this case includes an Aboriginal group, the Shuswap Indian Band, that supports the development.[95]

Moldaver and Côté desired to include the Ktunaxa claim under the banner of religious freedom given the significance of Qat'muk, but they were unwilling to protect the space given the need to balance the interests of other parties – notably another community of Indigenous Peoples – who have a financial interest in the land. Thus, even if the Ktunaxa section 2(a) claim met the limitations provided by McLachlin in the majority decision, it would appear that Qat'muk would not have received the protection desired by the Ktunaxa, because their claims would have still been subject to the conditions of public religion.

Thus far, we have explored the challenges of the shallow interpretation of religious freedom and the conditions of public religion for the possibility of Indigenous religious freedom in Canada. This chapter largely explored the expectations of the section 2(a) and section 35(1) religious freedom claims of Indigenous Peoples, but there is more to these frameworks. Given our attention to procedural expectations in this chapter, I have largely treated sections 2(a) and 35(1) as somewhat similar means of seeking legal redress on matters of cosmologically significant space. However, the challenges of these legal frameworks extend well beyond the expectations for public religion that seem to stretch uniformly across both section 2(a) and section 35(1) claims. The fundamental freedom of conscience and religion and Aboriginal rights are very different legal frameworks with competing and often contradictory foundations and case law. In addition to the issues of the depth of religious freedom and the expectations of public religion, it is necessary to now explore sections 2(a) and 35(1) in greater detail to understand how these frameworks further complicate the possibility of Indigenous religious freedom in Canada.

chapter three

Religions Plus? Competing Frameworks of Indigenous Religious Freedom

In 1966, H.B. Hawthorn edited a two-volume report for the government titled *A Survey of the Contemporary Indians of Canada: Economic, Political, Educational Needs and Policies*. The primary thrust of the report was to advocate for Indigenous Peoples to be recognized as "Citizens Plus." The opening of what has come to be known as the Hawthorn Report explains, "The right derives from promises made to them, from expectations they were encouraged to hold, and from the simple fact that they once occupied and used a country to which others came to gain enormous wealth in which the Indians have shared little."[1] Hawthorn found support for the position in an earlier Committee Report from 1961, which stated, "The advancement of the Indians towards full acceptance of the responsibilities and obligations of citizenship must be without prejudice to the retention of the cultural, historical and other economic benefits which they have inherited."[2]

It is unsurprising that the Indian Chiefs of Alberta title their response to the 1969 White Paper "Citizens Plus." The Alberta Chiefs stipulated in their first counter policy to the White Paper, "We say that the recognition of Indian status is essential for justice."[3] They go on to stipulate that most Indigenous Peoples wish to stay within Canada, but that they must retain their special rights.[4] Throughout the 1960s and 1970s the emphasis rested on the "plus" to secure Indigenous rights as a means of protecting the cultures and institutions of Indigenous Peoples. It is this political pursuit of special status that is embodied in the recognition and affirmation of Aboriginal rights in the Constitution Act of 1982. The exact contours of Aboriginal rights would need to be defined, but the basic framework for Indigenous rights is now protected by the highest law in the country. Indigenous Peoples are citizens, in that they possess the same rights as all other Canadians, and "plus" in the respect that they possess special rights related to their occupation and existence on Turtle Island prior to European colonization.

On the matter of religious freedom, Indigenous Peoples possess the freedom of conscience and religion guaranteed under section 2(a) of the Charter of Rights and Freedoms. As "Aboriginal Peoples," they possess cultural rights, including religion, under section 35 of the Constitution. Theoretically, Indigenous Peoples possess the fundamental right to freedom of religion along with Aboriginal rights that provide protections specific to Indigenous Peoples and their religious traditions.

The problem is that the courts have yet to read Charter right and Aboriginal rights together to construct a sort of "religions plus" framework for the protection of Indigenous religious traditions. The law's interpretation has been such that Charter rights and Aboriginal rights conflict with each other in both nature and application. In part, the Ktunaxa Nation raised this very concern during their 2014 case before the BCSC, only to have the matter passed over in the BCCA decision.[5] And while the SCC did not address the relationship between section 2(a) and section 35(1), we can deduce some conclusions based on the reasons of the majority. My intention here is to pursue and extend the Ktunaxa claim that there is a significant and impactful difference between the law's response to section 35(1) and section 2(a) claims.

To begin, I comparatively assess the foundations, interrelated interpretations, and qualifying standards of the two competing frameworks of rights to Indigenous religious freedom. In these opening sections, I highlight the potential and limitation of each frame and the tensions between the two before returning to *Ktunaxa Nation v. British Columbia* to demonstrate the challenges created by those differences.

Foundations and Interpretations

Section 35(1) of the Constitution Act reads, "The existing aboriginal and treaty rights of the aboriginal peoples of Canada are hereby recognized and affirmed."[6] The text of the Constitution is not specific as to the nature of Aboriginal rights. Instead, the courts have been responsible for defining the foundations of section 35(1). *R. v. Van der Peet* is a critical decision in this activity. Chief Justice Lamer stipulated, "Aboriginal rights arise from the prior occupation of land, but they also arise from the prior social organization and distinctive cultures of aboriginal peoples on that land."[7] The central question in this case was how the court may determine Aboriginal rights. On this, Chief Justice Lamer wrote, "The test for identifying the aboriginal rights recognized and affirmed by s. 35(1) must be directed at identifying the crucial elements of those pre-existing distinctive societies. It must, in other words, aim at identifying the practices, traditions and customs central to the aboriginal societies that existed in North America prior to contact with the Europeans."[8] The court provided several steps and factors in the application of the integral-to-a-distinctive-culture test. First, the chief justice explained, the court must be sensitive to the unique perspectives of Indigenous Peoples. The court stipulated that this perspective must be included with respect to the location of Aboriginal rights as a construct of Canadian law. In other words, Indigenous claims to sovereignty as an Aboriginal right will not be considered by the court. Ultimately, Lamer explains that this limitation speaks to the purpose of Aboriginal rights as a means of reconciliation between Indigenous Peoples, whose use and occupation of the land predates European settlement, and assertions of Crown sovereignty.[9]

Legal scholar Brian Slattery, in his article "The Generative Structure of Aboriginal Rights," argues that section 35 rights are understood as a panoply of interconnected generic, intermediate, and specific rights, generative in nature, historically rooted, contemporarily focused, and future-oriented. Generic rights stem from the time of Crown assertions of sovereignty over the traditional territories of Indigenous Peoples. It is understood that at that time, the Crown assumed certain responsibilities to help to reconcile the tension between its assertion of sovereignty and the pre-existence of Indigenous Peoples on the same territory.[10] Generic rights provide abstract categories of rights universally applicable to all Indigenous Peoples, related to their physical and social existence prior to European contact. Slattery identifies several generic rights, including rights to cultural integrity, self-government, honourable treatment from the Crown, and ancestral territory.

Within generic rights are intermediate rights, which continue to operate at an abstract level while serving several functions that help bring focus to the legal framework. For example, Slattery explains, "the right to practice a religion arguably qualifies as an intermediate generic right because spirituality and the performance of religious rites have always been central to Indigenous societies, a matter acknowledged in relations between the Crown and Aboriginal peoples, notably in the ceremonies attending diplomacy and treaty-making."[11] In this sense, religion can be understood as a subcategory of the abstract right of cultural integrity, while providing some direction on the specific rights related to culture in particular cases. While Slattery's categorization of rights is his own interpretation of the law, one can see this kind of reasoning as early as 1990 in *R. v. Sioui* and in the decisions in the *Ktunaxa Nation* case, both of which are discussed below.

For Slattery, intermediate rights are crucial since they help to identify what aspects of the societies of Indigenous Peoples "rise to the level of constitutional significance" and the scope and generative potential of the rights associated with such aspects.[12] Importantly, the question is one of constitutional significance and not the integrality of the cultures of Indigenous Peoples. This constitutional significance is based on intersocietal law – that is, the Indigenous and Crown laws that governed their relationship with each other. Slattery stipulates, "There is little evidence that intersocietal law ever supported a right to sleep or joke, but much that attests to a right to gain a livelihood."[13] Regardless, the important point here is that not all aspect of Indigenous cultures are deemed "integral" – a benchmark set in *Van der Peet*.

The roots of Aboriginal rights in intersocietal law, in theory, set them in conversation with, rather than fully encompassed within, the parameters of the common law. After all, common law is rooted in European law while Aboriginal rights ought to be to some extent rooted in the legal traditions of both Indigenous Peoples and the Crown. In *R. v. Sparrow*, the court inferred that Aboriginal rights are *sui generis*. Chief Justice Dickson and Justice La Forest write, "Courts must be careful to avoid the application of traditional common law concepts of property as they develop their understanding of the 'sui generis' nature of aboriginal rights."[14] Here, the court affirms the importance of including Indigenous perspectives for defining the contours of specific Aboriginal rights. Dickson and La Forest continue, "While it is impossible to give an easy definition of fishing rights, it is crucial to be sensitive to the aboriginal perspective itself on the meaning of the rights at stake."[15] John Borrows argues that the practical application of Aboriginal rights has tended to ignore the rich and diverse legal traditions of Indigenous Peoples, despite the underlying premise that they be included in the framework.[16] The fact that this remains an issue speaks to broader concerns related to the inclusion of Indigenous Peoples in decision-making processes, but, for now, the point is simply to identify a foundational element of Aboriginal rights that the upper court itself has acknowledged.

Section 35(1) also affirms and recognizes existing treaty rights. While treaties may contain specific rights, they continue to operate on the same premise as Aboriginal rights insofar as they gesture towards the contemporary reconciliation of assertions of Crown sovereignty and the pre-existence of Indigenous Peoples and institutions on the same land. This was best articulated in *R. v. Sioui*, where members of the Huron-Wendat First Nation challenged provincial legislation that prevented them from carrying out religious rituals in a Quebec provincial park. The respondents asserted that a 1760 treaty provided them with the right to practice their customs and religion. However, the treaty made no explicit reference to the space in which the exercise of customs and religion could be carried out. Ruling in favour of the Huron-Wendat First Nation in the SCC, then justice Antonio Lamer wrote, "For a freedom to have real value and meaning, it must be possible to exercise it somewhere."[17] He went on to state, "Protecting the exercise of the customs in all parts of the territory frequented when it is not incompatible with its occupancy is in my opinion the most reasonable way of reconciling the competing interests."[18] Foundationally, treaty rights are rooted in the desire for reconciliation, just as are broader Aboriginal rights.

As noted in the previous chapter, *R. v. Sparrow* stipulates that Aboriginal rights are subject to limitations. Restrictions, however, are based not in that which can be demonstrably justified in a free and democratic society – a restriction to which Charter rights are subject – but rather in the context of reconciliation and the honour of the Crown.[19] Recall that in *Sparrow*, a Musqueam man came before the courts for the use of a drift net that exceeded the length of the fishing licence provided to his community. The court unanimously agreed that Sparrow had an Aboriginal right to fish but ordered a retrial to determine whether the restrictions imposed were justifiable. According to the SCC, justifiable legislative infringements must uphold the "honour of the Crown and be in keeping with the unique contemporary relationship," and be in the pursuit of "compelling and substantial" reasons.[20]

Section 2(a), on the other hand, is firmly rooted within a Western legal framework. It is also founded on more abstract theoretical ideals rather than the historical and practical foundation of reconciliation (as articulated by the SCC in its commentary on Aboriginal rights). On a theoretical level, religious freedom is a critical feature of liberalism. In *Free to Believe: Rethinking Freedom of Conscience and Religion in Canada*, legal scholar Mary Ann Waldron argues that a free and democratic society is only possible with the protection of fundamental freedoms. She writes, "A weakening of any of the fundamental freedoms means a curtailment in the process of democratic conversation, a reduction in the opportunity for social change, and a limitation on citizens' free participation in our society."[21] For political philosopher Will Kymlicka, Charter rights, such as those of section 2(a), help to preserve the necessary cultural context for an individual or community to pursue their own definition of the good life, a cornerstone of liberalism.[22] Putting aside the elevation of liberal democratic principles into the realm of neutral universalisms for a moment, Waldron and Kymlicka tell us something about the theoretical underpinnings of religious freedom in a Canadian context. Freedom of religion is an important right for all people to engage in both self-determination and self-development. The manner by which these theoretical aspirations are interpreted and applied is, of course, a different matter.

On one hand, section 2(a) has been interpreted as a matter of equality, consistent with the theoretical underpinnings of freedom of conscience and religion. The court has described religion as a "constructively immutable" component of an individual's identity.[23] On the other hand, freedom of conscience and religion has been interpreted by the courts as a liberty, subject to restrictions in a free and democratic society. Legal scholar Richard Moon insists that the court has adopted a "weak standard" that easily allows for infringement under the *Oakes* test.[24] Despite the relatively broad definition of religion offered in *Amselem*, courts have tended to favour belief over practice. In what Moon calls an observation rather than an assertion, the court expressed the following in *Trinity Western University v. British Columbia College of Teachers*: "The freedom to hold beliefs is broader than the freedom to act on them."[25] In this case, the court determined that individuals have the right to hold homophobic beliefs rooted in a particular Christian understanding of sexuality, while outward practices of those beliefs may be justifiably limited. This decision embodies the tension between liberty and equality in rulings on section 2(a) claims.

This restriction on action is also a manifestation of the cultural underpinnings of religious freedom in Canada, which understands the freedom as predominantly a private right. Benjamin Berger explains, "The personal or private is protected space, the space in which interest and preference can guide conduct and, most crucially, the space over which the state has the weakest claim to authority. The public, by contrast, is the domain of state power and, concomitantly, governed by the demands of public reason over personal interest or preference."[26] As noted in the previous chapter, a publicly intelligible discursive legitimation is required in the public realm as a condition of religion in secular, liberal democracies. When "choice and preference" become the discursive foundations, the private sphere has been entered "and reason is no longer the guiding principle."[27] In this sense, the limits of religious freedom under section 2(a) are bound by cultural assumptions regarding the public-private divide, which manifest in the conditions of public religion.

The emphasis on belief is a constraint that has been tied back to Protestant and (interconnected) liberal epistemologies. While the current legal order may best be described as post-Protestant in nature, it is important to call attention to the residually Christian aspects of an emphasis on belief. As indicated by J.Z. Smith, the concept of religion took a significant turn towards belief after the Protestant Reformation, as if the intellectual component was privileged and external components were peripheral.[28] Donald S. Lopez, in his study of the term "belief," traces the pervasive emphasis on belief back to Christian theological debates. He writes, "The accumulated weight of this discourse has resulted in the generally unquestioned assumption that adherents of a given religion, any religion, understand that adherence in terms of belief."[29] Lopez asserts that the dominance of Christian Europe, especially in the study of religion and classification of "world religions," tended to focus on belief or belief and practice, "those deeds motivated by belief."[30] It is "belief," Lopez argues, that is "perhaps the most common term we use to describe religion to one another."[31] He writes, "The problem ... [is] whether religion *must be* represented as something that derives from belief, as something *with* external manifestations that can ultimately be traced *back to an inner assent* to a cognitive proposition, as a state of mind that *produces* practice."[32] Elizabeth Shakman Hurd adds, "In normalizing subjects for whom believing is taken as the universal defining characteristic of what it means to be religious, and the right to believe as the essence of what it means to be free, [secular states] exclude other modes of living in the world, as bodies in communities and in relationship to which they are obliged."[33]

In his contribution to *Politics of Religious Freedom*, Webb Keane explains that this attention to belief speaks to the larger cultural discourse of rationalism and discursive legitimation associated with modern secular states. It is important to remember that secular spheres are, like the law, culturally informed and carry with them particular sets of ethics, morals, and protocols. Keane writes,

> According to this moral narrative, modernity is a story of human libera-
> tion from a host of false beliefs and fetishisms that undermined free-
> dom in the past. It is a narrative in which freedom as such is pitted
> against certain forms of religion, such that their elimination (and, in
> some versions, replacement with the religion of sincere beliefs but, in
> others, with no religion at all) is a condition for the fuller realization
> of human agency. Those who persist in their fetishisms are not merely
> behind the times; by denying the agency that is properly theirs, they can
> even undermine the gains made by others, such as secular liberals, over
> the course of that long struggle.[34]

In this sense, the tendency for religious freedom to embody a more restricted freedom of belief is the product of the confluences of Protestant thought and secular ideals aligned with modernity. Keane draws our attention to the fact that the emphasis of belief over practice is not just an act of balancing – which reads the law as a neutral arbiter of competing claims – but an act of control in a desire to make the world in a particular way. In Canada, this bias emerges in the negotiation between equality and liberty, and not in the definitional parameters of religion offered in the SCC.

The interpretive parameters of religion are far less restrictive under section 35(1). As noted above, under section 2(a) the courts are more than willing to protect belief but not necessarily practice. Under section 35(1), practice was explicitly considered in *R. v. Sioui*, when the court practically observed that a right requires land on which it may be exercised. This reading of religion under section 35(1) challenges the cultural underpinning of the public-private divide ingrained with the jurisprudence on section 2(a). For this reason, it appears that section 35(1) is a more inclusive frame-work, as it escapes some of the trappings of the Eurocentric roots of section 2(a). Part of the reason for the potential of section 35(1) relates to the theoretical nature of Aboriginal rights as founded in intersocietal law. The relationship between Indigenous Peoples and the land is one of which the SCC is acutely aware, determining that such a relationship is *sui generis* and should be understood in conversation with the common law tradition (though this is often not the case).

There is an important difference in how infringements are justified under sections 2(a) and 35(1). In both cases, the courts will seek accommodation and even outright protection if the exercise of the right has little impact on Crown interests. But it is only under section 35(1) where consultation is mandated. Under the Aboriginal rights framework, infringement, if approved, is ideally done in consultation between the state and Indigenous Peoples. The court, for its part, weighs in when the accommodations are deemed unsatisfactory by Indigenous Peoples. At the foundation of consultation is the honour of the Crown, which refers to the Crown's obligation to recognize and respect the rights of Indigenous Peoples, who consist of unconquered communities in existence long before Europeans came to the continent.[35]

While I provide a separate analysis, drawing on different sources and arriving at different conclusions, it is appropriate for me to acknowledge that I share many of the same critical observations of John Borrows in "Living Law on a Living Earth: Aboriginal Religion, Law, and the Constitution." Borrows examines the theoretical potential of the Constitution to protect Anishinaabe religion. Borrows argues for a reading of Anishinabek law alongside the Canadian constitutional order to provide insight into the human relationship with a living Earth.[36] For Borrows, the moral community must extend to include the land, which results in certain rights and responsibilities. This is a major divergence from common law perspectives on land.[37] While Borrows sees potential in section 2(a), he argues that the requirement to treat the land as a living entity stretches the Charter beyond its "cultural context," rendering the right "unproductive" for Anishinabek peoples.[38] Borrows, too, emphasizes the potential value of section 35(1) in the obligations it demands upon the state but, ultimately, he believes the constitutional order has a long way to go before recognizing the significance of a living Earth.[39]

Qualifying as a Right

In *R. v. Van der Peet*, Chief Justice Lamer explained, "The claimant must demonstrate that the practice, custom or tradition was a central and significant part of the society's distinctive culture."[40] He further stipulated, "The court cannot look at those aspects of the aboriginal society that are true of every human society (e.g., eating to survive)."[41] In *Van der Peet*, the court understands the investigation of Aboriginal rights as a historical endeavour located at the time of contact. According to this decision, Aboriginal rights today refer to specific customs, practices, and traditions continuous with pre-contact societies of Indigenous Peoples. John Borrows is critical of the *Van der Peet* decision. He writes, "When constitutional limits are placed on spirituality's development, the law stoops even lower. It denies Aboriginal people protection of the inner means to cope with the physical impoverishment that often developed as a result of European contact."[42] He continues, "This culturally biased categorization diminishes Aboriginal religion's substance. It severely decreases the protection available for Aboriginal practices in the modern world and degrades the court's role as a champion of 'human rights.'"[43]

The courts qualified the historically located understanding of Aboriginal rights present in *Van der Peet* in subsequent decisions. In *R. v. Sappier, R. v. Gray*, the subject of harvesting timber for non-commercial use among the Mi'kmaq and Maliseet was brought before the court.[44] The court determined "that the jurisprudence weighs in favour of protecting the traditional means of survival of an aboriginal community."[45] Here, Slattery argues, the court effectively acknowledges the intermediate generic right of sustenance. However, the court firmly understands sustenance as the historical means of sustenance of the Mi'kmaq and Maliseet and not sustenance in general, but this does not mean that such practices must continue to be acted upon as they were prior to contact with Europeans. On this, Justice Michel Bastarache writes,

> If aboriginal rights are not permitted to evolve and take modern forms,
> then they will become utterly useless. Surely the Crown cannot be

suggesting that the respondents, all of whom live on a reserve, would be limited to building wigwams. If such were the case, the doctrine of aboriginal rights would truly be limited to recognizing and affirming a narrow subset of "anthropological curiosities," and our notion of aboriginality would be reduced to a small number of outdated stereotypes. The cultures of the aboriginal peoples who occupied the lands now forming Canada prior to the arrival of the Europeans, and who did so while living in organized societies with their own distinctive ways of life, cannot be reduced to wigwams, baskets and canoes.[46]

The specific measures of these rights can only be determined on a case-by-case basis, since all Indigenous Peoples possess unique cultural forms. Despite this nuanced reading of *Van der Peet*, the historical requirement is not bypassed in *Sappier/Gray*.

As a set of rights that are, at least theoretically, in conversation with the Euro-Canadian legal tradition, Aboriginal rights are not individual rights but rather collective rights. In a case on Aboriginal hunting rights, *R. v. Sundown*, Justice Peter Cory stipulated, "Any interest in the hunting cabin is a collective right that is derived from the treaty and the traditional expeditionary method of hunting. It belongs to the Band as a whole and not to Mr. Sundown or any individual member of the Joseph Bighead First Nation."[47] This too is rooted in the reconciliatory nature of Aboriginal rights, for such rights are based on a nation-to-nation relationship and not an individual-to-state one. Any right granted to an individual of a particular First Nation could be read as the exclusion of other members of that First Nation who possess the same rights, as noted by Justice Cory in the *Sundown* case.[48]

On the matter of section 2(a), the court has demonstrated a growing uneasiness with talking theology or assessing the authenticity of religious claims. The depth of one's individual sincerity is the relatively easy benchmark established in *Amselem*. Given its significance for my argument here, I quote Justice Iacobucci at length:

Assessment of sincerity is a question of fact that can be based on several non-exhaustive criteria, including the credibility of a claimant's testimony ... as well as an analysis of whether the alleged belief is consistent with his or her other current religious practices. It is important to underscore, however, that it is inappropriate for courts rigorously to study and focus on the past practices of claimants in order to determine whether their current beliefs are sincerely held. Over the course of a lifetime, individuals change and so can their beliefs. Religious beliefs, by their very nature, are fluid and rarely static. A person's connection to or relationship with the divine or with the subject or object of his or her spiritual faith, or his or her perceptions of religious obligation emanating from such a relationship, may well change and evolve over time. Because of the vacillating nature of religious belief, a court's inquiry into sincerity, if anything, should focus not on past practice or past belief but on a person's belief at the time of the alleged interference with his or her religious freedom.[49]

The court, of course, still must "talk theology" to some degree when assessing proportionality. The courts must determine the real impact government action may have on a religious community. If they say that it impacts a community minimally, they have made an assertion about the value of some aspect of a religion. What the court does not do, however, is judge the authenticity or historical roots of any particular religion. Section 2(a) embraces the fluid and adaptive and even potential spontaneous nature of religious experience even if it is significantly constrained to belief in its application.

On matters of religious freedom, the most obvious distinction between sections 35(1) and 2(a) is the way in which courts recognize whether a particular activity or belief passes the threshold of being a valid claim. Under section 2(a), sincerity is the benchmark. Here, courts seek to avoid playing the role of religious expert by allowing individuals to define themselves as religious people. Under section 35(1), the court must take on the role of anthropologist, historian, and archaeologist to assess the legitimacy of a communal claim to religious identity. In this sense, section 2(a) is favourable. Despite the fact that the court has demonstrated flexibility in the assessment of the integral-to-a-distinctive-culture test (as we see in *Sappier/Gray*), the religious right is still historically located. New revelations, important for the development and maintenance of

Indigenous religions (discussed in the next chapter), are not protected under the section 35(1) framework. Under section 2(a), the court in *Syndicat Northcrest v. Amselem* specifically removed history from the assessment process, whereas under section 35(1), sincerity is not a pivotal subject under consideration.

One of the more striking differences between section 2(a) and section 35(1) is the subject of communal rights. There is a tendency to emphasize the individualistic nature of rights frameworks in liberal democracies. Canada, though, has demonstrated a tolerance and even embrace of group rights in its history. Aboriginal rights is the obvious example, but rights for the protection of separate schooling are also protected in section 29 of the Charter.[50] In *Loyola High School v. Quebec*, the court determined that section 2(a) applied to a Québécois Catholic community as a group.[51] What may surprise some observers is that the particularly noteworthy distinction of section 35(1) is that it is actually *limited* to group rights and not that section 2(a) is constrained to individual rights (which is, in fact, not the case). This has serious implications. For instance, if a sacred knowledge keeper is privy to information to which no one else has access, their knowledge could be considered individual. A claim of a violation of Aboriginal rights may then fall outside the realm of section 35(1), as was the case in *Ktunaxa Nation v. British Columbia*.

Ktunaxa Nation v. British Columbia

On one hand, section 2(a) provides a rubric for the fundamental freedom of conscience and religion for all Canadians, though the court continues to struggle with the delicate balance of individual freedoms in a diverse democratic society. Section 2(a) is a freedom rooted primarily in belief and, to a limited extent, practice. Under this framework, the court acknowledges the sincerity of belief rather than its authenticity. The reason for this is that the court has recognized the dynamic nature of religion. The court seeks to determine whether a particular belief or practice is significant to an individual (or community), not the authenticity of that particular element within a given religious tradition. At the same time, wider societal interests and accompanying legislative actions of certain objectives limit section 2(a) when those interests are considered "pressing and substantial." While scholars have criticized the courts for, at times, the ease with which infringement is justified in section 2(a) cases, the underpinnings of public interest and human equality are important features of liberal democratic states.

On the other hand, "religion" operates within section 35(1) as an intermediate generic right related to the distinctive cultures of Indigenous Peoples. This right is best understood as an intermediate cultural right operating with the same foundations and limitations as any other Aboriginal right. Using *Van der Peet* as the definitive case on the generic right, culture refers to the customs, traditions, and practices integral to the distinctive traditions of Indigenous Peoples. From Slattery's perspective, "the right to practice a religion has a uniform scope, which does not vary from one Aboriginal people to another. However, the particular activities, rites, and institutions protected by the right differ from group to group, depending on their specific religious outlook."[52] Slattery's terms "activities, rites, and institutions" are offered as examples of the kinds of cultural elements related to the broader generic and intermediate rights rather than a definitive list of specific rights. These rights are collective, historically locatable, and *sui generis*. In *Ktunaxa Nation*, the BCSC describes these as "spiritual rights."[53]

In 1991, Glacier Resort Ltd proposed the construction of a year-round ski resort near Invermere, British Columbia. At the outset, the Ktunaxa/Kinbasket Tribal Council (KKTC) expressed the necessity of consultation and accommodation since the proposed resort fell within their land claims territory. The KKTC also expressed concern that the resort may have serious implications for their cultural heritage and religion. Recall from chapter 1, the Ktunaxa know the area as Qat'muk and consider it the home of the Grizzly Bear Spirit. While the area is only used in a limited manner for ceremonial reasons, the space holds cosmological significance, giving meaning to Ktunaxa ceremonies and identity. Glacier was granted rights to the region in 1993 and the province, through the

Commission on Resources and Environment, determined that a resort was an acceptable use of the space. Following the commission approval, a ten-year environmental assessment took place, concluding in 2004.

Several reports were created over the course of the review, including one by the Environment Assessment Office titled "First Nations Socio-Economic Assessment: Jumbo Glacier Resort Project, A Genuine Wealth Analysis." This report makes it clear that religion is an important and sensitive subject warranting more attention. A portion of the report cited by the court reads, "The expressions of the sacred and 'priceless' value of the Jumbo/Quatmu by many of the First Nations people should not be underestimated. As economists, we could interpret this situation as a revealed preference of no development under any circumstances with an 'infinite price' tag."[54] Following the environmental assessment, Glacier was able to come to terms with the Shuswap Band but not the Ktunaxa. At this time, the KKTC, which was representing both groups, disbanded and the Ktunaxa Nation continued consultation with the resort company. Concerns regarding the sacredness of the space were raised again in a gap analysis in 2006 after Glacier and the Ktunaxa were unable to reach an agreement. Following a series of workshops on land use, the minister of Forests, Lands, and Natural Resources was led to believe that Glacier and the Ktunaxa were close to an agreement.

Early in 2008, the Ktunaxa rejected an accommodation proposal from the minister on financial grounds without reference to spiritual matters. However, a second accommodation proposal put forth by the minister was rejected with reference to the sacredness of the space. The Ktunaxa then proposed further consultation to address their concerns, not specifically mentioning the sacredness of the site as a main point of discussion. The minister accepted this proposal, stipulating that the pending issues were matters of interest and that the project could move forward while consultation continued. In June 2009, the minister met with the Ktunaxa and their council, where they voiced their concern that consultation on the subject of the sacredness of the site had not been fulfilled.

They explained that sacred knowledge was considered secret and only possessed by certain individuals in the community. The minister agreed to extend consultation to hear from the Elder specified by the Ktunaxa. In September 2009, the Ktunaxa, along with Chris Luke, Sr, the knowledge keeper identified earlier that year, articulated that no middle ground was possible and that any movement of the Earth would violate the sacredness of the site. This position was articulated again in 2010 in the *Qat'muk Declaration*.[55] Included with this declaration was a statement on stewardship principles associated with the space.

In 2012, the minister approved the master development plan for the ski resort. In his justification for this decision, the minister made a number of important statements regarding the religious claims of the Ktunaxa. The minister found that the Crown had fulfilled its obligation of consultation and sought reasonable accommodation of the spiritual concerns of the Ktunaxa. The "no middle ground" position was weakened, according to the minister, because knowledge of the inviolability of the site was not widespread among the Ktunaxa. The minister also felt there was little evidence to support the inviolability position under the integral-to-a-distinctive-culture test set out in *Van der Peet*. This test would require proof on the part of the Ktunaxa that the right would have been exercised prior to assertions of Crown sovereignty. Additionally, the minister concluded that since practices took place mainly on the reserve and one other site, continued access to portions of the controlled recreation area was sufficient accommodation.[56]

The task before the court was to determine whether the minister had violated the Ktunaxa Nation's rights under sections 35(1) and 2(a). On the subject of section 35(1), the Crown did not object to the fact that it had an obligation to consult with and accommodate the Ktunaxa Nation, whose traditional lands were affected by the project. The question was whether the Crown had done enough, in particular with respect to the cultural rights protected under section 35(1). While I take up this subject in greater detail in chapter 5, it is important to note that the current framework for consultation and accommodation is, as Chief Justice McLachlin appropriately identifies, about due process and not outcome.[57] The amount of accommodation granted is based on the severity of the potential infringement on Aboriginal rights. This process does not grant First Nations veto power.[58] In addition, rights cannot be framed as a demand on the state that dictates they are unable to carry out a particular activity.[59] As noted in chapter 2, section 35(1) is subject to the politics of compromise and negotiation.

The test for the existence of Aboriginal cultural rights under section 35(1) was, as mentioned, set forth in *Van der Peet*. Within this framework, the Ktunaxa must prove that their spiritual practices and beliefs associated with the space predate European contact. In other words, in order to be granted significant accommodation under section 35(1), the Ktunaxa must prove that the resort seriously violates a pre-contact practice or belief related to the location of the proposed resort.

The BCSC took issue with the Ktunaxa claim on the subject of the inviolability of the space as a pre-contact perspective. The "no middle ground" position was, in the court's view, raised too late in the process to indicate that it was a belief that predated the Crown assertion of sovereignty. Justice Savage writes,

> The evidence discloses that the Ktunaxa are secretive in their spiritual beliefs. However, there is no evidence that the specific belief at issue here, namely that a development in the nature of the Proposed Resort is fundamentally inimical to Ktunaxa religion, is one which was not revealed earlier because of secrecy concerns. In other words, the spiritual belief on which the "no middle ground" position is based is of recent understanding rather than being a longstanding belief that was kept secret. This belief is first explained in the affidavit of a single knowledge holder. The ancillary affidavits do not suggest that this position stems from concerns or teachings learned from any other knowledge holders ... [There] is no suggestion that the "no middle ground" position reflects a specific belief of ancient or earlier origins.[60]

Later in the decision, Savage affirmed the sacredness of the site to the Ktunaxa, but stipulated that most of the actual ceremonies take place on two sites and that the continued access to the region by Glacier will provide them opportunity to continue their spiritual beliefs and practices.[61]

On the section 35(1) claim, the court did not consider the "no middle ground" position, arguing that it was not consistent with communal or pre-contact customs and traditions of the Ktunaxa Nation. It is clear that the court took on the task of anthropologist, historian, and even theologian in assessing the exclusion of the "no middle ground" position. However, it is important to note that the land was an integral part of the section 35(1) discussion, even if it was only about ceremonially specific sites. It is also important to note that the very nature of a comment on Aboriginal rights recognizes the fact that Indigenous Peoples were here prior to the existence of European settlers.

On the matter of religious freedom, the main question the court sought to answer was whether the master development agreement infringes the Ktunaxa section 2(a) right. Savage agreed that this was a matter of religion, even if certain revelations were quite new. He writes, "Nor, in my view, is recent revelation necessarily inconsistent with a genuinely held religious belief. I accept ... that the Ktunaxa's spiritual beliefs and practices are sincere and have a nexus with religion."[62] In contrast to the section 35(1) claim, this included the "no middle ground" position.

Earlier in the book, I asked readers to set aside a claim made by the BCSC: "The otherwise lawful use of land by others is not a form of coercion or a constraint on freedom of religion."[63] This "lawful use by others" clause substantially differentiates section 35(1) claims from section 2(a) claims. The BCCA, which focused almost exclusively on the section 2(a) claim of the Ktunaxa Nation, provided a troubling clarification of the ahistorical reading of Charter rights. Following an assertion that religion is something that finds its appropriate home in the private sphere, Justice Goepel writes, "In essence, the Ktunaxa submit that s. 2(a) includes within its ambit the freedom to, on the basis of an asserted religious belief, control (or at least modify) the behaviour of others on their own property, so as to preserve, to the fullest extent possible, the vitality of their religious community."[64] Here, the court effectively distils religion from the domain of power, reconceptualizing the claim to a violation of religious freedom in a colonial context of dispossessed lands into a private imposition of restrictions on the part of the Ktunaxa Nation on public land. Referencing the SCC decision in *Loyola High School v. Quebec*, where the court found that the teaching of Catholic values in a Catholic high school was protected under section 2(a) since no demands were made on non-members, Justice Goepel made the following claim: "It is not, in my view, consonant with the underpinning principles of the Charter to say that a group, in asserting a protected right under s. 2(a) that implicates the vitality of their religious community, is then capable of restraining and restricting the behaviour of others who do not share that belief in the name of preserving subjective religious meaning."[65] Possessing a right rooted in equality, the Ktunaxa have the right to believe whatever they choose, but when it comes to the practice of that belief, liberty is limited. Given the size of the area in question, Goepel went as far to assert that support of the Ktunaxa claim may violate the Charter rights of other Canadians, as if a Catholic high school and Qat'muk are commensurable.

For their part, the Ktunaxa argued that sections 2(a) and 35(1) are so different that justification cannot be assessed in the same manner in both cases. The court felt this matter was a non-issue, stipulating that the minister's consideration of Charter implications would have added little to the case.[66] Goepel clarified, "This is neither the rejection nor the acceptance of the Ktunaxa assertion that the balancing of *Charter* values with statutory objectives is fundamentally different than the balancing of asserted but unproven Aboriginal rights with competing societal interests."[67] In effect, the court sidestepped the discussion altogether.

The Supreme Court decision offers little clarification in the way of a comparison between section 2(a) and section 35(1), since the majority denied that the object of belief is protected under section 2(a). Despite this, the SCC continued to affirm striking differences between the two legal frameworks. Despite rejecting the section 2(a) claim altogether, Chief Justice McLachlin declared that the sincerity of the Ktunaxa claim and the "no middle ground" position were beliefs worthy of protection under section 2(a) (even if the object of belief was not).[68] In contrast, the SCC affirmed the minister's choice to reject accommodations of the "no middle ground" position. The chief justice wrote, "The Minister did not have evidence that the Ktunaxa were asserting a particular practice that took place in Qat'muk prior to contact. The Late-2009 Claim seemed designed to require a particular accommodation rather than to assert and support a particular pre-contact practice, custom, or tradition that took place on the territory in question."[69] In this sense, the diachronic nature of the Ktunaxa religion is recognized under section 2(a) and rejected under the Aboriginal rights framework because of the supposed newness and individual nature of the revelation, a subject to which I return in the next chapter.

Recall that the chief justice limited the scope of religious freedom to belief and the manifestation of belief.[70] McLachlin justified this limitation by citing several international mechanisms on religious freedom, including the Universal Declaration of Human Rights and the International Covenant on Civil and Political Rights, among others.[71] Unsurprisingly, McLachlin uses these Western legal documents to justify the Western contours of the Charter right. In contrast, reconciliation and the honour of the Crown are cited as foundational principles of section 35(1) claims.[72] The Ktunaxa witnessed the strengths, weaknesses, and tensions of sections 2(a) and 35(1) claims first-hand. Brought together before the courts and yet read separately, the limitations of each framework were troubling and unmistakably clear.

Conclusion

Ktunaxa Nation v. British Columbia provides important insight into the tensions and limitations of two legal frameworks that do not seem to work together, despite addressing the same content. When section 2(a) is pushed to its colonial limits within its Euro-Canadian common law framework, section 35(1) offers opportunities of redress incapable of realization under the Charter protection. At the same time, when section 35(1) is pushed to its historicized limit, section 2(a) offers necessary correctives. Together, the frameworks ought to be a sort of "religions plus," in line with the desires of H.B. Hawthorn and the Indian Chiefs of Alberta. Demands for authenticity under one framework are challenged by the prioritization of sincerity in another. While colonialism is recognized as a reality of the modern Indigenous-state relationship in one, it is denied in another. From *Amselem* to *Van der Peet* and *Sioui* to *Trinity Western*, the tensions are not subtle. It would appear that Indigenous Peoples are either just citizens or just a specially protected group, but not both.

Some readers of the SCC decision in *Ktunaxa Nation* may be surprised that the United Nations Declaration on the Rights of Indigenous Peoples is not mentioned in the chief justice's list of binding and non-binding international mechanisms on religious freedom.[73] It is less surprising – as I noted in *Policy Options* shortly after the SCC decision – when we realize that, under the Charter, Indigenous Peoples are *not recognized* as Indigenous Peoples to which the Crown possesses reconciliatory responsibilities in the context of the colonial occupation of Indigenous territories.[74] This is a significant limitation of section 2(a). While the Charter right to freedom of conscience and religion appears more than capable of addressing the challenge of diversity, it is overwhelmingly limited by all other challenges presented in the introduction to this book. At this time, we can leave section 2(a) behind as both hollow and useless for the protection of the cosmologically significant spaces of Indigenous Peoples. Having cast aside section 2(a), our attention must now turn to critical features of section 35(1). We begin with the challenge posed by diachronic and diverse cultures in the context of the integral-to-a-distinctive-culture test as outlined in *R. v. Van der Peet*. The rejection of the "no middle ground" position from consideration under section 35(1) in the *Ktunaxa Nation* case raises important questions about how lived religious traditions are treated by the state.

chapter four

Dealing with Diversity Poorly and the Gustafsen Lake Standoff

Since the seventeenth century, Indigenous Peoples of North America have lived within colonial structures that attempted to regulate nearly every aspect of their lives.[1] Central to this project were the false stereotypes of Indigenous Peoples. To be an "Indian" meant one was uncivilized and incapable of participating in politics or owning land. To be an "Indian" and not a Christian meant one was untrustworthy and without a sense of morality. As noted earlier, attitudes towards Indigenous Peoples began to change following the Second World War as many countries, including Canada, embraced principles of individual freedom and human rights. The adoption of an official policy of religious freedom was particularly important given the state's previous efforts to destroy Indigenous religious traditions. As I have discussed throughout this book, the state accepts the fact that Indigenous religious traditions are important facets of contemporary life for Indigenous Peoples in Canada; however, this does not mean that pervasive stereotypes of Indigenous Peoples and their religious traditions do not continue to complicate and disturb Indigenous-state relations.

Two interconnected problems persist. First, the state understands Indigenous religious traditions as relics of the distant past, which means that the state does not recognize these traditions as diachronic (i.e., undergoing continual historical change) in nature. Second, given the fact that the state fixes Indigenous religious traditions historically, outsider observations of heterogeneity and diversity, and internal debates of authenticity and authority, pose unique problems for the legal protection of Indigenous religious traditions, ceremonies, and spaces. In other words, the state, in its formal dealings with Indigenous Peoples, does not indicate that it fully grasps or recognizes the complexity of contemporary Indigenous religious traditions, and this misunderstanding of or failure to recognize the complexity of Indigenous religions has negative consequences for the future of those religions.

The focus of this chapter is twofold. First, I contrast the diverse and diachronic nature of Indigenous religious traditions with a colonial discourse that, for the most part, portrays them as homogeneous and fixed in a historical past. In this colonial activity, many Euro-Canadians – more importantly state representatives – reject the "newness" of Indigenous religions that have developed through, in the words of Tracy Leavelle, "contact and combination"[2] and the natural processes of development and diversification. Second, related to this exclusion, I examine how the identification of state-instituted Indigenous political representation as religious authorities may perpetuate stereotypes of homogeneity and ignore cultural change and difference. My purpose here is not to make a normative claim regarding state-instituted Indigenous governance but rather, more simply, to identify diverse perspectives on Indigenous leadership, through prominent Indigenous scholars, intertribal communities, and religious communities, and to highlight how these views, at times, may conflict with each other.

The failure to grasp or recognize difference is not simply a nuisance but a component of colonial discourse that determines agency-subjectivity and power. The state cannot equate "authentic" Indigenous religions with historically located traditions if it wishes to understand when Indigenous religious traditions are present and important. Nor can it necessarily rely on the bureaucratic structures *it* has created to regulate Indigenous-state relations for an answer. We have already been introduced to the challenge of diversity through Winnifred Fallers Sullivan and her testimony in the *Werner* case, discussed at the outset of this book. Recall that Sullivan claimed it was impossible to capture the diversity of the American religious landscape in any singular legal construct, as each individual may practice their tradition differently. Even if there are those who claim they are knowledgeable in the ortho-doxy of a tradition, practitioners may respectfully disagree.

To lay the foundations for this argument, we begin with an examination of the complexity of cultural difference in the con-text of the colonial discourse. Through Homi Bhabha's influential work *The Location of Culture*, I identify the dominating and com-mon colonial "stereotype" and "fixity" in the interpretation of diachronic "cultures of survival." Through Bhabha, the political implications of this discourse are identifiable, referencing Indig-enous scholar Taiaiake Alfred and his congruent criticism of con-temporary Canadian state praxis and Indigenous leadership. Following this, I examine the state's tendency to authenticate Indigenous Peoples and their religious traditions through historici-zation and the problem with this practice, especially in the context of a modern revival of Indigenous religions. Given the broad range of Indigenous religious traditions, and the ceremonies that exist among the many varied and diverse communities of Indigenous Peoples on Turtle Island, the second half of this chapter focuses on one ceremony as an exemplary case: the development and spread of the Sun Dance and its complicated transmission and translation for some Indigenous Peoples. We conclude with an analysis of the Gustafsen Lake Sun Dance and subsequent standoff in the inte-rior of British Columbia in 1995. The Sun Dance demonstrates the diachronic nature of Indigenous religions in a persisting colonial discourse and the potential dangers of rejecting and marginaliz-ing the newness of Indigenous spiritual practices and affiliations. Claims of violations of religious freedom initiated the tension at Gustafsen Lake, and the state's reluctance to acknowledge religion as an important component of the confrontation and its persistent attempts to deal with elected Secwepemc leaders, whom the Sun Dancers did not recognize, exacerbated the situation. Further com-plicating meaningful dialogue was the state's coordinated attempt to silence and discredit occupiers.

This chapter takes a noticeable turn from the legal focus of the previous chapters. It is important to remember that the courts are the final option for Indigenous Peoples on matters of religious freedom. It is only when there is a failure on the part of the state to recognize and protect Indigenous religions that cases come before the courts. The courts, for their part, assess whether compromise, negotiation, and discursive legitimation have been offered in the process that triggered a religious freedom concern in the first place. The court itself has its own challenges when it comes to Indigenous religious freedom, but the continuing impact of colonialism manifests internally in how the state and society view and understand Indigenous religions. For this reason, this chapter moves from the courtroom to the barricade, another site of the Indigenous-state relationship.

The Politics and Complexity of Cultural Difference

The support of a nation-to-nation relationship may help to address some of the broader issues of injustice identified within contemporary Indigenous-state relations, but what of the more specific subject of cultural difference within the communities of Indigenous Peoples? This question is crucial, for it speaks to a tension that arises when specific identity claims collide with the political power that comes with a consolidated claim to national identity. Or, as Homi Bhabha put it, the promotion of one nation with a singular homogeneous, repeating culture is a product of "cultures' own structured demand for imitation and identification."[3] However, culture is not predictable, consistent, and static. As Bhabha argues, culture is "an uneven, incomplete production of meaning and value, often composed of incommensurable demands and practices, produced in the act of social survival."[4] In a colonial situation, Bhabha argues, the culture of survival stands in contrast to prevailing myths of national culture. He writes, "The transmission of *cultures of survival* does not occur in the ordered *museé imaginaire* of national cultures with their claims to the continuity of an authentic 'past' and a living 'present.'"[5] Even in these "cultures of survival," however, there exists diversity and change. In other words, minority cultures in a colonial context, such as those of Indigenous Peoples, are heterogeneous modes of resistance.

In the introduction to *The Location of Culture*, Bhabha asks the following question: "How do strategies of representation or empowerment come to be formulated in the competing claims of communities where, despite shared histories of deprivation and discrimination, the exchange of values, meanings and priorities may not always be collaborative and dialogical, but may be profoundly antagonistic, conflictual and even incommensurable?"[6] Bhabha contends that colonial discourse understands the difference of the "Other" as a homogeneous, "recognizable totality" existing without change or complexity.[7] These important tools of "stereotype" and "fixity" frame cultures of the "Other" as both unchanging and repetitive and backwards and disorderly. He argues that this positioning of culture is "continually under threat from diachronic forms of history and narrative, signs of instability."[8] The result is that minorities in "the opinion of the liberal public sphere ... are relegated to a distanced sense of belonging elsewhere."[9]

The imposition of concepts of "stereotype" and "fixity" are particularly devastating for communities of Indigenous Peoples. In effect, colonialism supports a "teleology" where "the native is progressively reformable" and a visible separation between the colonial power and the colonized, "which, in denying the colonized the capacities of self-government, independence, [and] Western modes of civility, lends authority to the official version and mission of colonial power."[10] This understanding of "native" populations translates into systems of governance both within and over the community. Bhabha writes,

By "knowing" the native population in these terms, discriminatory and authoritarian forms of political control are considered appropriate. The colonized population is then deemed to be both the cause and effect of the system, imprisoned in the circle of interpretation. What is visible is the necessity of such rule which is justified by those moralistic and normative ideologies of amelioration recognized as the Civilizing Mission or the White Man's Burden. However, there coexist within the same apparatus of colonial power, modern systems and sciences of government, progressive "Western" forms of social and economic organization which provide the manifest justification for the project of colonialism ... It is on the site of this coexistence that strategies of hierarchization and marginalization are employed in the management of colonial societies.[11]

It is exactly this perspective of state-sanctioned structures of governance that leads Mohawk philosopher Taiaiake Alfred to reject the systems of governance enacted by the Canadian government. Alfred writes,

> The fact is that neither the state-sponsored modifications to colonial-municipal models (imposed in Canada through the Indian Act ...) nor the corporate or public-government systems recently negotiated in the North constitute Indigenous governments at all. Potentially representing the final solution to the white society's "Indian Problem," they use the co-operation of Native leaders in the design and implementation of such systems to legitimize the state's long-standing assimilationist goals for Indigenous nations and lands.[12]

Alfred continues by asserting that very little has changed in the way of Euro-Canadian perceptions of Indigenous Peoples as primitive, backwards, and in need of help. Alfred contends that the state selectively engages only those Indigenous Peoples that conform to the persistent colonial project of "civilizing" Indigenous Peoples. He argues that the state manipulates "lines of cleavage" within the Indigenous identity to legitimate its own systems of control. Alfred acknowledges a diversity of perspectives but qualifies those diverse identifications with the colonial encounter and the level of decolonization of consciousness one has undergone. He identifies these points on the "spectrum of identity" as follows:

1. The traditional nationalist represents the values, principles, and approaches of an Indigenous cultural perspective that accepts no compromise with the colonial structure.
2. The secular nationalist represents an incomplete or unfulfilled Indigenous perspective, stripped of its spiritual element and oriented almost solely toward confronting colonial perspectives.

3. The tribal pragmatist represents an interest-based calculation, a perspective that merges Indigenous and mainstream values toward the integration of Native communities within colonial structures.
4. The racial minority ("of Indian descent") represents Western values – a perspective completely separate from Indigenous cultures and supportive of the colonial structures that are the sole source of Native identification.[13]

Stereotypes of an uncivilized people help to both legitimate colonial power and illegitimate Indigenous diversity. Alfred claims that the state seeks Indigenous Peoples from the latter two categories, ignoring those in the first two. He believes that seeking change within the system is naive and a proven method of failure.

In many ways, Alfred is describing what Bhabha calls the "singularity of difference" perpetuated by colonialism.[14] Bhabha contends that scholarship urgently needs to address these singularities, which postcolonial theorists call the homogenization of the "Other." In his chapter "How Newness Enters the World," Bhabha explains that the complexity of difference is an important aspect of "agency in a form of the 'future' where the past is not originary, where the present is not simply transitory."[15] He continues, "The 'newness' of migrant or minority discourse has to be discovered *in medias res*: a newness that is not part of the 'progressivist' division between past and present, or the archaic and the modern; nor is it a 'newness' that can be contained in the mimesis of 'original and copy.'"[16] This "newness" may even be a point of contestation within communities.

One may wonder how to discern the "newness" Bhabha speaks of in relation to the culture(s) from within which it emerges. Tradition still plays an important role in "newness." He explains, "The 'right' to signify from the periphery of authorized power and privilege does not depend on the persistence of tradition; it is resourced by the power of tradition to be reinscribed through the conditions of contingency and contradictoriness that attend upon the lives of those who are 'in the minority.'"[17]

Unlike Bhabha, I am not concerned with the "creation of agency through incommensurable (not simply multiple) positions" in the discourse of minorities.[18] Rather, my intention is much simpler and modest. Colonial discourse tends to homogenize and fixate the "Other" (such as Indigenous Peoples), and that act has manifested itself in particular structures of power and governance. Minority communities and their cultures are neither homogeneous nor fixed in a historical past that has already written their futures. If one understands agency as intimately connected to self-determination, and self-determination is an important facet of justice, then matters of diversity and homogenization require attention.

With respect to the subject of justice for Indigenous Peoples in contemporary Canada, two important and interconnected points of interest emerge from Bhabha's analysis of diversity. The first point concerns the perpetuation of stereotypes of an "imaginary Indian" that simultaneously dominates Indigenous Peoples through its own implemented systems of governance and confirms the value and worth of its own colonial ambitions of superiority and universality. The second is the treatment of Indigenous religions and ceremonies as static, unchanging traditions of the past as opposed to diachronic components of a culture of survival.

The "Imaginary Indian" and Indigenous Religious Traditions

In 1899, the government of Canada enlisted poet Charles Mair to carry out negotiations pertaining to Treaty 8. He remarked that the Indigenous Peoples he met in northern Alberta were not the "Indians" he had come to imagine. Instead, Mair wrote,

> There presented itself a body of respectable-looking men, as well dressed and evidently quite as independent in their feelings as any like number of average pioneers in the East ... One was prepared, in this wild region of forest, to behold some savage types of men; indeed, I craved to renew the vanished scenes of old. But, alas! One beheld,

instead, men with well-washed unpainted faces, and combed and common hair; men in suits of ordinary store-clothes, and some even with "boiled" if not laundered shirts. One felt disappointed, even defrauded. It was not what was expected, what we believed we had a right to expect, after so much waggoning and tracking and drenching and river turmoil and trouble.[19]

In the opening chapter of *The Imaginary Indian: The Image of the Indian in Canadian Culture*, historian Daniel Francis juxtaposes Mair's account and his own modern-day encounter with Indigenous Peoples. Francis recalls that he came to realize his preconceived notions of "Indians" were simply untrue. He contends that he did not come to imagine "Indians" in isolation but instead amidst a culture in which "public discourse about Native people still deals in stereotypes." "[Euro-Canadian] views of what constitutes an Indian today are," Francis asserts, "as much bound up with myth, prejudice and ideology as earlier versions were."[20] The "imaginary Indian" is a pervasive myth rooted deep within the Euro-Canadian colonial past that manifests both in popular perceptions of Indigenous Peoples and in state legislation. In particular, Francis points to the perception that Indigenous cultures were primitive and undeveloped while Euro-Canadian culture was superior. As a result, government policies and residential schools sought to correct Indigenous Peoples in accordance with popular prejudice. The space in which these cultures engage each other is contingent upon power. Francis argues that the group that "enjoys advantages of wealth or power or technology ... will usually try to impose its stereotypes on the other."[21] He concludes that as long as the state continues to deal with an "imaginary Indian," they are silencing the voices of real Indigenous Peoples.

The pervasive myth of Indigenous Peoples who exist in some far-off past is a perception that continues to dictate state decisions regarding Indigenous religions in both Canada and the United States. In particular, there is an overwhelming assumption that Indigenous cultures are historical rather than modern.

Vine Deloria Jr wrote the following regarding historicization and authenticity for Native American religions:

> In denying the possibility of the continuing revelation of the sacred in our lives, federal courts, scholars and state and federal agencies refuse to accord credibility to the testimony of religious leaders, demand evidence that a ceremony or location has always been central to the belief and practices of the tribe, and impose exceedingly rigorous standards on Indians who appear before them. This practice does exactly what the Supreme Court avows is not to be done – it allows the courts to rule on the substance of religious belief and practice. In other words, courts will protect a religion if it shows every symptom of being dead but will severely restrict it if it appears to be alive.[22]

Building upon Deloria's argument, Tracy Leavelle argues that perceptions of Indigenous religions as historical artefacts continue a legacy of colonialism that understands Indigenous religions as primitive and misguided. Leavelle concludes that the state ignores, marginalizes, and dismisses contemporary forms of Indigenous religions altered by "contact and combination."[23] The state has proven it is willing to protect "pure" forms of Indigenous religions despite the fact that their very nature is diachronic.

Deloria argues that the problem rests in a pervasive perception of religion as historically located, where doctrines are established and canons are closed.[24] This is not the case for Indigenous religious traditions. A recent example is the Sioux Valley Dakota Nation in Manitoba, whose spiritual leaders discovered a ceremonial Sun Dance site in Birds Hill Provincial Park in 1999. With support from the province, the Sioux Valley Dakota practiced the ceremony from 2000 to 2007. Mark Ruml, a religious studies scholar who both studied and participated in the Birds Hill Park Sun Dance, shows how Indigenous religious traditions continue to evolve and change today. In the case of the Birds Hill Park Sun Dance, for example, the sacredness of a site grows as a community establishes their connection to the land. From the moment elders chose the site to the first dance, Ruml writes, there is "a process of increasing sanctification."[25] This evidence, that Indigenous Peoples are discovering (or creating) new sacred sites, suggests that the state's protection of only pre-contact Indigenous cultures, outlined in *R. v. Van der Peet*, could have serious implications for forms of religious practice developed long after colonization. There is a contradiction between law and the actual practices of Indigenous Peoples. This contradiction has led to the loss of the cosmologically significant space of Indigenous Peoples, as demonstrated in the previous chapters, and armed conflict, as demonstrated in the following pages.

In addition to new practices emerging within particular communities, the meanings of traditional practices are also highly susceptible to change. The fact that Indigenous religions are experiential rather than canonically closed is a distinction and a serious concern of which contemporary practitioners of Indigenous religions are astutely aware. In an article on the Indigenous Knowledge Documentation Project,[26] Ruml notes that participants were concerned that the documentation of their teachings and beliefs may be misunderstood as authentic when in fact meanings, interpretations, and teachings may change from day to day. Elders echoed this concern. Ruml writes, "Although oral expression may place limits on a felt understanding of 'Truth,' the written form serves as a further reification."[27] Ruml concludes that one should understand investigations of Indigenous religious traditions as snapshots rather than absolutes.

In addition to the very nature of Indigenous religions as experiential, contact has resulted in cultural change and loss among many communities of Indigenous Peoples. In particular, the effects of and responses to Canadian assimilation policies regarding Indigenous cultures led to the loss and alteration of many Indigenous religious beliefs and practices. For example, Indigenous Peoples on the West Coast altered their Potlatch practices in many ways to disguise traditional customs.[28] Displacement, dispossession, and resource development continue to force Indigenous religions to respond to the ever-present effects of colonialism.[29] Those communities that experienced cultural loss have begun to relearn their traditional practices and beliefs. For some this has meant the repatriation of cultural artefacts, while for others it has meant relying on colonial writings to piece together their cultures.[30] Put simply, conceptions of "pure" and untainted forms of Indigenous spiritual practices and beliefs are both fictional and ahistorical. Indigenous religions, like all religions, continue to transform and develop both internally and in response to external forces.

Following the Second World War migration to the cities, the construction of intertribal urban community centres, Indigenous-run schools, and even prisons provided for sites of cultural sharing, renewal, adoption, and adaptation. This process of social and cultural revitalization is explicitly evident in the United States and just as important, although less obvious, in Canada.[31] Historian Ken Coates writes, "Pan-Indigeneity is one of the most important religious and spiritual phenomena observable among Indigenous populations today."[32] Both Indigenous and non-Indigenous Peoples have criticized intertribal spiritual practices as non-traditional and therefore not authentic. Coates responds by stating that the "emergence of shared spiritual traditions is ... a fairly logical outgrowth of social and demographic change. The practices provide a symbolic and practical identifier for Indigenous people and a recognizable means of asserting Aboriginality to non-Indigenous Peoples."[33] In other words, one could understand intertribal religious communities as the outgrowth of a culture of survival.

In Canada more specifically, Reginald Bibby and James Penner conclude that a revitalization of Indigenous religions is particularly prevalent among Canadian Indigenous youth.[34] Marc Fonda writes, "The increasing interest among scholars of religion, increased numbers of books being written on the subject, and the fact that Aboriginal spiritual thinking and epistemologies are promoted in national Aboriginal organizations" is evidence that Canada is amidst a revitalization of Indigenous religions.[35] This revitalization is particularly important for public policy, Fonda argues, given the demonstrated connection between "cultural continuity" and well-being. However, the state's primary means of gathering information on its citizenry is, in Fonda's analysis, inadequate to recognize this revitalization. He criticizes census practices for assuming a lineage of belief determinable by the religion of the previous generation and allowing for only one choice in the field of religious beliefs.[36] In many ways, the census reflects the larger limitation facing contemporary Indigenous religions. It understands them as unchanging, singular, and unaffected by contact and combination.

Scholars suggest these revitalization movements may be inherently political.[37] For instance, Naomi Alderson writes, "There has been a tremendous growth of Native Spirituality across Indigenous Canada, and this growth has occurred, significantly, in tandem with the larger, more overt political recuperative process."[38] The "rise of pan-Indian spirituality" not only presents what Fonda describes as "evidence of vital and thriving cultures that are adopting to different conditions of life, different situations, times, and technologies," but also evidence of the importance of both understanding and protecting contemporary forms of Indigenous religions regardless of the contentious debates in existence among some Indigenous Peoples.[39] As Fonda concludes, there is still a lot of research to be conducted on the "varieties, characteristics," and "politics" of the revitalization of Indigenous religions.[40]

Despite the colonial and historical actions of Christian churches, the widespread adoption of Christianity by Indigenous Peoples adds even more complex layers to the subject of religious diversity within and among communities of Indigenous Peoples.[41] In *Inuit Shamanism and Christianity: Transitions and Transformations in the Twentieth Century*, Frédéric B. Laugrand and Jarich G. Oosten chart the dynamic interplay and adaptive nature of both Christianity and traditional Inuit practices in the North.[42] At the same time there are cases of serious division between Christianity and traditional Indigenous religions. One case occurred in 2011 in Oujé-Bougoumou, Quebec, where a Cree community collectively decided to tear down a sweat lodge that one of their community members had erected on the reserve. The predominantly evangelical Christian community also issued a ban of all forms of Indigenous religions.[43] Thus, Indigenous religions are extraordinarily complex and subject to internal debate and dissent in response to both internal and external factors, like all religious traditions.

Diversity and the Sun Dance Ceremony

In his review of European academic work on the Lakota Sun Dance, Dale Stover expresses a concern regarding historicization. He writes,

> For traditional Lakota people the contemporary Sun Dance signifies the continuation of and identification with the traditional ways of ancestral generations, whereas for European American culture it represents the epitome of "otherness," the imagined "primitive" world of Indigenous America before European contact. Lakota Sun Dancing carries this double marking because it emphatically represents an embodied spirituality that is, on the one hand, deeply characteristic of Indigenous traditions and is, on the other hand, at profound odds with a Eurocentric modernism that dualistically segregates the religious experience of the subjective self from the objective, embodied realities of the world. European American descriptions of Lakota Sun Dancing typically manifest the predilection of the metropole for assigning to Indigenous rituals only those meanings that conform to modernist categories of thought.[44]

Stover examines three studies of the Sun Dance that focus on the authenticity of the ceremony, as opposed to the aspects that make up its contemporary forms. Moreover, given the fluid, adaptive nature of Indigenous religious traditions, there is an inherent difficulty in any general examination of the Sun Dance ceremony. A historical study of the ceremony does provide evidence of the adaptive and experiential nature of the Sun Dance, but it does not dictate its modern forms. In other words, studying a "historical" Sun Dance does not determine the authenticity of the ceremony, despite the fact that scholarship has tended to do just that. Recall the concern raised by interviewees of the Indigenous Knowledge Documentation Project: documentation does not denote authenticity.

Within the region where the Sun Dance originated, Great Plains communities such as the Cheyenne and Lakota have oral traditions that trace the ceremony to time immemorial. While European scholarship acknowledges that the origins of the Sun Dance certainly extend deep into the unwritten histories of North American civilizations, prevailing Western scholarship holds that the ritual may have first emerged among the Plains Algonquians at the beginning of the eighteenth century. Regardless, the ceremony then spread throughout the Great Plains to communities in contemporary Canada and the United States, including the Arapaho, Ankara, Assiniboine, Blackfeet, Cheyenne, Comanche, Crow, Eastern Dakota, Gros Ventre, Hidatsa, Kiowa, Lakota, Mandan, Ponca, Plains Cree, Plains Ojibwa, Sarsi, Shoshone, and Ute.[45]

Colonialism and the move to reserves affected the Sun Dance ceremony. Joseph Jorgensen contends that the contemporary form of the Sun Dance is one "born of misery and oppression" persisting in a context of misery and oppression.[46] Although his analysis should not be broadened to include all communities, Jorgensen points to a significant change among the Wind River Shoshone, for example, who saw the meaning of the Sun Dance move away from the purposes of "insuring successful bison hunts and warfare to an increased concern over illness and community misery."[47] He argues that similar patterns emerged among the Ute. Legislation banning the ritual in both Canada and the United States during the first half of the twentieth century meant that further changes were required of the ceremony. For example, some communities chose to hide in plain sight, conducting traditional ceremonies on officially recognized Euro-Canadian holidays.

Put bluntly, there is no singular form of the Sun Dance. It has developed differently in each community in response to internal and external forces. For example, one of the most well-known practices of the Sun Dance is the piercing ritual that involves tearing of flesh as an act of self-sacrifice, the embodiment of pain and suffering, the dismantlement of egos, the initiation of visions, and the attainment of power, among other things. However, some groups, such as the Kiowa, did not include the piercing practice within their Sun Dance ceremony.[48]

To make claims regarding a Lakota, Kiowa, or Ute ceremony today is problematic given the fact that, even among communities where the ceremony is historically locatable, it can be distinctly intertribal in nature. In his study of the Oglala Lakota religious identity, Paul Steinmetz notes that multiple Sun Dances occur on the reserve each year, involve participants from outside the Lakota Nation, and emphasize "Indian identity" rather than tribal identity.[49] Eventually, Sun Dances began to take place in locations where practitioners had not traditionally performed them. Amidst the 1995 Sun Dance at Gustafsen Lake, Jorgenson explained to *Vancouver Sun* readers that they should not be surprised to see the ritual – which originated and developed among Plains communities – emerge in places where it had not historically been part of Indigenous religious practice. Referencing the Navajo of Arizona and the Paiutes in Nevada and Oregon, Jorgenson contends that following the standoff at Wounded Knee, South Dakota, in 1973, a new religious movement began to spread across North America that emphasized redemption through spirituality. Young Indigenous Peoples embraced traditional practices such as the Ghost Dance and Sun Dance because, as Jorgenson explained, they offer relief from personal problems, a more defined identity, and a sense of honour.[50]

The American Indian Movement (AIM), which led the violent standoff at Wounded Knee, is an excellent example of an intertribal organization that has been politically active against state-sponsored Indigenous leadership and religiously committed to the Sun Dance ceremony. One of the AIM leaders at his trial for Wounded Knee expressed how his religious convictions confirmed through the Sun Dance ceremony provided him and others with the courage to stand up in defence of Indigenous Peoples and protest elected leadership.[51] One of the most notorious AIM members, Leonard Peltier, controversially convicted by a US federal court of killing two Federal Bureau of Investigation agents during a 1975 shootout in Pine Ridge, South Dakota, wrote an autobiography entitled *Prison Writings: My Life Is My Sun Dance*.[52] In the book, he details the important role the Sun Dance played in providing him with identity and strength in his struggle for Native American freedom.[53] Since 1990, AIM has held an annual Sun Dance ceremony in its home state of Minnesota, but AIM's ties to the Sun Dance go back to nearly the origin of the movement.

Splitting the Sky and Transmitting the Sun Dance Ceremony

The AIM is an even more appropriate example when one considers that the 1995 Gustafsen Lake Sun Dance leader, Splitting the Sky (1952–2013), was a member and regional leader of the American Indian Movement in the 1980s. As discussed, a number of important structural and organizational changes have led to even greater diversity within the Sun Dance ceremony. Further adding to the complexity of Indigenous religious traditions is the manner by which practitioners learn about religious traditions today. One generation does not necessarily pass these traditions on to the next, as the Canadian census assumes. Uniquely transmitted religious traditions or ceremonies do not make them any less authentic for practitioners. The story of Splitting the Sky's encounter with the Sun Dance is one illustration of how some Indigenous Peoples may learn religious traditions and practices in modern-day Canada.

Splitting the Sky is a Mohawk born and raised in New York State. His childhood memories are mostly of his experiences in foster homes and various state-sponsored housing and correctional facilities. The state took him from his mother at a very young age and he only briefly remembers spending some time with his grandmother on the Tonawanda Indian reserve just outside of Buffalo. By his own admission, he spent most of his early life partying and getting into trouble without any real sense of identity or direction. He spent the 1970s in prison following an attempted robbery conviction and the subsequent conviction of killing a prison guard during the 1971 Attica prison riot. During this time, he began to come "into awareness historically of [his] own roots as an Indigenous person, as a Mohawk Native."[54] Literature, rather than first-hand accounts of Indigenous heritage, provided him with the foundations of his identity. His studies began with Dee Brown's *Bury My Heart at Wounded Knee*. Later, he encountered *Lame Deer: Seeker of Visions*, *Black Elk Speaks*, and Elliot Silverstein's film *A Man Called Horse*, which first informed his knowledge of the Sun Dance. He recounted to me his feelings of watching Richard Harris act out the Sun Dance ceremony in *A Man Called Horse*:

> And this guy is standing there and all of the sudden I see them cut his chest in two places and then they put the hooks in ... All of the sudden drumming, the beat became fast and furious. And this was totally exciting me. And ... all of the sudden they start pulling him up and everyone who's there looking at it says "Oh, man, look at this. This is incredible! Look what they're doing, this ritual." And I thought to myself, "Jeez, if a white man can do that, I can do that."[55]

After discussing the impact of *Bury My Heart* and *Black Elk*, he remarked, "Anyways, that being the basis of my search because I was pretty much, you know, in the foster homes and boarding schools, residential schools, and most of my life was spent away from my Native heritage." Following a prison-cell revelation in the mid-1970s, which he interpreted through Eastern philosophy, he became fascinated with the power and strength that, he believed, he could attain through religious belief and experience.[56]

After being pardoned from his conviction stemming from the Attica riot, Splitting the Sky met AIM members at a rally on the Washington Mall in 1980. They invited him to participate in the Sun Dance ceremony, which he claimed was central to the AIM and its appeal to him and other members. He stated,

> The Sun Dance eventually became part of the essential ceremony in the movement throughout all North America and all four directions. It helped us to create a pan-Indigenous movement – very key. Which is why historically when the cavalry came in and the generals and the criminals came in, the first ones they wanted to kill was the spiritual leaders of these very ceremonies. And that's why these spiritual leaders were always first designated to be killed and/or co-opted. If they could not be bought off they were killed instantaneously because that was a source of power.[57]

Within a year of becoming involved with AIM, Splitting the Sky was on his way to South Dakota to participate in his first Sun Dance. The ceremony at Gustafsen Lake was his sixteenth.

Splitting the Sky's life story is an exemplary case demonstrating how Indigenous Peoples are formulating, learning, relearning, and teaching their religions in the wake of outright state-sanctioned attempts to eradicate Indigenous cultures. His interpretation of the Lakota origin of the Sun Dance and Black Elk's teachings is that Indigenous ceremonies, in general, are sources of community strength that can help to unify Indigenous Peoples and combat the genocide brought on by the colonial experience. During his fifth Sun Dance ceremony, while suspended in the sacred arbour, he articulated that a vision and journey to the spirit world gave him an understanding of how one could attain strength, unity, and freedom. He recounted,

> I started crying, in my heart it felt like I was crying. And then I could see, I looked into the sky and the whole sky was this face of this great powerful thunder and lightning being. And I said to him, "spiritual father, are you the power, the thunder and the lightning being?" And it just smiled at me, this beautiful smile, almost like a Mona Lisa smile on a great powerful warrior in the sky ... I began to sob, not through my face but my heart was sobbing and I wept like a child and I totally broke down, my ego was broke down. I had a momentary vision that said "prepare for hard times to come but don't worry, the powers are with you," and then there was just these thousands of eagles that were flying in the spiritual realm, all around ... It helped me see, at that point, on physical levels, that this world does not stop here.[58]

Through the Sun Dance, he reported that he was able to establish a connection between past, present, and future generations. He was also able to transcend a fear of death that, in turn, gave him the courage to engage in defensive stances with those who threatened "his nation, his extended family."[59]

He conducted his first two Sun Dances in South Dakota in 1980 and 1981 and then returned to the East Coast to continue the ceremony in Port Tobacco, Maryland, roughly 35 miles (60 kilometres) outside of Washington, DC. The land on which they conducted the ceremony received a blessing from Leonard Crow Dog, a well-known Lakota Medicine Man, a member of the AIM, an occupier at Wounded Knee, and a supporter of a pan-Indigenous community. With the location of the dance in such close proximity to the capital, and with support of the AIM, the ceremony attracted new participants from across the country. Splitting the Sky eventually made his way to Canada in 1993 and participated in a Sun Dance in Saskatchewan. He then sought out another Sun Dance after relocating to Hinton, Alberta. There he met Percy Rosette, who had been conducting ceremonies at Gustafsen Lake in British Columbia since 1990.

Splitting the Sky's spiritual journey and rediscovery of traditional Indigenous religions is an exemplary story of the pan-Indigeneity that emerged in the second half of the twentieth century. Traditional Indigenous religious practices and beliefs provided him with a sense of identity, determination, and purpose that may have otherwise been unrecognized and undeveloped during his early troubled life. His story is not unique. He spoke of many others who came to Maryland, experienced the Sun Dance for the first time, and returned to their homelands to continue the practice. Even at Gustafsen Lake, a young Anishinaabe from Ontario, James "OJ" Pitawanakwat, participated in the ceremony for the very first time and expressed an attraction and appreciation for Indigenous religious practices following the standoff.[60]

The Gustafsen Lake Sun Dance Ceremony and Occupation

In 1990, a group of Indigenous Peoples began conducting a Sun Dance in the interior of British Columbia at Gustafsen Lake. Through visions, Percy Rosette, a Secwepemc man from the Esk'etemc First Nation, and others discovered the Sun Dance site and the burial grounds they believed to be nearby. Rosette approached the owner of the area at Gustafsen Lake to ask for permission to hold a Sun Dance on the grounds. Lyle James, an American rancher who held title over the land for his cattle company (since 1972), entered into a verbal agreement with Rosette to use the area for a period of four years under the condition that the Sun Dancers would not erect any permanent structures. Gustafsen Lake (or Ts'peten for local Indigenous Peoples) was a popular camping and fishing area for Indigenous and non-Indigenous alike, so allowing the ritual to take place was of little consequence to James. The Sun Dance drew participants from both Canada and the United States, attracting between four and five hundred people in the first two years. Rosette would take the title "Faith Keeper," responsible for protecting the sacred Sun Dance site. Members of the local elected Secwepemc leadership admitted that they were not familiar with the ceremony before Rosette and John Stevens, a Nakoda Medicine Man from Alberta, brought it to the British Columbia interior. Indeed, the Sun Dance is not traditional to that area.[61]

In 1994, the Sun Dance continued as usual despite the fact that Rosette's initial agreement with Lyle James had ended the previous year. James visited the site after the completion of the ceremony to find that Rosette and his partner Mary Pena had taken up residence at the lake. Unknown to James at the time, Rosette and Stevens had enlisted the aid of Bruce Clark, a lawyer and veteran activist for Indigenous land rights. Rosette had been involved in researching land claims for the Secwepemc and had discovered that the land on which the Sun Dance was taking place had been part of a larger tract of land whose rightful owner, in Rosette's view, was the Secwepemc Nation and not the James Cattle Company. Rosette claimed that local leadership had intentionally lost the evidence he had collected. As early as 1992, elected Secwepemc leaders were having problems with the Sun Dancers. One member of the Cariboo Tribal Council[62] commented that he was concerned with the fact that the Sun Dancers were "mixing religion and politics" in their preparatory meetings.[63]

Central to the standoff to occur later that year was Clark's petition to Queen Elizabeth II, dated 3 January 1995 and signed by both Rosette and Stevens. Clark's petition is an exercise in Canadian and British jurisprudence and international law, arguing for third-party adjudication over unceded Indigenous lands within the contemporary boundaries of the Canadian state. The petitioners attested that because of the illegal usurpation of land by the federal government, Indigenous Peoples, under the current tribal system, were facing "serious mental harm," as defined under the 1948 United Nations' Convention on the Prevention and Punishment of Genocide, leading to "prejudiced rates of mortality." The plaintiffs identify themselves as "The Tribal System Natives of the Sun-Dance (central), the Potlatch (western), and the Feast of the Dead (eastern) traditions."[64] Representatives of Indigenous religious traditions sought restitution from the Queen rather than elected First Nations leadership. The attorney general of British Columbia stopped the petition at the provincial level and did not forward it to Ottawa.[65]

Royal Canadian Mounted Police (RCMP) were involved early in 1995 to mediate what they had determined to be a civil matter. After chasing grazing cattle from the Sun Dance site in the previous year, occupiers erected a fence around the sacred arbour to protect the space from defecating cattle.[66] On 13 June, out of fear that the Sun Dancers were trying to stake out territory, James presented the Sun Dancers with an eviction notice. Although James argued that the serving of the notice was quite formal, Sun Dancers contended that ranch hands were responsible for a number of violations towards their religion, including the interruption of ritual preparation, the photographing of Sun Dancers in preparation, and the desecration of a sacred spear on which ranch hands impaled the eviction notice. The violation of sacred objects and religious practice was complicated by the fact that the ranch workers were allegedly brandishing weapons and stated it would "be a good day to string up some red niggers."[67]

A press release of 17 June, signed by the self-proclaimed "Defenders of the Shuswap Nation," outlined the events of 13 June and the various violations to their sacred site that took place at the hands of the James Cattle Company. Fearing the suppression of their religious ceremony, they offered an open invitation to all Sun Dancers "to come to Gustafsen Lake and ensure that this Sun Dance [would] be held as planned to sustain [Original Peoples'] inheritance and religious freedom."[68] Conceptualized within the context of the colonial experience, the attempted eviction on the part of James and the response of the RCMP to engage as anything more than passive mediator at this early juncture contributed to the perception among occupiers that their religion was under attack.

On 17 June, the Sun Dancers met with representatives of the James Cattle Company and locally elected leaders from the Cariboo Tribal Council. At the meeting, the parties supposedly reached an agreement that would allow the Sun Dance to occur in early July, after which point occupiers would vacate the site.[69] The Sun Dancers rejected the resolution and issued a press release on 18 June, identifying themselves as the "defenders of the Gustafsen Lake Sacred Grounds" and affirming that the space was non-negotiable. They stated, "It is our belief that the presence of the ancestral powers on this land will ensure that our struggle will be victorious."[70] Asserting their belief in the spiritual significance of the Sun Dance site, the defenders again confirmed their intention to ensure that the ritual take place, despite the perceived attempts to suppress the ceremony.[71] Splitting the Sky later stated that the Sun Dancers might have left the site after the ceremony if it were not for the persistent violations to their preparations.[72]

On 28 June, Stephen Frasher of the *100 Mile Free Press* published an article highlighting a primary concern of the situation at Gustafsen Lake that observers would later forget. In his article, "Is Gustafsen Lake a Sacred Site? Or More?," Frasher identifies the important connection between land disputes and religious practice for Faith Keeper Percy Rosette, noting the divide between the "traditionalists" and elected Secwepemc leadership. He concludes, "Preventing the Sundance itself, [occupiers] say, would be an infringement of religious freedom and human rights."[73]

In the early stages of the occupation, three Indigenous RCMP constables were involved in the mediation of the civil dispute between James and the Sun Dancers. They were responsible for maintaining some form of security for the site and were active in setting up meetings between the competing parties. Splitting the Sky invited Constable Wood in mid-June to attend the ceremony. Constable Andrew attended the opening day of the ceremony and reported that there were no problems at the site. Sun Dancers took Constable Findley on a tour of the burial grounds and sacred arbour before they invited him to participate in prayer and a cleansing sweat with the Sun Dancers. Findley expressed in his notes that he had established a good rapport with the occupiers and that the presence of eagles upon their concluding handshakes was a good sign.[74] Wood, Andrew, and Findley believed that a meeting established for late August would have resolved the situation if not for the occupiers' discovery of the Emergency Response Team (ERT) on 18 August, which marked the transition of the situation from an occupation to a standoff.[75] After the 18 August incident (discussed in detail below), the RCMP asked the three Indigenous officers who had been working the case not to visit the camp, despite their apparent recognition of some overlapping metaphysical frames. Wood eventually quit the RCMP. Andrew and Findley later expressed their frustrations with the RCMP for ignoring them during the later stages of the occupation.[76]

One of the greatest detriments to recognizing the important role religion played at Gustafsen Lake was the combined efforts of local Secwepemc leadership and the media, both of which, to varying degrees, advocated for dismissing the validity of the religious beliefs of the Sun Dancers. The early introduction of mixing politics and religion, which upset Tsq'escenemc chief Antoine Archie, led him to research the Sun Dance practice that had begun occurring in Secwepemc territory in 1990. Archie explained in a July 1997 interview that the elected Secwepemc leadership challenged those at Gustafsen Lake by claiming that the "real Sun Dancers" told them they needed to take a break.[77] Newspapers picked up the story of the Sun Dance as a modified import that challenged the occupiers' right to stand in defence of the land.[78] Additionally, the public assertions by local leadership that there were no burial sites on the premises and that the land held no specific spiritual significance were some of the most damaging statements in understanding the important role religion played in the dispute.[79]

Amidst much controversy and criticism, the Sun Dance began on 2 July with protection from the RCMP.[80] The strong political nature of the occupation led many to believe that the religious beliefs at Gustafsen Lake were less than genuine. On the day the Sun Dance began, a news article in the *100 Mile House Free Press* reported a local

Sun Dance Elder as condemning the militancy of the Sun Dancers, arguing the occupiers were "part and parcel of the Confederacy movement for sovereignty under the umbrella of the Sun Dance."[81]

When occupiers invited local media, who had been covering the Sun Dance since 1993, into the camp in late June to view the site, Steven Frasher noted that the things Splitting the Sky spoke to them about were "entirely different than anything [the media had] heard associated with Gustafsen Lake before." In his interview with Susan Lambertus, he explained that despite the speech they received on jurisdiction and rightful ownership of the land, there was no evidence provided to support their claims, and he interpreted the tour of the Sun Dance grounds and alleged burial site as a ploy to "create their spin on the situation." Observing Splitting the Sky and Rosette speaking during the tour, Frasher recalled that Rosette was uncomfortable because "for him it was a Native spiritual thing." Frasher also noted that Splitting the Sky and the militant faction of the group "would have to latch [their] cause to take whatever legitimacy they could from what Percy was doing," a claim he and other reporters had been asserting since the beginning of the occupation.[82]

Rumours of gunfire and armament at the camp started to surface in July and early August. The RCMP initially dismissed ranch workers' claims of gunfire. This changed when the RCMP apprehended two of the Sun Dance participants fishing illegally in the Fraser River and found an assault rifle in their truck. The RCMP decided not to go to the media with their decision to intensify their investigation of the occupiers for fear that it "would give them the audience" they wanted.[83] Instead, they intended to send in a reconnaissance team to gather information before removing the occupiers, despite the fact that the Indigenous officers mediating the situation had already set up a meeting for later that month.[84]

The Standoff

On 18 August, occupiers discovered and shot at an ERT sent to conduct reconnaissance on them, officially beginning the standoff. Four hundred RCMP officers and four armoured personnel carriers (APCs), supplied by the Canadian military under Operation Wallaby, converged on 20 square acres outside of 100 Mile House to confront nearly two dozen armed people. On 25 August, the Cariboo Tribal Council invited National Chief of the Assembly of First Nations Ovide Mercredi to mediate and end the standoff. The RCMP told Mercredi that he had two days, during which time they would continue planning alternative procedures for removing the occupiers. Media coverage of the first meeting reported that Mercredi was largely unsuccessful despite his comments to the contrary.[85] Following the first meeting, the RCMP cut off media access and cell phone communication with the occupiers. The RCMP did not permit media to enter the camp for Mercredi's second meeting. Mercredi noted afterward that the meeting consisted mostly of those at the camp voicing their frustrations regarding the RCMP action.[86]

In her comprehensive study of the media and Gustafsen Lake, Susan Lambertus explains the significance of the RCMP action:

> The RCMP's strategies of barricading the primary road to the camp and cutting off the camp's ability to communicate with anyone other than law enforcement personnel probably had the strongest influences on the [negative] media characterizations [of the occupiers]. The RCMP did not likely anticipate at the time that these common law-enforcement practices would result in the escalation of stress inside the camp, the altering of news-gathering processes, and the magnification of the RCMP's power to interpret the event to the media. These outcomes increased the risk of violence as well as the potential for media distortion.[87]

For the RCMP, the actions were a preventative measure against violence and a means to cut off any instructions received from either Splitting the Sky, who left the camp shortly before the standoff, or Bruce Clark, the lawyer consulted by Splitting the Sky and Rosette. For the camp, it was a sign that the RCMP was setting the stage to storm the site. The RCMP began the confrontation as mediators; however, by August, they had taken on an oppositional role. In addition, the media became almost completely dependent on the RCMP to provide or deny them information. On the afternoon of

27 August, reports that two ERT officers encountered gunfire from the camp ended any further chance of Mercredi returning to the site to mediate.[88]

In addition to setting up barricades around the occupation site, the RCMP confiscated video footage of and released by the occupiers. On 23 August, the RCMP seized the documentary *Defenders of the Land*, shot by non-Indigenous occupier Trond Halle, from the Canadian Broadcasting Corporation (CBC). On 6 September, they confiscated the CBC's footage captured earlier in the standoff when the news agency had access to the camp. In both cases, the RCMP considered the video footage of occupiers to be evidence in a criminal investigation.

According to facts later publicized at trial, the RCMP also fabricated stories that contributed to negative public characterizations of those in the camp.[89] The day before the RCMP seized the second video footage, they reported an incident of gunfire between occupiers and police vehicles. At the trial, it became clear that within 24 hours of the incident, the RCMP could not confirm occupiers had shot their vehicles. The forensic evidence identified towards the end of the standoff suggested that a tree branch might have hit the vehicle, but the RCMP did not retract any statements regarding the alleged attack by occupiers.[90]

On 7 September, the Secwepemc Nation held a meeting involving all seventeen of their bands. The purpose of the meeting was to establish a team of Indigenous intermediaries to bring the standoff to a peaceful resolution. The Secwepemc Nation invited the RCMP and media as guests, asking them to adhere to their agenda and to attend only those portions of the meeting for which they had given permission. The view of the communities of Indigenous Peoples in the area was that Gustafsen Lake was an Indigenous issue that would be resolved through Indigenous means. Once they were able to access the camp, the intermediaries were able to provide a different perspective on the occupiers and the conditions at the lake. Chief Nathan Matthew of the Simpcw First Nation, chairperson of the Shuswap Nation Tribal Council, expressed his concern regarding the public depiction of occupiers at the camp. The *Vancouver Sun* quoted Matthew stating that the camp had transformed from "a defence-oriented camp to a peace camp."[91] BC attorney general Ujjal Dosanjh responded acerbically in the *Victoria Times Colonist*, "Peace camps do not have AK-47s."[92]

Shortly after these comments, on 11 September, an extensive firefight took place between the RCMP and occupiers. The incident involved the APCs on loan from the Canadian military and thousands of rounds of ammunition. The incident began when RCMP detonated an "early warning device" buried in an access road to the camp, blowing out the front axle of a truck carrying occupiers. Non-Indigenous occupier Suniva Bronson was the only individual shot and wounded during the confrontation. The three occupants of the truck were heading to get water for the Indigenous intermediaries set to arrive that afternoon. Whether the occupiers knew the RCMP had tightened the camp perimeter the day before, cutting off access to the well and firewood, remains unknown. The next day, Matthew clarified his comments regarding the "peace camp," stating that he wanted to remind people of the site's significance as ceremonial Sun Dance grounds.[93]

The portrayal of the occupiers following the firefight was the "most vilifying" of all the news coverage.[94] The RCMP took the opportunity to enact a smear campaign[95] identifying the names and criminal records of the occupiers. The RCMP worked out the media strategy on 1 September but seized the opportunity following the firefight to enact the plan. According to Lambertus, "The success of the 'smear campaign' rested on the RCMP's knowledge of the kind of news that would have the greatest appeal, their knowledge of news production practices, and their authority as the most important media source."[96] The RCMP contrasted negative characterizations of the occupiers with positive assertions regarding their own actions. The occupiers were officially violent criminals.[97]

After an incident on 12 September, in which ERT officers shot at an unarmed occupier, a shift in the approach by the RCMP turned their attention back to the religious aspect of Gustafsen Lake. On 13 September, the same day a spiritual leader from the local Penticton Indian Band (of the Okanagan Nation Alliance) was able to bring someone out of the camp, the RCMP arranged for Dakota spiritual leader Arvol Looking Horse to enter the site. Amidst a religious ceremony the occupiers agreed to leave the camp after three days. However, the RCMP stifled the progress made by Looking Horse when they coerced CBC radio to broadcast a message to occupiers from elected chief Antoine Archie, ensuring their safety if they surrendered. The RCMP stated that the occupiers requested the assurance from local leadership, but following the broadcast, reporters and supporters of the occupiers questioned the choice of Chief Archie given the occupiers' stance towards elected leadership.[98] Looking Horse, unaware of the RCMP plan, criticized the police for not giving him enough time.[99]

On 17 September, Medicine Man John Stevens led the twelve remaining occupiers out of the camp, ending the standoff. Two days afterward, the media discovered that at least three weeks earlier Splitting the Sky had provided two names to the RCMP who could act as mediators in the conflict: Looking Horse and Stevens. RCMP corporal John Ward confirmed for reporters the existence of Splitting the Sky's list of mediators. However, he denied that the RCMP ignored the importance of religion in the conflict and told reporters it was "not a big deal." He continued, "We knew about these people. We had a list of them. It was a matter of when we were going to use them, plain and simple."[100]

Splitting the Sky's choice to recommend Looking Horse and Stevens as mediators in the conflict is important because it speaks to the foundational purpose that drew occupiers to the site. It also speaks to the point Chief Matthew made following the firefight that Gustafsen Lake was a sacred ceremonial site. Splitting the Sky offered this perspective on the mediators: "John Stevens had the total respect of everyone. So, if John Stevens says 'go for it,' then all right, we went with his protection and the spirits that walk with him. And, if he says it's time to quit then it's time to quit ... What John Stevens says goes. That's it. That's the law. He was the keeper of that Sun Dance, the Medicine Man for the Sun Dance."[101] Splitting the Sky thought Chief Arvol Looking Horse deserved an opportunity to mediate since he is a respected Lakota spiritual leader and the nineteenth-generation holder of the sacred pipe of the White Buffalo Calf Woman.[102] Splitting the Sky concluded his interview by reaffirming the authority of Stevens at the Sun Dance grounds.

The RCMP charged eighteen people in the Gustafsen Lake standoff. The most serious of the sixty charges laid was attempted murder, but the most serious conviction was "mischief causing danger to life." The trial lasted ten months, beginning 8 July 1996 and ending on 27 May 1997. In his statement to the court before it found him guilty of "mischief causing danger to life," James Pitawanakwat defended his stand at Gustafsen Lake: "Ceremonies like the Sun Dance need to be protected from cultural genocide. This is the basis for my resistance. We are not militants or terrorists. We are warriors to our people. Our families. Our generations yet to come."[103] In addition, Pitawanakwat's statement emphasizes a concern made explicit in pre-ceremony press releases; namely, Indigenous religion was under attack at Gustafsen Lake.

Conclusion

In this chapter, we stepped beyond the law to provide some insight as to how diachronic cultures, new revelations, migratory activities, contested leadership, and the compounding and interrelated factors of contemporary politics and colonialism complicate the discourse on Indigenous religious freedom. Indigenous religions, rooted in tradition, are fluid, responding to both internal and external factors, just as all religions do. In addition, communities of Indigenous Peoples are internally diverse, as is the case in all cultural groups. This fact is particularly prevalent in intertribal movements that cut across the boundaries of nation and tribe. However, while cultures continue to change and diversify through innovation, contestation, and revelation, the integral-to-a-distinctive-culture test – central to Aboriginal rights – defines a limited understanding of Indigenous cultures, restricted by state-constructed hierarchies and the evidence-based prerequisite of existence prior to contact. Of course, there is no indication that the Ts'peten Defenders sought recognition under the Aboriginal rights framework. This is unsurprising given that they rejected elected Indigenous leadership and the authority of the Canadian state to participate as anything more than an interested party, the facilitators of cultural genocide. Nevertheless, the case offers important insights into the potential dangers of the marginalization, dismissal, misunderstanding, and outright suppression of Indigenous religions – a reality that seems to be supported under the current Aboriginal rights framework.

For the Ts'peten Defenders, armed reoccupation of Gustafsen Lake was the means by which they sought to bring attention and resolution to their concerns. Blockades and barricades are a reality of contemporary Indigenous-state relations, particularly when other forms of redress are unavailable, unacknowledged, or ineffective.[104] However, for those communities of Indigenous Peoples who accept (and are included under) the Aboriginal rights framework, the recognized and affirmed duty of the state to consult and accommodate Indigenous Peoples is a preferred mechanism by which the impacts of state actions on Indigenous cultures may be addressed. We now turn from one central feature of Aboriginal rights – the integral-to-a-distinctive-culture test – to another, the consultation doctrine, to explore its limitations for the protection of Indigenous religious freedom.

chapter five

The Duty to Consult and Accommodate

Following the Second World War, Indigenous Peoples made it clear that if they were to emerge from the systemic oppression of colonialism, Canada needed to provide access for Indigenous Peoples and their perspectives in the decisions and structures affecting their communities. The message was clear: Indigenous and non-Indigenous Canadians must reformulate the foundations of law and politics to include Indigenous Peoples and their perspectives.

Inclusion requires that the state confront Canada's colonial heritage, correcting continuing injustices. As noted earlier in the book, Canada has taken several important and positive steps in the past fifty years that allowed Indigenous Peoples into the governing structures that once excluded them. Indigenous suffrage in 1960 brought Indigenous Peoples into the wider polity, and the constitutional recognition of Aboriginal rights distinguished them as distinct peoples deserving of their own seat at the constitutional negotiating table. More recently, the inclusion of Indigenous voices and perspectives in decision-making processes is now a standard of Canadian constitutional, political, and legal discourses.

In this chapter, I examine the complexity of the contemporary Indigenous-state relationship as demonstrated in the duty to consult and accommodate. Through the theoretical lens of communicative democracy, we can better understand what the Canadian state is attempting in the consultation doctrine. At the same time, communicative democratic theory provides insight into the limitations of the doctrine without self-reflective analysis of the state's own place in its relationship with Indigenous Peoples. The promotion of deliberation to broaden social knowledge among relationally autonomous groups, to include minority narratives and perspectives, and to promote learning and understanding among diverse communities, is without purpose if the interests of one group impede the ability of another "to actively engage in the world and grow."[1] As will be demonstrated at the outset of this chapter, communicative democracy requires a separation between deliberative parties and the formal regulation of procedures. Civil society and the state are complementary, but the tension between these two spheres provides for the framework of democratic justice. Merging these two complementary spheres tends to tip the balance of power in one direction, restricting either self-determination or self-development.

In many ways, the state understands the fundamental concern of Indigenous Peoples. Government decision-makers have actively sought to implement a new relationship founded on the principles of deliberation and inclusion, important political ideals on the path to correct social, cultural, economic, and political domination; but that recognition is limited by the state's unwillingness to reflect honestly on its own location in the Indigenous-state relationship.

In an attempt to bring some clarity to this matter, I explore the legal challenges that have helped to define the modern consultation doctrine, but I ultimately move beyond the court, where consultation actually occurs. The chapter concludes with a review of the Voisey's Bay negotiation in Newfoundland and Labrador in the late 1990s. The case is a relatively successful application of communicative democratic principles, providing an exemplary precedent in the search for a more just relationship.

Communicative Democracy and the State

The purpose here is not to develop a new theory of deliberative democracy or to provide an overview of the extensive literature on the many debates and discussions among its proponents and critics.

Rather, the purpose of this section is to answer three important questions: (1) Why is inclusive deliberation so important in a just democracy? (2) What is the place and role of the state in deliberative politics? (3) How can deliberative politics extend to include multiple political jurisdictions and, in such a case, what is the role of the state? Following the political philosopher Iris Marion Young, I use the term "communicative democracy" rather than the more popular terms "deliberative democracy" or "discursive politics." The reason for this is that Young's theory best describes the ideal principles of the modern Indigenous-state relationship. In this theory, narrative, rhetoric, teaching, and learning are promoted in decision-making processes instead of universalized procedures of communication.[2] The communicative democratic approach helps to foster the inclusion of minority communities and, through its procedures, legitimate formal decision-making processes. In addition to Iris Marion Young, I draw on the work of Jürgen Habermas, who "is responsible for reviving the idea of deliberation in our time, and giving it a more thoroughly democratic foundation."[3] Young's and Habermas's discussions of deliberative democracy also provide elucidation on the contentious role of the state in deliberative processes.

Why is inclusive deliberation so important in a just democracy? Young argues that justice requires that individuals be self-determining. "Self-determination," Young writes, "consists in being able to participate in determining one's action and the condition of one's action; its contrary is domination."[4] Democratic societies that exclude individuals from participating in decisions affecting their lives, and from the conditions in which those decisions are made, "do not live up to their promise."[5] From the communicative democratic perspective, practical reason and sovereignty reside in procedural action oriented towards understanding. In other words, justice resides in the communicative activity of deliberating parties, unlike in the case of liberalism, where justice resides in the balanced governmental output of constitutionally established rights.[6] The result of liberalism is a form of domination where individuals are no longer able to participate in the decisions or structures that affect their lives. By contrast, communicative democracy requires self-determination for justice.

The argument that liberalism is unjust is particularly appropriate in the Canadian context. Dale Turner dedicates the first half of *This Is Not a Peace Pipe* to a criticism of "White Paper" liberalism, Alan Cairns's *Citizens Plus*, and Will Kymlicka's *Multicultural Citizenship*. Turner argues that these three approaches to Indigenous Peoples and the state share a common conclusion. He writes, "They do not recognize that a meaningful theory of Aboriginal rights in Canada is impossible without Aboriginal participation."[7] Put another way, they develop a framework of Aboriginal rights in Canada while effectively ignoring Indigenous Peoples' participation in the development of that construction. The application of rights imposes conditions and may even affect deliberation. For Turner, then, only when people are able to participate in the decisions that affect them can they be self-determining individuals in a just society.

For reasons that will become more apparent when I address the next question, deliberation is necessary to address the potential corruption of a state-centred conception of justice. In communicative democracy, participants engage each other with the knowledge that they are answerable to each other. Young argues that, in order to address the real correlation between socio-economic power and political power that leads to exclusion, marginalization, and the preservation of privilege, democracies ought to promote greater inclusion in decision-making processes. She writes, "Participants arrive at a decision not by determining what preferences have greatest numerical support, but by determining which proposals the collective agrees are supported by the best reasons."[8] Deliberating parties will reject or refine proposals based on proper dialogical examination. Young outlines four normative ideals to help guide deliberation. They are (1) the *inclusion* of all affected parties in the process of discussion and decision-making; (2) a *political equality* that promotes free and equal expression without domination or coercion; (3) a *reasonableness* of participants who seek insight and understanding of different perspectives with at least the initial intention of reaching an agreement regarding collective problems; and (4) a *publicity* to which participants are required to express themselves in the "plural public-speaking context" in a way that "all those plural others" can understand.[9]

Deliberation must be inclusive to be effective. Even when individuals have access to processes of decision-making, they may encounter internal forms of exclusion where the dominant mood finds minority views "are so different from others' in the public that their views are discounted."[10] In contrast to many deliberative political theories, Young argues that deliberative processes should not restrict political communication (i.e., the use of rhetoric, figurative language, emotion, etc.).[11] Many advocates contend that this process goes beyond mere speech and response to transform "the preferences, interests, beliefs, and judgements of participants."[12]

One way to combat the issue of what Young terms "internal exclusion" is through the adoption of *narrative* as a communicative ideal. Young writes, "Storytelling is often an important bridge in such cases between the mute experience of being wronged and political arguments about justice. Those who experience the wrong, and perhaps some others who sense it, may have no language for expressing the suffering as an injustice, but nevertheless they can tell stories that relate a sense of wrong."[13] Narrative also helps to address ignorance, false understandings, or stereotypes that one group may have of another. It can help to foster a better understanding of the "practices, places, or symbols" held by diverse communities and the reasons why they value and give priority to them.[14] Here, Young turns specifically to communities of Indigenous Peoples as an illustration. She writes, "Indigenous people in Anglo settler societies ... too often encounter incredulity, mockery, or hostility from whites, when they try to make major political issues out of holding or regaining control over a particular place." She continues, "The meanings and values at stake here cannot be explained in universalizable arguments. Those facing such lack of understanding often rely on myths and historical narratives to convey what is meaningful to them and why, to explain 'where they are coming from.'"[15] Deliberation in a plural society requires a mode of communication that speaks to the fact that different groups possess uniquely situated values that inform their perspectives on matters of justice and public interest. Narrative allows individuals to present their concerns in a more effective manner. Listeners of narrative not only learn about other groups but also learn to situate their own values in relation to others. This communicative ideal helps to broaden social knowledge and promote inclusion through education. Inclusive deliberation is necessary for self-determination and non-domination in a democratic society.

What is the place and role of the state in deliberative politics? Communicative democracy does not forgo the state in favour of deliberation among those in civil society. Instead, the state is "a subsystem specialized for collectively binding decisions."[16] The deliberative process points the activities of the subsystem and its administrative power in specific directions. Relationally, deliberative power generates from the public sphere, the periphery of the nucleus that is the state. Deliberations pass from the periphery into the nucleus of administrative processes in order that the state may formally institute them. Law and politics, in Habermas's view, help to reduce the social complexity of a large, diverse society. He writes, "The basic rights and principles of government by law can be understood as so many steps toward reducing the unavoidable complexity evident in the necessary deviations from the model of pure communication."[17]

The state also functions as an important institution for the promotion of justice by providing the buttresses against oppression. According to Young, one should understand justice as both self-determination and self-development. She writes,

> Self-development means being able actively to engage in the world and grow. Just social institutions provide conditions for all persons to learn and use satisfying and expansive skills in socially recognized settings, and enable them to play and communicate with others or express their feelings and perspective on social life in contexts where others can listen. Self-development in this sense certainly entails meeting people's basic needs for food, shelter, health care, and so on. It also entails the use of resources for education and training. Self-development does not depend simply on a certain distribution of materials goods. Using satisfying skills and having one's particular cultural modes of expression and ways of life recognized also depend on the organization of the division of labour and the structures of communication and co-operation.

While self-development is thus not reducible to the distribution of resources, market- and profit-oriented economic processes particularly impinge on the ability of many to develop and exercise capacities. Because this is so, pursuit of justice as self-development cannot rely on the communicative and organizational activities of civil society alone, but requires positive state intervention to regulate and direct economic activity.[18]

The state acts as the formal institutor of structures that allow plural publics of self-determining people to engage each other in a way that promotes learning and combats institutional oppression. While the state and civil society are complementary, there is a tension between the deliberative public and the state because there is a tension between "participating in one's action and determining the condition of one's action" and actively engaging and growing in a diverse world.[19] Self-determination without the formal and centralized regulations of the state may lead to competition and selfishness among plural publics, while a state without a deliberative public sphere may fail "to take account of individual, group and local differences."[20] In other words, communicative democracy promotes "relational autonomy" in which "persons [can] pursue their own ends in the context of relationships in which others may do the same."[21] The state provides the context and ensures formal regulations to bring attention to the relationships among diverse peoples.

This formal procedure of self-development must still adhere to communicative power despite its location in the political sphere. Habermas writes, "The constitutional state does not represent a finished structure but a delicate and sensitive – above all fallible and revisable – enterprise, whose purpose is to realize the system of rights *anew* in changing circumstances, that is, to interpret the system of rights better, to institutionalize it more appropriately, and to draw out its contents more radically."[22] In some cases, the state may reverse the circulation of power, generate decisions from within, and project them outward into the periphery. In this case, Habermas contends, "the only decisive question concerns which power constellations these patterns reflect and how the latter can be changed. This in turn depends on whether the settled routines remain open to renovative impulses from the periphery."[23] In other words, the decisions from within the administrative nucleus must be susceptible to the deliberative processes of the public sphere to maintain legitimate democratic authority. The periphery is not responsible for formally instituting its deliberations – that is the responsibility of the administrative nucleus. According to Habermas, one should not view this role for the periphery as incapacitation. He writes, "The administration does not, for the most part, itself produce the relevant knowledge but draws it from the knowledge system or other intermediaries."[24] Ideally, deliberation among affected parties translates from communicative power into legislative and legal power. Those within the nucleus of formal power do enter the public domain of communicative procedures, but they may do so "only insofar as they make convincing contributions to the solution of problems that have been perceived by the public or have been put on the public agenda with the public's consent. In a similar vein, political parties would have to participate in the opinion- and will-formation from the public's own perspective."[25] The ability of the deliberative public to influence the political sphere may seem difficult, but power shifts from the political to the communicative with the greater vibrancy of affected peoples (i.e., the public). The state and deliberative politics are interwoven. In a complex society, the state may act as formal administrator, ultimate decision maker, and participant in the deliberative process, but only insofar as it acknowledges the communicative power of the deliberative public as the cornerstone of a just democracy.[26]

How can deliberative politics extend to include multiple political jurisdictions and, in such a case, what is the role of the state? In the final chapter of *Inclusion and Democracy*, Young analyses three popular arguments – the positivist, nationalist (assimilationist and separationist), and associative – that have framed how nation-states have conceptualized their responsibility to justice as limited to its own citizenry. She criticizes these three arguments for assuming a limited state-centred justice rather than arguing in favour of it. She contends, "Obligations of justice extend globally in today's world."[27] Natural resources, land, and environmental protection are among the points of interdependence across borders and jurisdictions. Just as with the "relational autonomy" of self-determining citizens in a state, which supports the self-development of all, deliberative politics can extend to international and multi-jurisdictional relations. With respect to the latter relationship, "many peoples [who] suffer at the hands of nation-building efforts to suppress or assimilate culturally distinct peoples ... claim a right of self-determination as a means to throw off the yoke of cultural imperialism and gain some control over resources as a base for the life and development of their people."[28] These aspirations for self-government within existing state jurisdictions, notably made by Indigenous Peoples across the world, provide a unique challenge to modern conceptions of state sovereignty. "Despite unjust conquest and continued oppression, however, few Indigenous Peoples seek to establish an independent, internationally recognized state with ultimate authority over matters within a determinately bounded territory. For the most part Indigenous Peoples seek greater and more secure autonomy within the framework of a wider polity."[29] Young contends that one should understand these claims as non-domination rather than non-interference. On one hand, distinct peoples have the right to self-determination through their own governance in which they can determine their own goals and ways of life. On the other hand, interdependence is an undeniable reality of the modern world, and distinct political institutions must be accountable to each other. Just as regulations are required for the deliberative operation of civil society, regulations are also required to guide the procedures of deliberation among multiple jurisdictions and states. As in the case of civil society and the regulations of the political sphere, those involved in international or multi-jurisdictional relations must also be involved in the creation of those regulations. Young stipulates,

> Understood as non-domination, self-determination must be detached from territory. Given that a plurality of peoples inhabits most territories, and given the hybridity of peoples and places that characterizes many territories, institutions of governance ought not to be defined as exclusive control over territory and what takes place within it. On the

contrary, jurisdictions can be spatially overlapping or shared, or even lack spatial reference entirely.[30]

Deliberative processes can be extended to global relationships both within and outside of a nation's borders. However, there is a problem with this theory of global relationships. Young recognizes that there is a difficulty "of trying to apply a principle of self-determination as non-domination in a world where state sovereignty remains and where its hegemonic interpretation remains non-interference."[31] If nations move into the periphery in international relations, what will enforce the formal regulations instituted to promote self-development among a differentiated global community? Ideally, strong global institutions would be the proper adjudicator of human rights and self-development, but when one understands self-determination as non-interference, the state has typically retained the dual role of self-interested party and decision maker. Young proposes international and overlapping regulatory bodies to determine the standards of engagement between citizens, organizations, and governments and to de-territorialize "some aspects of sovereignty" and reposition them within the deliberative process.[32]

Democracy requires deliberation to be just. Justice requires that affected peoples possess the ability for both self-determination and self-development. The tension and separation of the self-determining peoples, on the one hand, and the regulatory institutions, on the other, are required so that a diverse society can be reasonably just (i.e., relational autonomy). Domestically, internationally, or within overlapping jurisdictions, democratic legitimacy rests in the deliberations of the plural publics only in that they may deliberate upon the regulations that guide those deliberations and in that an external mediator formally institutes those regulations. Domestically, the state carries out the role of mediation and leaves deliberation to civil society. In international or domestic nation-to-nation relationships, the mediator ought to be a third party to maintain separation between the periphery and the nucleus. In a world where most states understand sovereignty as non-interference, deliberative processes often fail at the regulatory level – particularly within Indigenous-state relations.

The Consultation Doctrine

Battles at the barricades or in the courts are not the ideal location for healthy Indigenous-state relations. However, blockades have been helpful in bringing matters to the attention of the courts, and the courts have been helpful in determining some of the failures of the Canadian state's relationship with Indigenous Peoples. This process has helped to establish some guidelines for an improved Indigenous-state nation-to-nation relationship. The consultation doctrine legally obligates the state to consult and accommodate Aboriginal Peoples affected by government projects. The SCC has defined the duty of the Crown to consult and accommodate Indigenous Peoples as an Aboriginal right protected under section 35(1), although the court did not begin to provide a definition of the doctrine until 2004.[33] Ultimately, the consultation doctrine embodies communicative democratic principles of inclusive deliberation. However, the state's complicated role as both participant and administrator has led to problems of domination in the assessment of the deliberative process and the implementation of decisions.

Legal scholar Dwight Newman summarizes the duty to consult and accommodate from the three landmark cases that brought definition to the doctrine.[34] The consultation doctrine is not contingent upon established Aboriginal rights or title but is rather easily triggered based on minimal knowledge of Crown interference on potential or established Aboriginal or treaty rights. Based on the potential impact of the project, consultation may require a simple notification or a degree of accommodation. The scope and level of accommodation will be determined in accordance with the impact of the project. Where Aboriginal title has not been established, the SCC has made it clear that consultation does not entail a veto power. If the government fails to adequately consult Indigenous Peoples, it may result in injunctions against the project, but most commonly courts will order the parties to continue dialogue on the matter.[35]

Newman argues that there are four identifiable and sometimes overlapping frameworks motivating the doctrine (depending on each individual case). The relatively easy triggering of the doctrine and the fact that Aboriginal rights do not need to be established prior to consultation are emblematic of the most common theoretical foundation put forth for the duty: the honour of the Crown. In *Haida Nation v. British Columbia*, Chief Justice McLachlin wrote,

> Put simply, Canada's Aboriginal peoples were here when Europeans came, and were never conquered. Many bands reconciled their claims with the sovereignty of the Crown through negotiated treaties. Others, notably in British Columbia, have yet to do so. The potential rights embedded in these claims are protected by section 35 of the *Constitution Act, 1982*. The honour of the Crown requires that these rights be determined, recognized and respected. This, in turn, requires the Crown, acting honourably, to participate in processes of negotiation. While this process continues, the honour of the Crown may require it to consult and, where indicated, accommodate Aboriginal interests.[36]

The consultation doctrine is a positive step forward in ensuring dialogue between Indigenous Peoples and the Canadian state, but the state's emphasis on itself acts to diminish the power and place of Indigenous Peoples in those conversations. Additionally, McLachlin's statement on Crown honour speaks to one of the central issues with the consultation doctrine: its internal tension. Crown honour simultaneously acknowledges Indigenous Peoples as unconquered and asserts Crown sovereignty over land.

Newman argues that the second theoretical approach is results-based, with a focus on the scope and level of accommodation provided. Here, we see the complicated role of the state begin to limit the effectiveness of the consultation doctrine. Newman holds that "circumstances in which governments wished to develop certain lands for significant economic development purposes would, on this account, reasonably give rise to a more attenuated duty to consult in relation to proposed government activities on those lands."[37] The spectrum of circumstances could result in the prioritization of state or economic interests over those of Indigenous Peoples given a large enough state project. This philosophy of the doctrine, on its face, expresses a state-centred conception of justice that bases its legitimacy, to return to Habermas, on the "output of government activities that are successful on balance."[38] If we interpret this in multi-jurisdictional terms, it is the self-determination of the state dictating the regulations of self-development for itself and its citizenry. In either case, the state has overridden procedures of deliberation.

Newman also identifies that the court understands that the consultation doctrine embodies an ongoing process of reconciliation. In *Haida Nation*, McLachlin explains,

> The jurisprudence of this Court supports the view that the duty to consult and accommodate is part of a process of fair dealing and reconciliation that begins with the assertion of sovereignty and continues beyond formal claims resolution. Reconciliation is not a final legal remedy in the usual sense. Rather, it is a process flowing from rights guaranteed by s. 35(1) of the *Constitution Act, 1982*. This process of reconciliation flows from the Crown's duty of honourable dealing toward Aboriginal peoples, which arises in turn from the Crown's assertion of sovereignty over an Aboriginal people and *de facto* control of land and resources that were formerly in the control of that people.[39]

At the foundation of the consultation doctrine is Crown sovereignty – this is, after all, where consultation "begins." Newman contends that an ends-based result could even render ongoing dialogue unnecessary. The duty to consult provides for the inclusion of Indigenous voices, but not necessarily in a meaningful way. It does not adequately address the subject of power in those consultations necessarily constituted by the colonial encounter. In part, the process seeks a more honourable relationship, but the application of this doctrine favours a state-centred distribution of rights without reference to relations of power. Maybe even more important, as Newman explains, is that the state ultimately decides when their actions trigger a duty to consult and the extent of that consultation. Even in its ideal application, the consultation doctrine has yet to include deliberative processes in the formation of its regulations.

Newman argues that the duty to consult requires a degree of reasonableness that satisfies the honour of the Crown. By reasonableness, Newman refers to the state's "consultation spectrum," which dictates the level of consultation based on the strength of an Aboriginal claim. The doctrine may require the state at least to provide notification and at most to provide accommodation. Accommodation is subject to the balance of convenience characteristic of modern liberal democratic societies as discussed in chapter 2. Newman, who recognizes that the doctrine needs time to develop, argues that despite criticisms regarding the lack of power held by Indigenous Peoples in the procedure, the potential benefits have yet to become clear.[40] He writes,

> Consultation embodies the possibility of genuinely hearing one another and seeking reconciliations that work in the shorter-term while opening the door for negotiations of longer-term solutions to unsolved legal problems. Those potentially engaged with consultations, whether governments, Aboriginal communities, or corporate stakeholders, ought to bear in mind not only their doctrinal legal position but the longer-term prospects for trust and reconciliation that will enable all to live together in the years ahead.[41]

The optimism Newman demonstrates towards the consultation doctrine is quite similar to the normative ascriptions of Indigenous political thinkers on the subject of good Indigenous-state relations, such as those put forth by John Borrows or Dale Turner.[42] The purpose is to effect change at a foundational level, where social knowledge is developed and power changes on a fundamental level rather than shifting from one party to the other. For Newman, at the foundation of the doctrine, ideally, is the principle of listening rather than state-goal-based accommodation.

On a theoretical level, the consultation doctrine embodies many of the same principles and concerns raised in communicative democratic theory. It seeks reconciliation through greater inclusion and participation in decision-making processes. At times, it may even demand dialogue among affected parties. Ultimately, the consultation doctrine seeks to include Indigenous perspectives and voices in the decisions that affect their lives. It is only through a consultative process that the impact of a claim can be adequately understood. This is where narratives of injustice act as powerful tools in deliberation. The challenge is offered by the dual role of the state as both participant and administrator. As an interested party, its power to commence and set the rules of the deliberative process is troubling since it too makes the final decision.

Although there are three cases that have helped to define the modern consultation doctrine, I turn to one case, *Taku River Tlingit First Nation v. British Columbia*, to elaborate on the limits of the consultation doctrine in practice. The concerns of the Taku River Tlingit in response to the court's decision in favour of the government's approval of the Tulsequah Chief Mine Project help to demonstrate concerns regarding the subject of power in decision-making processes and the inclusion of Indigenous perspectives.

In 1994, Redfern Resources Ltd began the process of acquiring and reopening an old mine in north-western British Columbia at the meeting point of the Taku and Tulsequah Rivers (65 kilometres northeast of Juneau, Alaska, and 100 kilometres south of Atlin, British Columbia). The Taku River Tlingit were concerned about an access road to the mine that would run through their traditional territories. Under the BC Environmental Assessment Act (1995), Canada had a duty to consult with the Taku River Tlingit. In many cases, various acts of government trigger the duty to consult and accommodate. The courts only become involved once Indigenous Peoples participating in the consultation process express dissatisfaction with Crown decisions. In such a case, the court is responsible for determining whether the government adequately met its duty.

Once the state determines that an environmental assessment is required, it forms working committees to address the environmental concerns of the various parties. In this case, the Taku River Tlingit, the federal and provincial governments, the US and Alaskan governments, and the Atlin Advisory Planning Commission participated in the assessment process. The proponent creates a report based on public consultations and the information generated by the committees. The Project Committee may approve a report or instruct the proponent to include additional information.

In January 1997, the committee determined that Redfern's first report was deficient. The Taku River Tlingit were concerned with deficiencies of basic information regarding the impact of the access road, the protection of wildlife, and traditional land use. An additional report was prepared on Tlingit traditional land use upon recommendation from the committee. Redfern submitted a second report including the land-use study in November 1997. The Taku River Tlingit felt the land-use study required additional information, and the Environmental Assessment Office ordered an addendum to the report. In March 1998, the Project Committee submitted an additional recommendations report to the executive director. The Taku River Tlingit were the only members of the committee who disagreed with the recommendations report. They submitted their own report voicing their concern with the process and the recommendations. The executive director referred the project application to the ministers with the recommendations report and the Taku River Tlingit report.

The ministers granted project approval shortly thereafter. The Taku River Tlingit criticized the referral to the ministers because it did not adequately address their concerns or refer to the addendum regarding their traditional land use. In February 1998, they brought their concerns before the court on administrative grounds that the state failed to adequately consult and accommodate the Taku River Tlingit. The lower court agreed with the Taku River Tlingit, as did the Court of Appeal in 2002. In 2004, the Supreme Court of Canada overturned the decision of the lower courts.

The Taku River Tlingit felt their concerns were not included in the recommendations report and not acknowledged by the various BC ministries involved in the project.[43] They did not feel that their sustainability as a people, their Aboriginal rights, or the implications for pending treaty negotiations were adequately addressed. The judge who heard the Taku River Tlingit claim in the BCSC agreed that the final stages of deliberation appeared to exclude Taku River Tlingit participation. Justice Pamela Kirkpatrick was critical of the recommendations report for failing to mention the term "sustainability" given its significance for the Taku River Tlingit. In reference to the addendum that received no attention in the final report, Kirkpatrick emphasized the important connection between land, society, culture, economy, and governance that the recommendations report should have taken into consideration. In her reasons for judgment, she restated one of the central conclusions of the addendum:

> Impacts on traditional land use are impacts that affect the integrity and well-being of [Taku River Tlingit] institutions and the social and cultural well-being of the community. These links cannot be overstated. At bottom, they are the fundamental difference between the [Taku River Tlingit] and non-native society, in that their traditional institutions and system of governance are fashioned to a great extent from the very values their traditional land use supports.[44]

Kirkpatrick concluded, "It can be said ... that there was inadequate (and perhaps no) assessment of evidence produced by or on behalf of the Tlingits. In this respect, the decision was unreasonable."[45] Kirkpatrick ordered the parties to reconvene and deliberate on the concerns of the Taku River Tlingit and the reasons presented in her decision.

Affidavits provided additional information in support of the Taku River Tlingit claims to the court. They continued to assert their concerns regarding the correlation between the access road and the Tlingit connection to the land. One member wrote,

> One of the reasons I tend the trail is to make it possible for our people to stay on the land. That's my dream. That's why I do the work year after year. If a road goes over the trail or near the trail it takes the whole relationship with the land away. Redfern told me that the road will make it easier for us to access our lands, but I believe that really it will only make it easier for everybody else to access our land. Under our system, when one house or family manages an area in our traditional territory other families and houses respect that. But after the road is built everybody else will access our lands and they will not respect it the way we do.[46]

A Taku River Tlingit council member further expressed, "I told them when we saw the route that it would wipe out our migratory trails and history and that our Tlingit culture and traditions would follow."[47]

While waiting on Kirkpatrick's decision, Taku River Tlingit submitted a report to the Ministry of Forests titled *Ha tlatgi ha kustiyi: Protecting the Taku Tlingit Land-based Way of Life.* In this report, they reiterated the important connection between culture, land, economy, and society that they felt the access road and subsequent mitigations overlooked. They wrote,

> The natural resources of the territory affected by the proposed project form a substantial contribution to our domestic economy and the culture of our people. Our land-based way of life requires that we continue to maintain and strengthen our relationship to the land. This means that we have an ongoing responsibility to protect our trails, camps, villages, and spiritual connections to our land and our creator.[48]

In the view of the Taku River Tlingit, the recommendations report did not adequately address their intimate connection between land, animals, religion, economy, and culture. The land-use report and minority report expressed these concerns and called for further deliberation, but the government, according to the Taku River Tlingit, fully considered neither.

In a split decision, the BCCA upheld Kirkpatrick's ruling. The Crown's central argument was that it did not hold a fiduciary right to consult with First Nations who have yet to establish Aboriginal rights or title in court proceedings. On behalf of the majority, Justice Ann Rowles disagreed with the Crown's claim. She wrote, "To say ... that establishment of the Aboriginal rights or title in court proceedings is required before consultation is required, would effectively end any prospect of meaningful negotiation or settlement of Aboriginal land claims."[49] Reports during the assessment process and information provided throughout the first court case clearly established the potential impact of the project on the sustainability of the Taku River Tlingit ways of life. According to Rowles, the law requires the Crown "to ensure that the substance of the Tlingits concerns had been addressed."[50] The majority concluded that the Project Committee had gathered sufficient information regarding Tlingit concerns but that the ministers had not considered the evidence in its entirety. They instructed the ministers to reconsider their approval with respect to their decision and Tlingit concerns.

Justice M.F. Southin, dissenting, argued that the ministers had sufficiently consulted with the Taku River Tlingit prior to making their decision. She writes, "The right to be consulted is not a right of veto. To put it another way, the right to be heard, whether in this or any other process, and no matter how great the issue, is not a right to victory."[51] Southin concluded that a duty certainly exists without first establishing rights or title, but that the Taku River Tlingit claim that the ministers overlooked their perspective was overstated.

In 2004, the case went before the SCC and the decision of the lower courts was overturned. Like Southin in the BCCA, the SCC agreed that the Crown had a duty to consult with the Taku River Tlingit and that the process leading up to the ministers' decision satisfied their fiduciary duty. Chief Justice McLachlin explained, "Where consultation is meaningful, there is no ultimate duty to reach agreement. Rather, accommodation requires that Aboriginal concerns be balanced reasonably with the potential impact of the particular decision on those concerns and with competing societal concerns."[52] Based on the demonstrated potential economic, social, and cultural impacts on the Tlingit during the consultation process, the SCC believed that the honour of the Crown dictated that the state accommodate the Taku River Tlingit to some degree. The SCC determined that the extensive involvement of the Taku River Tlingit with the planning committee and various subcommittees inevitably affected Redfern's proposal. The SCC disagreed with the Taku River Tlingit, stating that the recommendations report sufficiently accommodated Tlingit concerns with the inclusion of mitigation strategies for future management of the road and the collection of information.

The concerns of the Taku River Tlingit and the decision by the SCC demonstrate a fundamental limitation regarding the modern relationship between Indigenous Peoples and the state. The consultation doctrine simultaneously promotes a deliberative democratic process where procedure determines authority and state-centred liberal decisions that seek to maintain balance by enforcing constitutional imperatives. In other words, the procedure legitimates the outcome, regardless of whether the outcome meets the satisfaction of Indigenous Peoples. The Taku River Tlingit felt that the planning committee and ministers did not fully understand or accommodate the importance of their "habitat."[53] The state has established a firm doctrine of consultation, but accommodation based on a spectrum analysis – that is, a sliding scale of accommodation based on state analysis of an Indigenous claim – remains too susceptible to acts of domination.

In 2008 and 2009, Aboriginal and treaty rights lawyer Maria Morellato completed two studies on Crown consultation policies and practices for the National Centre for First Nations Governance.[54] In both studies, she concludes that, in order to foster meaningful engagement, support reconciliation, and uphold the honour of the Crown, the most important policy change that the state needs to enact is joint decision-making processes on matters pertaining to Indigenous land. She continues, this "essential 'missing piece' undermines the legitimacy of any consultation and accommodation process and renders 'referrals' associated with Crown decisions affecting land and resources largely ineffective and dysfunctional."[55] Morellato identifies the sometimes contradictory founding principles of the consultation doctrine, arguing in favour of the underlying foundations of honour and reconciliation as opposed to teleological principles related to spectrum analysis.

The Crown has recognized that inclusion in decision-making is a concern within the consultation doctrine debate. In the past, British Columbia discussed limited joint decision-making processes but no policies emerged from those conversations.[56] In the government's 2011 guidelines for federal officials to fulfil the duty to consult, the government provides a series of guiding principles to enact change in Indigenous-state relations. The second principle provides the opportunity for consultation with Indigenous Peoples in decision-making if the government deems such a measure appropriate. The consultation directive of the third principle states, "Federal officials must be able to demonstrate in decision making processes that Aboriginal concerns have been addressed or incorporated into the planning of proposed federal activities."[57] The fourth guiding principle clearly outlines a communicative method of engagement. It reads,

> The Government of Canada and its officials are required to carry out a fair and reasonable process for consultations. A meaningful consultation process is characterized by good faith and an attempt by parties to understand each other's concerns, and move to address them ... Federal officials, during a consultation process, must reasonably ensure that Aboriginal groups have an opportunity to express their interests and concerns, and that they are seriously considered and, wherever possible, clearly reflected in a proposed activity. Aboriginal groups also have a reciprocal responsibility to participate in consultation processes. ... Federal officials must seek to develop processes that move beyond a project-by-project approach to consultation and move towards one that facilitates the inclusion of Aboriginal perspectives, timely decision making, integrates with and strengthens regulatory processes and promotes economic benefits for all Canadians.[58]

The eighth guiding principle stipulates that the government will "develop and maintain meaningful dialogue with its partners" (i.e., Aboriginal groups) to facilitate long-term relationships.[59] Often other policies and legislation such as the environmental assessment process will help to carry out these principles.

Despite the theoretical underpinnings of the doctrine as a step towards deliberative processes of joint decision-making, the Taku River Tlingit case remains a foundational case for the implementation of the duty to consult and accommodate. Decisions ultimately rest with the state because it is responsible for the interests of all Canadians. The guidelines for consultation read, "The duty to consult does not include an obligation on the Crown to agree with Aboriginal groups on how the concerns raised during consultations will be resolved."[60] There is an inherent tension between the reconciliatory foundation and implementation of the consultation doctrine. In certain circumstances the doctrine might call for joint decision-making but such is rarely the case.[61] Moreover, in the guidelines, the state portrays itself as a "partner" in conversation with others; but in implementation, the state asserts itself as a neutral mediator of competing claims.

Herein lies an unresolved tension when it comes to Canada's relationship with Indigenous Peoples: How can a state be both an interested partner and a neutral mediator? This tension is what makes the ideal form of the duty to consult and accommodate so difficult to implement. The fact that Indigenous Peoples may have different perspectives on land, governance, law, property, and religion renders deliberative processes even more important. Many of the foundational principles of the consultation doctrine emphasize the Canadian state's recognition of inclusion, the broadening of social knowledge, and the role of narrative in mending the oppressive and dominative Indigenous-state relationship that continues to be present today. However, the state has also shown that in moving towards a nation-to-nation relationship, it is unwilling to relinquish its role as both self-determining participant and mediator of self-development.

The Voisey's Bay Mine and Mill Project Negotiation

The consultation doctrine is not so rigidly defined that it offers no hope of redress for Indigenous Peoples. The challenge, to reiterate, is to reconcile the contradictory role of the state in the communicative process. We can find precedent in the Voisey's Bay Mine and Mill Project negotiations. In 1994, Vancouver-based mining company Diamond Fields Resources Inc. discovered a significant mineral deposit at Voisey's Bay in Labrador. The site is 35 kilometres southwest of the Inuit community of Nain and 79 kilometres northwest of the Innu village of Davis Inlet. At the time, both the Innu and Inuit claimed the area as their own unceded territory.[62] Diamond Fields, supposedly unaware of pending Indigenous land disputes in the area, accumulated more than 8,000 claims and set up exploratory drill sites without formally consulting the Inuit or the Innu. In February 1995, Diamond Fields' actions prompted a blockade and protest from the Innu Nation, resulting in $15,000 in damages from fires set at the exploration site. Innu leader Peter Penashue told reporters, "From the Canadian point of view, [the arson is] against the law ... But from international law, we feel we are within our rights because these are trespassers who have come into our lands."[63] In late June 1995, the Newfoundland and Labrador provincial government, responding to public pressure, took action to mediate the situation. They banned further claims to the Voisey's Bay area and instructed existing claim holders that they would require government approval before conducting operations in the region.[64] Reports of burial sites and other historical and culturally significant spaces did not stop Diamond Fields from moving forward with their project without any meaningful consultation with the Innu or Inuit. In *Mining, the Environment and Indigenous Development Conflicts*, Saleem H. Ali notes that Diamond Fields "clearly had little or no incentive to interact constructively with the native groups because their aim was mainly to sell the company to a larger mineral conglomerate."[65]

At a conference on the impacts of mining on Indigenous Peoples in Sudbury, Ontario, William Barbour, president of the Labrador Inuit Association (LIA), stated, "A lot of people look at [the Voisey's Bay mining project] as the greatest thing that's happened in North America in the last 30 years. But for a lot of us back in Labrador, this is going at a pace we've never seen ... We're said to be anti-development, but we're not. We just want it to be done properly and we want to have a say in it."[66] Early in 1996, the Innu Nation Taskforce on Mining Activity completed a report titled *Ntesinan, Nteshiniminan, Nteniunan (Between a Rock and a Hard Place)* in which it asserted that Diamond Fields should broaden their conception of the environment and commit themselves to an ongoing partnership with the Innu that involves meaningful participation in decision-making. The report also encouraged the Innu to continue protesting as a means to effect change if consultation was unsatisfactory.[67]

In August 1996, international Canadian mining giant Inco Limited purchased Diamond Fields for $4.3 billion, securing the Voisey's Bay claim. In the following month, the Voisey's Bay Nickel Company (VBNC), a wholly owned Newfoundland subsidiary of

Inco, filed for an environmental assessment under the Canadian Environmental Assessment Act. The environmental assessment process is a necessary and crucial step in the development of resource projects such as those at Voisey's Bay. Without clearance through the environmental assessment process, the project cannot move forward. Shortly after VBNC made this announcement, Canada, the provincial government, the LIA, and the Innu Nation entered an unprecedented agreement in the relatively short history of environmental assessments. Ali explains, they "successfully negotiated a memorandum of understanding (MOU) establishing a joint, four-party environmental assessment process for the project ... Instead of the federal minister making the final decision on the project, a panel would report to all four parties."[68] Participants signed the MOU on 31 January 1997. The minister for the provincial Department of Mines and Energy stated, "It is unique in that it is a four-party agreement on mining in the North ... It means that there's a harmonized process so there's one environmental impact assessment and that Aboriginal groups had and will continue to have full formal input." In the same report, the federal environment minister stated, "The harmonization process will ensure an efficient, effective and fair evaluation. One in which all interested individuals and groups will have an equal opportunity to express their views and concerns about the project."[69]

The MOU declared that the minister should select panellists from a list of nominations generated between the four groups.[70] Each group could nominate three individuals and the minister had to include at least one individual from each nomination list.[71] One of the primary responsibilities of this panel was to establish the guidelines for the environmental impact statement (EIS) that the VBNC must complete. Upon reviewing the project proposal and separate reports from both the LIA and the Innu Nation, the panel created draft EIS guidelines that they presented to the public. Step 4 in the review process reads,

> The Panel will carry out a comprehensive scoping exercise to explain the Review process, to help identify priority issues to be addressed during the Review, and to receive comments on the Panel's Draft EIS

Guidelines. The scoping exercise must include seeking Innu and Inuit views about traditional ecological knowledge to be used for [environmental assessment] purposes, how traditional ecological knowledge should be obtained and how it should be evaluated. The scoping exercise will be carried out through public meetings in the communities of Nain, Utshimasits, Sheshatshiu, Hopedale, Makkovik, Rigolet, Postville and in other locations in the Province as may be determined by the Panel. Oral comments received at public meetings will be considered by the Panel as fully as written comments.[72]

Once the panel accepts the EIS, the panel brings the report to the public again for comments. Step 9 in the review process reads, "Once the Panel determines that the EIS is sufficient to proceed to public hearings, it will schedule and announce the public hearings within 7 days. The Panel will attempt to schedule the public hearings to maximize the attendance and participation of the public, taking into account the seasonal activities and traditional practices of the Innu and Inuit."[73] In addition, the MOU states that virtually all material collected must be available in Innu-aimun and Inuktitut at the same time they are available in English. Some information must also be available in audio format. The panel conducted twenty scoping hearings throughout Labrador, and thirty-two public hearings following the completion of the EIS.[74]

The MOU explicitly called for the inclusion of Indigenous knowledge in the assessment of environmental impacts. To include traditional knowledge, VBNC would have to include the narratives of Inuit and Innu peoples. Throughout the EIS, VBNC intersperses Indigenous narratives to foster the inclusion of traditional knowledge. For example, in the introduction to the EIS, it reads,

VBNC is committed to the consideration of Aboriginal knowledge in the environmental assessment process. VBNC has incorporated Aboriginal knowledge into environmental planning and in this EIS document to the extent that such knowledge has been made available by Aboriginal peoples.

"Aboriginal knowledge means things like the knowing that you learn from hunting over the course of your life, and the kind of knowing that makes you want to respect the animal spirits, and how all these ways of knowing work together to help you understand and make predictions about the proposed mining project at Voisey's Bay."[75]

I have quoted the EIS in English above, but it is also available in Innu-aimun and Inuktitut. VBNC joined in partnership with the Innu Nation to better integrate Indigenous knowledge into the EIS and promote a holistic approach to ecology.[76] VBNC, along with their Indigenous partners, sought to demonstrate that actions affecting migration patterns and breeding grounds impacted not only animals but also the cultures, spiritual practices, and ways of life of the Indigenous Peoples in Labrador. For example, chapter 16 on caribou opens with an Innu narrative and proceeds to contextualize that information for the purposes of the EIS. It reads, "Hunting is more than food on the table. It is a fundamental part of who we are. It is part of our way of life. The animals we hunt are not just commodities. We believe that they are given to us by the animal masters, and that by hunting, we show respect for the land and all that it provides."[77] The EIS continues:

> Caribou are important to the residents of northern Labrador, particularly Innu and Inuit for whom it is a major part of their diet. Caribou are also the focus of many cultural activities of the region and are an important base of the traditional economy. The harvest of caribou is part of the social structure and culture of Labrador north coast communities.[78]

Notably, the cultural poignancy of the caribou for the LIA and Innu was clear and unmistakeable in the EIS. The prevalent inclusion of narrative throughout the report and the number of public panel meetings conducted demonstrate a commitment to inclusive, just proceedings. More important, however, is the fact that the LIA and Innu Nation were included as partners. The ability of Innu and Inuit governments to deliberate on the formal parameters of deliberation allowed for individuals within those communities to participate in a meaningful way. The third-party panel acted as administrator for the process and ultimately the LIA, Innu Nation, provincial, and federal governments were answerable to each other. In many ways, the Voisey's Bay negotiation accomplished what the liberal state often cannot: the deterritorialization of sovereignty.

Conclusion

Both the Canadian state and Indigenous Peoples have identified that a more just Indigenous-state relationship is a more inclusive, deliberative one. In the current context for Indigenous-state discussions – namely, the duty to consult and accommodate – communicative democratic theory helps to identify both the importance and limitations of the doctrine. The doctrine embodies principles of listening and narrative, central to the communicative process and integral to overcoming problems of cultural incommensurability. At the same time, the promotion of self-determination through inclusive participation in decision-making processes is only meaningful if no participant in those deliberations also holds the power to define the contours of deliberation and, in turn, mediate communication. The Canadian state often occupies an ambiguous role in Indigenous-state relations as both mediator and self-interested party or partner. The consultation doctrine, for the time being and despite its best intentions, does not provide Indigenous Peoples with the justice they desire.

The consultation doctrine seemingly indicates the state's recognition that justice requires the relinquishing of some power in the current Indigenous-state relationship. At Voisey's Bay, the affected parties (i.e., the government, the Innu, and Inuit) together formed a third-party panel of relatively unbiased experts to mediate the deliberative process based on jointly established guidelines. The Innu Nation and LIA did not have veto power at Voisey's Bay, and there is nothing to indicate that they sought such power. What they sought, and received, was participation and inclusion in decisions and processes of deciding. Whereas Voisey's Bay demonstrates the potential of consultation to overcome the prevailing issue of domination, the *Taku River* decision demonstrates how relinquishment is conditional upon the generosity of the state.

To be fair, the consultation doctrine and communicative democracy are cyclical and ongoing, at least from a theoretical perspective. Amy Gutmann and Dennis Thompson explain, "The open-ended nature of deliberation enables citizens or legislators to challenge earlier decisions, including decisions about the procedures for making decisions. Deliberative democracy's provisionality checks the excesses of conventional democracy's finality."[79] Once participants have committed to a form of deliberative engagement, the process of deliberation should inevitably allow participants to change the very structures of engagement. Of course this assumes that the subject of public debate is negotiable and its alteration will not unalterably impact any participant's deliberative location so that they can return to the process and continue discussion. In other words, the cyclical nature of the consultation doctrine is immaterial when the fate of cosmologically significant space is the subject of debate, making the first cycle of deliberation one of finality.

Two challenges are clear. First, the Habermasian notion of "neutral" public deliberative space is, as Asad argues, a fallacy. "The public sphere," he contends, "is *necessarily* (and not just contingently) articulated by power. And everyone who enters it must address power's disposition of people and things, the dependence of some on the good will of others."[80] Second, a particular group may be active participants in decision-making processes, but the "structures of possible action" regulate those decisions independently of Indigenous input.[81] Implementation or acceptance of those "western" structures, Asad contends, brings with them "specific forms of power and subjection."[82] Even if the state has allowed Indigenous Peoples into the decision-making processes, Asad would ask, "Who is its author, who is its subject?"[83]

Indigenous scholars have offered their thoughts on the feasibility of Euro-Canadian politics and procedure and there is no consensus. John Borrows argues that one can find correlations between Indigenous philosophies of law and politics and those of Euro-Canadian society.[84] For Borrows, the state and Indigenous Peoples can engage each other in a mutually respectful manner on a common ground. Borrows contends that Indigenous perspectives can also contribute to broadening the state's knowledge of a variety of issues. At a fundamental level, Borrows believes that the state and Indigenous Peoples can work together to overcome colonial structures. Dale Turner is critical of Borrows's assertions regarding commonalities but praises him, nonetheless, as a "word warrior" skilled and engaged in both Indigenous and European legal philosophies. Turner argues that Indigenous "word warriors," such as Borrows, need to engage in agonic political dialogue to attain political power and effect change at the foundations of Euro-Canadian legal-political understandings.[85] In both cases, these scholars promote the inclusion of Indigenous Peoples within colonial structures in order that they may alter systemic issues of power at their origin. At the same time, scholars such as Taiaiake Alfred, discussed in the previous chapter, call attention to the subjects of authorship and co-optation through acts of participation in Euro-Canadian legal and political structures.[86]

Of course, in order to be included, one must first be recognized. Aboriginal rights are only afforded to those who are recognized as "Indian, Métis, and Inuit." There are Indigenous Peoples who do not want to be recognized, or co-opted, in the Euro-Canadian legal order.[87] Some groups may choose to align themselves politically with traditional hereditary leadership or a broader religious community, such as that which occurred at Gustafsen Lake. At the same time, there are groups who want to be recognized and are not. Dwight Newman explains how the state has marginalized some Indigenous Peoples from consultation processes because they are not officially recognized. He recounts that the court rejected the province-wide Native Council of Nova Scotia because it contained some non-Mi'kmaq members. In 2007, the Alberta Energy and Utilities Board applied a ruling handed down in Newfoundland and Labrador earlier that year when they denied political recognition to four different parties. Newman explains that among these groups were "two groups attempting to constitute themselves from individuals of already existing Indian Act bands, of an individual not connected to an Aboriginal community, and of an elders' society not showing itself to be the corporate agent of a rights-bearing Aboriginal community."[88] Michael Ross points to the same issue for groups who have separated from recognized communities of

Indigenous Peoples, such as the Kelly Lake Cree Nation, discussed in the opening chapters of this book, and the Poplar Point Ojibway First Nation, as noted in the preface.[89] The courts contended that neither group possessed any rights to state consultation regarding developments on their land.[90] Thus, the state also acts as decision maker as to those who are allowed to participate in communicative processes of consultation.

Without dismissing issues of power and recognition, it does appear that communicative democracy and the consultation doctrine move towards an awareness of the challenge of incommensurability. Young's emphasis on narrative in the communicative process recognizes that not all experiences or stories can be verbalized, challenging all participants to abandon universalist notions of definitive commensurability. To return to Cordova, addressing incommensurability begins with "acceptance that there is the possibility of the other as *other* (and not simply as a distortion of oneself) ... One must be willing to accept the other as *equal*; that is, both parties have something to say and can provide their own explanations for their end of the dialogue."[91] Cordova's assertion seems to be shared by both Young in her definition of communitive democracy and Newman in his explanation of the consultation doctrine.

It should be no surprise that the 2017 SCC decision in *Ktunaxa Nation v. British Columbia* affirms the fragile position of Indigenous Peoples in the consultation doctrine. Citing *Haida Nation*, Chief Justice McLachlin wrote,

> It is true ... that the Minister did not offer the ultimate accommodation demanded by the Ktunaxa ... It does not follow ... that the Crown failed to meet its obligation to consult and accommodate. The s. 35 right to consultation and accommodation is a right to a process, not a right to a particular outcome ... While the goal of the process is reconciliation of the Aboriginal and state interest, in some cases this may not be possible. The process is one of "give and take," and outcomes are not guaranteed.[92]

The state has proven itself to be a self-interested party in the Indigenous-state relationship. The fact that Indigenous Peoples remain largely excluded from participating in the administrative structures that continue to influence their communities, cultures, and lives is an underlying cause of the persistent threat to Indigenous religious traditions. This is why many Indigenous Peoples have turned to international mechanisms, both binding and non-binding, to mediate or influence their persisting colonial relationship with the Canadian state.

chapter six

The Potential and Limits of International Mechanisms of Redress

In the past few decades, Indigenous Peoples around the world have come together in international forums to aid in the construction of a discernable international Indigenous rights framework. Most recently, the United Nations Declaration on the Rights of Indigenous Peoples (UNDRIP) was an important achievement in an area of international law that had received very little attention. While not binding, the declaration establishes an important benchmark for the treatment of Indigenous Peoples around the globe. It marks the beginning of a new era for Indigenous rights.

The UNDRIP is one of several mechanisms in place at the international level capable of addressing the subject of Indigenous religious freedom. Broader rights treaties on civil and political rights built on the foundational principles of the Universal Declaration of Human Rights (UDHR) provide general protections for religion and, more specifically, the religions and cultures of minority communities, while the International Labour Organization (ILO) Convention No. 169, the UNDRIP, and various mechanisms at the United Nations (UN) support the specific rights of Indigenous Peoples, including those related to religion.[1] Given the relative early stages of the development of a comprehensive Indigenous rights framework, the greatest critique of this means of redress is that it simply has not been tested. While ILO Convention No. 169 is a binding treaty, the low number of ratifications among member states renders its status relatively comparable to the non-binding UNDRIP.

Canada reluctantly endorsed the spirit of the UNDRIP in 2010, three years after most other UN member states. However, it is clear, even in the examples offered so far in this book, that the international mechanism for redress does appeal to some communities. The Ts'peten Defenders, the Innu Nation, and the Ktunaxa Nation appealed to international laws and declarations to gather strength for their claims of injustice. The state, for its part, has shown that it is susceptible to international pressure, after being found in violation of the International Covenant on Civil and Political Rights (ICCPR) by the UN Human Rights Committee. Canada has also officially invited the UN Special Rapporteur on the Rights of Indigenous Peoples to visit the country on two occasions. In this regard, it appears that the emerging international framework on Indigenous rights may hold value for Indigenous Peoples in≈Canada.

In this chapter, I hope to show both the potential extent and limitations of international Indigenous rights mechanisms. The use of international mechanisms as a source of pressure to enact change at the domestic level is the most effective use of the international rights framework on matters of Indigenous religious freedom. In many ways, the argument is a practical one. The primary mechanisms of the framework offer no means of redress at this time. What is particularly revealing about this analysis is the ways in which international mechanisms can affect and, at times, challenge state authority, including that of Canada. Given the findings in this book so far, it appears that the pursuit of international mechanisms may be a necessity for those communities claiming violations of their religious freedom. First, I offer a brief review of the history of Indigenous rights at the international level. I then turn to Canada's involvement with international Indigenous rights, beginning with *Lovelace v. Canada* (1981) and concluding with the most recent report of the special rapporteur on his visit to the country in 2013. I conclude with a brief examination of the avenues available at the Organization of American States, which Canada officially joined in 1990. In particular, the Hul'qumi'num claim before the Inter-American Commission on Human Rights offers a meaningful example of the capabilities of international mechanisms and their operation in the Canadian state as they relate to the rights of Indigenous Peoples and religious freedom.

The United Nations and the International Labour Organization

While international bodies, including the League of Nations, sought to address the discrimination of minorities following the First World War, the subject of issues pertaining to Indigenous Peoples were largely viewed as domestic in nature. Even with the creation of the United Nations and adoption of the UDHR following the Second World War, the trend remained relatively consistent. The exception came in 1957, when the International Labour Organization adopted Convention No. 107 on Indigenous and Tribal Populations. The ILO had been paying attention to the particular situations of Indigenous and tribal peoples while investigating the subject of slave labour. ILO No. 107 was a problematic convention, which embodied many of the same issues present in Canada's 1969 White Paper. The document encouraged the integration of Indigenous populations. One of the advocates foundational for the advancement of Indigenous rights at the United Nations, Augusto Willemsen Diaz, recalls that ILO No. 107 embodied ideas that "were contradictory to what we knew full well Indigenous Peoples were fundamentally seeking."[2]

Over the next two decades Diaz sought to provide a framework in which Indigenous Peoples could achieve a voice at the United Nations. Some communities acquired consultative status as nongovernmental organizations (NGOs), while others were afforded time to speak by other organizations, such as the Antislavery Society.[3] In 1977, Diaz – in cooperation with the Subcommittee on Decolonisation and against Racism, Racial Discrimination and Apartheid – helped to organize the Conference of NGOs on Discrimination against the Indigenous Populations in the Americas. A conference on Indigenous Peoples and land followed in 1981.[4]

From 1982 to 1984, a report on the discrimination of Indigenous populations was presented to the Sub-Commission for Prevention of Discrimination and Protection of Minorities. The study had been approved in 1971, and José Ricardo Martínez Cobo was assigned as special rapporteur for the study. The Sub-Commission heralded the Martínez Cobo Report as "a highly valuable contribution to the clarification of basic legal, social and cultural problems relating to Indigenous populations."[5] While the study touches on many subjects related to Indigenous religions, chapter 19 focuses on "religious rights and practices."

The chapter on religious rights rests predominantly on existing declarations and conventions on the protection of religious freedom. Four documents are commonly cited on this matter: the UDHR, the International Covenant on Economic, Social and Cultural Rights (ICESCR) of 1966, the International Covenant on Civil and Political Rights (ICCPR) of 1966, and the 1981 Declaration on Intolerance and Discrimination Based on Religion and Belief. The UDHR established the groundwork with Article 18:

> Everyone has the right to freedom of thought, conscience, and religion; this right includes freedom to change his religion or belief, and freedom, either alone or in community with others and in public or private, to manifest his religion or belief in teaching, practice, worship and observance.[6]

The ICCPR adopted the same language in its Article 18, establishing the clause as binding international law.[7] The 1981 Declaration sought to address discrimination and provides the most comprehensive rubric for the protection of religious freedom. The declaration is not a binding treaty, and it appears there is no discussion of one in the near future. The declaration did, however, provide elaboration on a human right that had not received the same kind of attention as many other rights.[8]

These international mechanisms may seem enticing given their separation from the unique cultural essence of Canadian law, but we must not forget that international law too is subject to the same critiques offered in the introduction of this book. Elizabeth Shakman Hurd explains how advocates of religious freedom ought to tread with caution into the world of international rights frameworks. She writes,

In its stronger forms, international religious freedom globalizes the secular state's power over the individual. Appearing as a guarantee of the
worth of the individual's own desires, it tells individuals and groups
how to be religious, modern, and free. In regulating religious activity
along particular lines, it privileges particular ways of being religious
as deserving protection by the state or other authorities. It singles out
authorized representatives of "believers" (and less often, "nonbelievers")
for legal protection, reinforcing divisions and hierarchies within and
between communities.[9]

In other words, declarations and conventions on religious freedom
at the international level are also fraught with cultural bias that
seeks to regulate a particular form of religion across the world.
Thus, the "epistemologically colonial" nature of law is something
of which we ought to be conscious. At the very least, recognition
of such a nature at the international level strengthens the need for
alternative frameworks for Indigenous Peoples rooted in global
indigenous legal discourses.

The Martínez Cobo Report cites the 1981 Declaration regularly,
pointing to corresponding domestic examples of the declaration
at work in the laws of particular countries around the world. In
a section titled "Special Problems of Indigenous Populations, De
Facto Situation," the report points to several examples where clear
instances of cultural bias leading to the discrimination of practitioners of traditional Indigenous religions are evident. For example,
the report cites the Indonesian constitution, which provides several clauses on the freedom of conscience and religion. One particularly noteworthy characteristic is the inclusion of belief in God,
a classic definitional limitation easily identifiable in the history of
the discipline of religious studies. The problem is that many Indigenous Peoples in Indonesia live animistic traditions. In turn, their
animistic beliefs are not protected by the constitution.[10] The report
explains that several countries specifically address Indigenous
religions in their constitutions including Guatemala and New
Zealand. [11] The report addresses states that have claimed that existing general religious freedom laws protect Indigenous religious
freedom equally. While Canada receives a mention in a footnote

for making such a claim, the case of the United States is where the report highlights how Indigenous religions may be discriminated against indirectly.[12] A source cited in the report explains that traditional Native American religious practices have been challenged in the United States through various laws not aimed at Indigenous religions, including burial restrictions, governance structuring, and drug usage. The source also cites the historical mistreatment of Indigenous religions, articulating that popular perceptions of Indigenous religions are often negative.[13] These statements draw attention to the continuing impacts of colonialism and cultural bias in matters of Indigenous religious freedom.

The report weighs in on the subject of the definition of "religion" as well. Following a brief comment on the historical confrontation between Indigenous Peoples and European colonizers, which manifested in the rejection of Indigenous religions from the category of "religion," the report suggests "perhaps a new horizon will be open" if religion, in whatever substance, is "recognized as performing essentially the same function and serving the same fundamental purpose."[14] Martínez Cobo's suggestion draws important attention to the subject of the construct of religion addressed in chapter 1 of this book. While his remark about the purpose and function of religion is a substantive statement, this kind of attention to the specific issues faced by practitioners of traditional Indigenous religions and the recognition of the connection between power and the parameters of what counts as religion are important lines of enquiry in this foundational study on Indigenous rights.

In 1982, Diaz, who had been working on the Martínez Cobo Report, secured a Working Group on Indigenous Populations (WGIP), which aimed to provide a forum for Indigenous Peoples to voice their concerns at the United Nations. The WGIP would quickly act to remove the consultative status requirement so that Indigenous Peoples could participate with greater ease.[15] In 1985, the WGIP committed to drafting a declaration on the rights of Indigenous Peoples. Indigenous Peoples participated in the drafting process of the declaration. Twenty-two years later, the UNDRIP, Resolution 61/295, was passed by the General Assembly in a vote of 143–4 with 11 abstentions. The four countries who voted against the UNDRIP included Australia, New Zealand, the United States, and Canada.

The subject of religion is specifically dealt with throughout the UNDRIP. Although it is wise to remember that to say that religion is unrelated to matters of resource development or self-government would effectively act to distil religion into a series of bits and privileges separating religion from the domain of power. Nevertheless, the specific clauses on religion have been cited by Indigenous Peoples appealing to the United Nations on matters of religious freedom. Some of the key articles include:

> 12.1. Indigenous Peoples have the right to manifest, practise, develop and teach their spiritual and religious traditions, customs and ceremonies; the right to maintain, protect, and have access in privacy to their religious and cultural sites; the right to the use and control of their ceremonial objects; and the right to the repatriation of their human remains.
>
> 12.2. States shall seek to enable the access and/or repatriation of ceremonial objects and human remains in their possession through fair, transparent and effective mechanisms developed in conjunction with Indigenous Peoples concerned.[16]
>
> 25. Indigenous Peoples have the right to maintain and strengthen their distinctive spiritual relationship with their traditionally owned or otherwise occupied and used lands, territories, waters and coastal seas and other resources and to uphold their responsibilities to future generations in this regard.[17]

The declaration is not binding, but it offers a framework for Indigenous rights at the international level. These articles on religious freedom address many of the specific challenges faced by Indigenous Peoples in countries around the world. The articles pertain to specific features of Indigenous religions and seek to address issues pertaining to the colonial context. Notably, "belief" is not mentioned in these articles of the UNDRIP.

Aside from the effectiveness of a non-binding international document such as the UNDRIP, some critics argue that the declaration does not go far enough on certain subjects. This is, in part, due to the intervention of countries such as Canada, among others, during the drafting process who sought to protect the autonomy of states. One of the most limiting statements in the UNDRIP is Article 46, which significantly limits the right to self-determination guaranteed under Article 3.[18] The final article reads as follows:

> 46(1). Nothing in this Declaration may be interpreted as implying for any State, people, group or person any right to engage in any activity or to perform any act contrary to the Charter of the United Nations or construed as authorizing or encouraging any action which would dismember or impair, totally or in part, the territorial integrity or political unity of sovereign and independent States.[19]

Former chairperson of the WGIP Asbjørn Eide explains that with the addition of this clause, important statements of cooperation between Indigenous Peoples and states were excised. He provides the example of the following sentence from the preamble which did not make the final draft of the UNDRIP: "Recognizing that Indigenous Peoples have the right freely to determine their relationships with States in a spirit of coexistence, mutual benefit and full respect."[20]

Another, more recent accusation of states and their interpretation of the UNDRIP has been termed "rights ritualism." The Expert Mechanism on the Rights of Indigenous Peoples (EMRIP) communicated this fact in their eighth plenary meeting in 2015. Its report defines "rights ritualism" as the affirmation of positive human rights while deflecting responsibility for human rights violations.[21] The matter was discussed in several forums in 2015, including an EMRIP expert group meeting about the potential for an optional protocol for the UNDRIP in January 2015.[22] This meeting discussed the possibility of an oversight committee to monitor the implementation of the UNDRIP. They argued that "rights ritualism," in particular, poses a significant problem for the realization of the UNDRIP. Here, EMRIP introduces the idea of a Convention on the Rights of Indigenous Peoples.[23]

Despite these issues, it is important to remember that there is still a great deal of ground covered in the UNDRIP. Eide reminds readers, "The Declaration remains a very ambitious text, going very far in justifying Indigenous Peoples' claims to far-reaching autonomy, control over lands, veto over development projects which the Indigenous consider undesirable, and far-reaching claims for restitution or compensation. It is indeed an historic document."[24]

While the declaration was being drafted, the ILO offered another convention on Indigenous and Tribal Peoples. ILO Convention No. 169 marked a significant shift from the classical liberal sentiments evident in Convention No. 107. The convention supported the self-determination and self-development of Indigenous and tribal peoples, specifically addressing the subject of religion in Article 5 and Article 7.[25] The major problem with the convention is that it has been ratified by only twenty-two countries, the majority of which are located in Central and South America. As we will see, it remains an important reference point for advocates of Indigenous rights given its binding nature.

There are several other mechanisms at work at the United Nations that offer Indigenous Peoples opportunities to voice their concerns at the international level. Most notably, the Permanent Forum on Indigenous Issues (PFII) has been meeting regularly since 2002. The PFII consists of sixteen elected representatives, eight from governments and eight from communities of Indigenous Peoples. While the PFII is only an advisory body, it embodies the spirit of equal partnership central to the broader Indigenous rights movement. Other important mechanisms include the special rapporteur on Indigenous issues and EMRIP, who report to the UN Human Rights Council. Most recently, the World Conference on Indigenous Peoples (WCIP), a high-level plenary meeting, brought together Indigenous Peoples and heads of state at the United Nations.

In sum, while there are few binding treaties in international law on the rights of Indigenous Peoples, there is a comprehensive Indigenous rights framework that continues to develop with the active participation of Indigenous Peoples around the world. Correspondingly, the framework on religious freedom continues to develop as well, including the above-mentioned documents cited by the Martínez Cobo Report, a special rapporteur on religion or belief, and a 1996 UN elaboration on Article 18 of the UDHR.[26] In other words, the viability and effectiveness of international mechanisms of redress are uncertain at this time, but there is certainly a great deal of time and energy being spent on these frameworks.

Canada and International Indigenous Rights

Canada's treatment of Indigenous Peoples has commanded the attention of the international community for quite some time. The most notable instance took place in 1981, when Sandra Lovelace brought a human rights complaint against the SCC's ruling on the subject of Indian status under the Indian Act. In 1973, the Supreme Court ruled that the requirements for status under the Indian Act were exempt from the Bill of Rights. Sandra Lovelace, a Maliseet women from New Brunswick, married a "non-Indian" (as defined by the act) in 1970 and, in accordance with section 12(1) of the Indian Act, lost her status as an Indian at this time. Her marriage eventually broke up, at which point Lovelace was unable to legally return to live on her reserve with her family. Lovelace appealed to the ICCPR, which had only become binding in 1976 for Canada. I discussed Article 18 of the ICCPR above, but this case was primarily concerned with equality rights guaranteed under Article 2 and the protection of minority cultures, addressed under Article 27. Based on the timing of the implementation of the ICCPR for Canada, the Human Rights Committee (HRC) could only consider the effects of the law, rather than the application of the law, which took place six years prior to the ICCPR coming into effect.

The HRC was particularly concerned with one claim offered by Lovelace. She explained one adverse effect of the court decision as follows: "The major loss to a person ceasing to be an Indian is the loss of the cultural benefits of living in an Indian community, the emotional ties to home, family, friends and neighbours, and the loss of identity."[27] The HRC saw this as a potential violation of Article 27 of the ICCPR, which reads,

In those States in which ethnic, religious or linguistic minorities exist, persons belonging to such minorities shall not be denied the right, in community with the other members of their group, to enjoy their own culture, to profess and practise their own religion, or to use their own language.[28]

The HRC determined that the interpretation of the Indian Act was a violation of Article 27.[29] For its part, the Canadian state communicated its concern with the interpretation of the law and cited that legislative proposals were being considered to amend the Indian Act and to provide greater autonomy for First Nations to determine membership in accordance with the Bill of Rights.[30] Eventually, in 1985, Bill C-31 would offer this correction to the Indian Act.

In her article, "Gender, Sovereignty, and the Discourse of Rights in Native Women's Activism," Joanne Barker succinctly explains how international mechanisms came to play an important role in addressing violations of Indigenous women's rights. She explains,

Lovelace v. Canada severely embarrassed Canadian officials as Canada was in the process of patriating from England. Had Canada not been so, Parliament would have probably paid only lip service to the HRC's conclusions. However, being found in violation of international human rights accords in their treatment of Indian women on the occasion of their patriation from the Crown and revision of their Constitution and Bill of Rights produced a unique situation in which Parliament and [the Department of Indian Affairs and Northern Development] felt compelled to save face by pushing the [National Indian Brotherhood] and band governments for an amendment to the Indian Act.[31]

The Lovelace case is foundational for Indigenous rights in Canada. Lovelace demonstrated how international mechanisms could be used effectively by appealing to the HRC. It also helped to emphasize the potential impact of international conventions on domestic policy. Most importantly, Lovelace provides an example of a successful use of international mechanisms of redress for Indigenous Peoples. Granted, the international pressure that pushed Canada to move quickly on the subject of equality standards in the Indian Act was certainly the result of a unique confluence of historically specific events. Nevertheless, the mechanisms exist and have worked. Whether it is superficial or a matter of engaging in "rights ritualism" is a subject beyond the scope of this chapter, but Canada has hosted the special rapporteur on two separate occasions. In 2003–4, Special Rapporteur Rodolfo Stavenhagen visited Canada and spoke with Indigenous Peoples, government officials, and academics. Stavenhagen offered several suggestions for the government based on his findings. Among these recommendations were the following:

• New legislation on Aboriginal rights based on the RCAP Report of 1996
• Ratification of ILO Convention 169
• Assurances that Aboriginal rights cannot be extinguished
• A study of new self-government agreements
• Updated domestic human rights standards[32]

In reference to the RCAP Report, Stavenhagen specifically addresses the dispossession of Indigenous lands and need for "places of cultural and spiritual meaning."[33]

In 2007, Canada chose not to endorse the UNDRIP for several reasons largely related to the perceived incongruence between the UNDRIP and the Constitution. Canada's discontent with the declaration lessened in the next few years. In 2010, they endorsed the spirit of the UNDRIP, reiterating their concerns as follows:

Although the declaration is a non-legally binding document that does not reflect customary international law nor change Canadian laws, our endorsement gives us the opportunity to reiterate our commitment to continue working in partnership with Aboriginal peoples in creating a better Canada.

In 2007, at the time of the vote during the United Nations General Assembly, and since, Canada placed on record its concerns with various provisions of the Declaration, including provisions dealing with lands, territories and resources; free, prior and informed consent [FPIC] when used as a veto; self-government without recognition of the importance of negotiations; intellectual property; military issues; and the need to achieve an appropriate balance between the rights and obligations of Indigenous Peoples, States and third parties. These concerns are well known and remain. However, we have since listened to Aboriginal leaders who have urged Canada to endorse the Declaration and we have also learned from the experience of other countries. We are now confident that Canada can interpret the principles expressed in the Declaration in a manner that is consistent with our Constitution and legal framework.[34]

While the government had announced its intention to endorse the UNDRIP earlier that year, it wasn't until 12 November 2010 that the endorsement became official. Three days later, on 15 November, the Ktunaxa Nation released the *Qat'muk Declaration* appealing to Article 12 and Article 25 of the UNDRIP, cited above.[35]

In 2013, Special Rapporteur James Anaya accepted an official invitation to visit Canada and review the situation of Indigenous Peoples in the country. In his conclusions, Anaya praised Canada's constitutional order and various initiatives taken by the federal government to alleviate many of the unequal social and economic conditions faced by Indigenous Peoples. Anaya also commended the government for its embrace of a reconciliatory approach in the form of the TRC, although he stressed that the initiative required an extension. Generally speaking, Anaya was very critical of the state, arguing that "daunting challenges remain" and many of the initiatives taken have been "insufficient."[36] Anaya recommended increased consultation with Indigenous Peoples on all matters affecting their lives, greater communication between all levels of government, special attention to education and housing, and investigations into the situation of missing Indigenous women and girls.[37] Anaya was critical of the "adversarial" position of the government when it came to treaty and land negotiations, stipulating that the government should demonstrate that Indigenous issues are indeed part of the public interest.[38] In relation to the duty to consult and accommodate, Anaya writes,

In accordance with the Canadian Constitution and relevant international human rights standards, as a general rule resource extraction should not occur on lands subject to aboriginal claims without adequate consultations with and the free, prior and informed consent of the Indigenous Peoples concerned. Also, Canada should endeavour to put in place a policy framework for implementing the duty to consult that allows for Indigenous Peoples' genuine input and involvement at the earliest stages of project development.[39]

Where his predecessor urged for the adoption of ILO Convention No. 169, Anaya points to the UNDRIP as a guiding document for Indigenous-state relations. He writes, "The United Nations Declaration on the Rights of Indigenous Peoples, which has been endorsed by Canada, provides a common framework within which the issues faced by Indigenous Peoples in the country can be addressed."[40] And, while the case is only briefly noted, the Ktunaxa Nation's claim to violations of their religious freedom is presented to the United Nations in the final report of the special rapporteur.[41]

The UNDRIP continues to remain a focal point for many Indigenous Peoples in Canada. In December 2014, New Democratic Party member of Parliament Romeo Saganash put forth Bill C-641. The bill sought to ensure that the laws of Canada were in accordance with the UNDRIP. The bill followed the WCIP, where Canada, along with other participants, affirmed the measures put forth in the UNDRIP. [42] The bill did not make it to a second reading in a vote of 149–131. The bill would have compelled Canada to report on its activities with Indigenous Peoples and demonstrate its compliance with the UNDRIP through 2036. The rejection of the second reading of Bill C-641 led National Chief Perry Bellegarde to state the following: "The same government that endorsed the UN Declaration on the Rights of Indigenous Peoples has now actively defeated a bill that would compel Canada to act on its endorsement." He continued, "This is a betrayal of Canada's commitments to First Nations and all its citizens. Canada consistently pretends to be a defender of human rights on the international stage while working to undermine those same rights here at home."[43]

While at the PFII, only a few weeks prior to the dismissal of Bill C-641, Bellegarde spoke at a session on human rights. He cited

Anaya's preliminary findings that the UNDRIP offers a framework for "justice, reconciliation and peace."[44] Bellegarde raised the subject of Bill C-641, calling attention to the Canadian government's opposition to the bill, particularly the subject of FPIC, which the government feels would implement veto power for Indigenous Peoples. The Assembly of First Nations (AFN) called for the PFII to emphasize the significance of the UNDRIP and called attention to violations of the UNDRIP (particularly the issue of rights ritualism) in member states.[45]

For its part, the Liberal government of Justin Trudeau has taken action in moving towards implementation of the UNDRIP. Canada officially adopted the declaration without qualifications in 2016 and the minister of Indigenous and Northern Affairs communicated the following at the 2017 PFII: Canada has called for a "working group to review all federal laws and policies related to indigenous peoples, to reverse the colonial and paternalistic approaches. This is about breathing life into Section 35 of Canada's Constitution which formally entrenches the rights of indigenous people in Canadian law, and yet for far too long has not been lived up to."[46] Whether this is an act of rights ritualism or a genuine attempt at reconciliation remains to be seen, but this book has demonstrated that it is not just those laws and policies related specifically to Indigenous Peoples that impede the possibility of Indigenous religious freedom.

Much like general statements on the potential for international Indigenous rights mechanisms, the situation in Canada is equally untested and unknown. History indicates that Canada will invite assessment from the international community and receive critique. At times, Canada has responded to international criticism. Whether the state ignores those recommendations, engages in rights ritualism, or meaningfully enacts positive change seems to depend on the particulars of each concern. Clearly, at this time, Canada has defined the limits of the applicability of the UNDRIP in its rejection of what it feels is incongruent with existing Canadian law. Despite this, many Indigenous Peoples have referred to the declaration and other mechanisms in their pursuits of justice.

The Hul'qumi'num Treaty Group, Canada, and the Inter-American Commission on Human Rights

In addition to the mechanisms in place at the United Nations, Canada is also involved in the Organization of American States (OAS). The OAS officially came together in its contemporary form in 1948. That same year, the OAS adopted the Declaration on the Rights and Duties of Man. A portion of the preamble speaks to the primacy of religion and culture. It reads,

> Inasmuch as spiritual development is the supreme end of human existence and the highest expression thereof, it is the duty of man to serve that end with all his strength and resources.
>
> Since culture is the highest social and historical expression of that spiritual development, it is the duty of man to preserve, practice and foster culture by every means within his power.[47]

Article III of the declaration offers a general statement on the right to "profess," "manifest," and "practice" a "religious faith."[48] Article XIII, more broadly, addresses the right to culture. The declaration also led to the creation of the Inter-American Commission on Human Rights (IACHR), established as an observer of human rights in the American states. In 1969, the OAS sought to construct a binding mechanism based on the 1948 Declaration. The 1969 American Convention on Human Rights did not receive universal endorsement and ratification by its member states. The convention includes the creation of an Inter-American Court on Human Rights, but the jurisdiction of the court is restricted to those states who have ratified the convention. Canada became a member of the OAS in 1990 after twenty-eight years of observer status. The 1990 ratification of the OAS Charter made Canada subject to the jurisdiction of the IACHR. Canada has not ratified the American Convention on Human Rights, so it is not subject to the jurisdiction of the Inter-American Court of Human Rights. For this reason, the IACHR and the duties and responsibilities set forth in the 1948 Declaration remain the primary mechanisms for addressing violations of human rights in the OAS. Like the UNDRIP, these mechanisms are non-binding.

The IACHR has demonstrated its concern for the rights of Indigenous Peoples as early as the 1970s. The commission established a rapporteur on Indigenous rights in 1990. In addition to addressing specific cases in its reports over the years, in August 2015 the IACHR called on member states to protect the rights of Indigenous Peoples, drawing particular attention to land rights and consultation.[49] Canada has received attention from the IACHR for several reasons, including issues related to Indigenous rights.[50]

As evidenced in the United Nations, the OAS has also been identified by Indigenous Peoples as a means of seeking redress for what they view as violations of human rights perpetrated by the Canadian state. One particularly revealing example is the Hul'qumi'num Treaty Group (HTG) case, submitted to the IACHR in 2007, approved in 2009, and heard in 2011. The HTG represents six First Nations located in British Columbia, on south-eastern Vancouver Island, the Gulf Islands, and the lower Fraser Valley. The HTG brought several complaints to the OAS regarding Canada's alleged violation of articles enshrined in the 1948 Declaration. The 2009 IACHR decision summarized the HTG claim as follows:

> The petition alleges that the State has violated the human rights of the HTG because of the absence of demarcation, established boundaries and recording of title deed to their ancestral lands; the lack of compensation for HTG ancestral lands currently in the hands of private third parties; the granting of licenses, permits and concessions within ancestral lands without prior consultation; and the resulting destruction of the environment, the natural resources and of those sites the alleged victims consider sacred.[51]

The HTG pointed to Article II addressing equality before the law, Article XXIII regarding property rights, and Article XIII, the aforementioned right to culture.[52]

The HTG claimed that in the nineteenth century, nearly 85 per cent of their ancestral lands were forcibly taken and redistributed to non-Indigenous Peoples. Despite this, their ancestral territories remained largely undeveloped. Through the twentieth century, they "hunted, fished, gathered food and practiced ceremonies and spiritual activities."[53] With growing development in preparation for the 2010 Olympic Games in Vancouver, the HTG claimed that access to their ancestral territories had been restricted. They claimed they were denied access to sacred sites and unable to perform their religious ceremonies.[54] As with previous cases discussed in this book, the HTG claim was triggered by the allotment of development permits on their ancestral territories.[55]

The HTG initially sought redress through the British Columbia Treaty Commission (BCTC). However, in their view, the failure on the part of the Canadian state to negotiate privately held land restricted their claim to an unsatisfactory 15 per cent of their ancestral territory. In addition to financial restrictions and regulations, they claimed that they were not being treated fairly under the law.[56] More importantly, they argued that "domestic legislation does not provide for adequate and efficient remedies to serve the specific claims of the petitioners."[57]

The state disagreed with the HTG claim. In addition to the BCTC processes, the state, for its part, had offered to enter into negotiations with the HTG and reiterated that there are financial support structures available for Indigenous land claims processes. The state argued that "a final agreement can give Indigenous Peoples the authority to preserve their cultural interests inside and outside of the ancestral lands agreed upon in the negotiating process."[58] The state proceeded to discuss several domestic mechanisms of redress available to the HTG, stipulating that the Charter protects the right to equality before the law and religious freedom. The state further stipulated that the HTG claim to violations of religious freedom was "not properly developed."[59] In the state's opinion, the IACHR should dismiss the claim of the HTG based on procedural protocols regulating the exhaustion of domestic remedies prior to admission to the IACHR.[60]

In its ruling on the admissibility of the HTG claim, the IACHR found in favour of the petitioners. The IACHR was supportive of the BCTC process but decided that the timeline for treaty processes and the limited scope of the BCTC process makes the HTG claim admissible before the IACHR. The commission writes,

The IACHR notes that the third exception to the requirement of exhaustion of domestic remedies applies due to the unwarranted delay on the part of the State to find a solution to the claim [i.e., fifteen years]. Likewise, the IACHR notes that by failing to resolve the HTG claims with regard to their ancestral lands, the BCTC process has demonstrated that it is not an effective mechanism to protect the right alleged by the alleged victims. Therefore, the first exception to the requirement of exhaustion of domestic remedies applies because there is no due process of law to protect the property rights of the HTG to its ancestral lands.[61]

The IACHR further stipulated that another exemption to the exhaustion criteria is met "when it is evident from the case file that any action filed regarding that complaint had no reasonable chance of success based on the prevailing jurisprudence of the highest courts of the State."[62] This is a striking critique of cornerstones of the domestic mechanisms of redress for Aboriginal rights in Canada.

On 28 October 2011, the HTG, with support from fourteen amicus briefs from organizations such as the AFN and Amnesty International, met with the state before the IACHR to provide additional testimony and arguments on the matter. The HTG stressed the undisputed fact that "the Hul'qumi'num peoples have lived, subsisted and worshipped upon their ancestral territories ... since time immemorial."[63] They also stressed the fact that their claim before the IACHR was based on current human rights violations rooted in the historical narrative of the dispossession and redistribution of their ancestral lands by the Canadian state. Their task before the IACHR was not to address the nineteenth-century subject of dispossession but rather the twenty-first-century issue of human rights violations. The privatization of much of the ancestral territories and subsequent industry activities (predominantly forestry) has not changed the fact that the Hul'qumi'num peoples "continue to rely upon these lands ... their waters and their resources for their cultural identity, integrity and survival."[64] The HTG requested the demarcation of their ancestral territories or, alternatively, compensation. In the twenty minutes allotted to the HTG, an Elder spoke on behalf of the group, detailing some of the specific violations of human rights taking place on his ancestral territory in the recent past. The Elder pointed to several locations that are no longer available to the Hul'qumi'num peoples. He called attention to the destruction of cultural sites, disruptions with traditional religious ceremonies, and the desecration of burial sites.[65] The Elder concluded his testimony by drawing attention to the interconnectedness of land development, the environment, and the health and well-being, physical and spiritual, of Hul'qumi'num peoples.

For their part, representatives of Canada stressed the complexity of contemporary treaty-making processes, stipulating such processes do take time. Canada dedicated a substantial portion of its allotted time to addressing the admissibility issue resolved two years earlier, affirming the domestic mechanisms at work in the Canadian state. Of particular note is the act of distillation undertaken by the government. At the 2011 hearing, Canada declared the following:

> The key to the allegations of the violations to the American Declaration in this petition appears to be the allegations in respect to property. In essence, the HTG alleges that Canada must demarcate the land contained in its claim to ancestral territory and that it should have done so long ago. All other allegations of the petitioner flow from this central issue.[66]

While Canada did stipulate that they take issue with all allegations, concluding with a clear articulation that they had not violated the HTG rights to culture or freedom of religion, their reading of the petition effectively sidesteps the important issue of religion as articulated by the HTG.

The case remains before the IACHR and the HTC claim in the BCTC remains at Stage 4, awaiting an agreement in principle, as it was in 1997. The acceptance and assessment of the claim before the IACHR is an important decision in itself. Understandably, it is the admissibility of the claim that Canada took greatest issue with even after admissibility had been approved. The extension of the jurisdiction from an international human rights body into matters that have not proceeded through domestic means of legal and political redress provides a very visible opportunity for Indigenous Peoples in Canada to voice their concerns to the international community. The decision also provides for third-party adjudication of conflicts between Indigenous Peoples and the Canadian state by a body external to the colonial context of Canada's legal and political landscape.

The OAS, like the United Nations, is an important means of defining minimum standards, a source of external pressure on states, and a mechanism that allows Indigenous Peoples a forum outside of domestic spheres to voice claims to the violations of their rights. While decisions of the IACHR are not binding, as noted earlier, this HTG decision is important for the analysis presented in this book. If the Supreme Court decisions cannot adequately address Indigenous religious freedom based on embedded and prevailing culturally specific understandings of religion, this may be viewed as a means of bypassing the domestic mechanisms discussed in earlier chapters.

Conclusion

Benjamin Berger explains that while international law has its own culture, it is a culture that is disconnected from the legal cultures which bodies like the HRC or IACHR are asked to judge. For Berger, the location of legal decisions within a specific cultural history provides a greater sense of authority in the domestic sphere, where international decisions, disconnected, appear "more aspirational than legal."[67] Despite this, the aspirational tone of international decisions can be impactful. In her book, *Global Indigenous Politics: A Subtle Revolution*, Anishinaabe political scientist Sheryl Lightfoot contends that while international mechanisms are non-binding, they are forcing paradigmatic shifts in how Indigenous rights are conceptualized internationally. In turn, this subtle revolution in international relations reverberates in related discourses around sovereignty and territoriality, among others.[68] In the same vein, Kristen A. Carpenter and Angela R. Riley contend that international rights frameworks have helped to recentre and refocus the subject of Indigenous rights in domestic legal spheres.[69]

Domestically, in its final report, the TRC expressed its commitment to the UNDRIP as "the framework for reconciliation at all levels and across all sectors of Canadian society."[70] Thus, while international mechanisms are non-binding, this does not nullify their effectivity for the protection of Indigenous rights or, more specifically, matters of Indigenous religious freedom in Canada. The forward trajectory of an expanding Indigenous rights framework emphasizing the international, rather than domestic, nature of Indigenous rights has been an important conceptual shift that opened up international law as a means of redress. Remember that the Indigenous rights framework is relatively new. In addition to expanding, the boundaries and limits of the framework are being tested and debated regularly, and this will continue into the foreseeable future.

Mechanisms offered by the United Nations, the Organization of the American States, and the International Labour Organization provide sources of pressure and benchmarks for standards on the matter of Indigenous rights. Special rapporteurs, expert mechanisms, permanent forums, working groups, and commissions remain vigilant. And, while the UNDRIP specifically addresses the subject of religion, Indigenous Peoples can also find support for their claims in the American Declaration, ILO Convention No. 169, and the set of 1966 covenants. In Canada, Indigenous Peoples have proven effective in engaging with these various mechanisms over the past few decades.

While the state remains the ultimate authority, international pressure provides support for Indigenous Peoples at work in Canada striving for the protection of their own rights. In many ways, the emerging rights mechanisms for Indigenous Peoples at the international level offer a structural framework for mediation that properly locates the state in a position outside of the regulatory nucleus of society, as discussed in the previous chapter. The process is equally stifled in the international sphere as it is in the domestic sphere, given the fact that the final decision to act on the recommendations of the mediating party or not continues to rest with the state. Regardless, the potential for international redress appears promising, even if measurable results lie beyond the immediate future.

Conclusion

Challenges for Reconciliation

On its face, the Constitution and its Charter appear like valuable mechanisms for Indigenous religious freedom, but Indigenous Peoples have encountered serious challenges in both the right to freedom of conscience and religion and Aboriginal rights. The courts have made it clear that neither section 2(a) nor section 35(1) are capable of including the depth of religion, which has serious impacts on the existence of Indigenous religions themselves. And, while the Charter right is more than capable of overcoming the challenge of diversity that impedes section 35(1), it is burdened by the challenges of the homogenizing discourse of equality, Canada's heritage, and its denial of the colonial history of the seizure of the traditional territories of Indigenous Peoples.

Meaningful consultations and accommodations as mandated by the law also appear promising, but this too has been problematic for Indigenous Peoples. Challenged by a lack of control over cosmologically significant spaces – an issue related to assertions of Crown sovereignty – Indigenous Peoples are forced to enter into public dialogue that is subject to the conditions of public religion, a product of the Christian heritage of Canada. This opens cosmologically significant spaces to the politics of compromise and negotiation without consideration of the incommensurability of options, choices, and cultures. International mechanisms may, at some point, provide more than hope and pressure, but for the time being the self-ascribed sovereignty of the Canadian state diminishes their impact.

In its mandate to expose broader obstacles to the contemporary Indigenous-state relationship, the TRC, in its final report, offered ninety-four calls to action for reconciliation, spanning issues from the welfare of Indigenous children to the training of public servants to citizenship tests for newcomers to Canada. Unsurprisingly, the TRC was attuned to many of the broader issues impacting Indigenous-state relations that intersect with the theoretical and practical concerns raised throughout this book. In the remaining pages, I would like to draw connections between the specific analysis I have offered on Indigenous religious freedom and the broader project of reconciliation as communicated by the TRC. In particular, the commission's attention to the subjects of education, self-determination, and the foundations of a new Indigenous-state relationship help to draw out these important connections.

Newness, Diversity, and Education

One of the greatest challenges identified by Winnifred Fallers Sullivan in *The Impossibility of Religious Freedom* is the matter of a diversified religious landscape both within traditions and outside of them. For religious peoples and their communities, these are natural outgrowths of a lived religious experience that fosters dialogue, debate, change, and division. For marginalized and oppressed communities, according to Homi Bhabha, the dynamic and fluid nature of culture is an important facet of survival. Despite such facts, *Van der Peet* and popular conceptions of Indigenous religions tend to locate Indigenous traditions historically. While *R. v. Sappier/R. v. Gray* provided some much needed clarification on *Van der Peet*, the historical fixity of Indigenous religions remains.

The TRC is acutely aware of such realities. With specific attention to the existence of Indigenous legal traditions, the commission credits John Borrows and his book *Canada's Indigenous Constitution* when they write, "In applying Indigenous law and diplomacy to facilitate reconciliation, we must remember that legal traditions are never static. Traditions become irrelevant, even dangerous and discriminatory, if they do not address each generation's shifting needs."[1] On the subject of the revitalization of Indigenous law, the TRC recounted a narrative shared by a Mi'kmaq Elder at the TRC's Knowledge Keeper Forum of 2014. Elder Stephen Augustine shared the Mi'kmaq concept of "making things right" using the analogy of a tipped canoe. He spoke, "We'll make the canoe right and ... keep it in water so it does not bump on rocks or hit the shore ... [When we tip a canoe] we may lose some of our possessions ... Eventually we will regain our possessions [but] they will not be the same as the old ones."[2] The TRC goes on to claim the following: "The Mi'kmaq idea for 'making things right' implies that sometimes, in certain contexts, things can be made right – but the remedy might not allow us to recapture what was lost. Making things right might involve creating something new as we journey forward."[3] The TRC goes on to offer several examples from various communities of Indigenous Peoples across Canada to emphasize that each community possesses their own unique, contemporary traditions.

Recognition and respect for diversity begin with education. The TRC, in the opening to a chapter dedicated to education, asserts, "Much of the current state of troubled relations between Aboriginal and non-Aboriginal Canadians is attributable to educational institutions and what they have taught, or failed to teach, over many generations." The TRC goes on to affirm that education is a key to reconciliation.[4] Where there has been a noticeable absence of Indigenous Peoples and their narratives in schools and public forums historically, the problem is compounded by the fact that religion more generally has been significantly marginalized in the Canadian educational landscape. Sociologist David Seljak argues that policymakers and most of the Canadian public have been content with the de-Christianization and subsequent removal of all religion in public schools in its push towards a multicultural polity. He argues that a multicultural Canada "lacks credibility when its school system, an important state-controlled vehicle of socialization into a common Canadian culture, values, and social institutions for young people, ignores or suppresses a key element in the identity of so many citizens." Canada has "raised a generation of religiously illiterate students."[5] On this, the TRC's sixty-fourth call to action reads as follows: "We call upon all levels of government that provide public funds to denominational schools to require such schools to provide an education on comparative religious studies, which must include a segment on Aboriginal spiritual beliefs and practices developed in collaboration with Aboriginal Elders."[6] As the TRC notes on several occasions, the responsibility of reconciliation resides in all Canadians. The above call to action addresses a very specific issue: the lack of understanding of Indigenous religions in Canada. Seljak, however, draws our attention to an even deeper-seated issue related to secularization that, yet again, compounds matters for Indigenous religious freedom.

In many ways, the TRC calls attention to misunderstandings facilitated by a failure to listen. Listening is a critical feature of reconciliation. In fact, the commission expressed its concern that reconciliation is impossible "without listening, contemplation, meditation, and deeper internal deliberation."[7] The commission writes, "Canadians have much to gain from listening to the voices, experiences, and wisdom of Survivors, Elders, and Traditional Knowledge Keepers."[8] To borrow from Kathleen Absolon, just as we must begin with acts of "storying and re-storying," so too must the process of reconciliation.[9]

Recall that Viola Cordova reminds us that the act of listening to understand cannot be premised upon the desire to see a distortion of one's self. The commission, for its part, is conscious of the fact that communication requires the recognition of difference. For example, on the subject of reconciliation, the TRC explains, "Although Elders and Knowledge Keepers across the land have told us that there is no specific word for reconciliation in their own languages, there are many words, stories, and songs, as well as sacred objects such as wampum belts, peace pipes, eagle down, cedar boughs, drums, and regalia, that are used to establish relationships, repair conflicts, restore harmony, and make peace."[10] The TRC also called attention to non-verbal cultural modes of communication that may be equally important among Indigenous Peoples, such as the practice of silence.[11] As noted by Cordova, communication is far more complex than the words we use.

The TRC's call to action on education extends to politicians, lawyers, and law students, who the TRC assert should be educated in "appropriate cultural competency training," the UNDRIP, and Indigenous legal traditions.[12] These calls to action could potentially help to draw attention to cultural difference and incommensurability. Importantly, it may help to expose what Benjamin Berger calls the "conventional story" of law as a neutral arbiter of competing claims as a fallacy.[13] The call for education also extends to the media, who have played a role in escalating tensions and violence, as they did at Gustafsen Lake. On this, the TRC asserts, "The media has a role to play in ensuring that public information both for and about Aboriginal peoples reflects their cultural diversity and provides fair and non-discriminatory reporting on Aboriginal issues."[14] Despite calls for greater accountability in the media in the RCAP Report, the TRC reports that little has changed in media's role in inhibiting reconciliation.[15] This, too, returns us to the subject of education. In *Lethal Legacy*, J.R. Miller explains that in cases of standoffs, in particular, "politicians, journalists and ordinary citizens understood neither how nor why the crisis of the moment had arisen, much less how its deep historical roots made it resistant to solutions."[16] In this sense, the challenge facing Indigenous religious freedom is a pervasive issue related to education, which is tied to processes of secularization, the realities of lived religious traditions, and the resonating impacts of colonialism.

Indigenous Self-Determination and Consent

Unsurprisingly, the colonial legacy of the Doctrine of Discovery – that is, assertions of Crown sovereignty and the denial of self-determination for Indigenous Peoples on their traditional territories – and its continuing impact occupies a central place in the TRC's report as a serious challenge for reconciliation.[17] The TRC affirmed the need for the privileging of Indigenous self-determination, a call to action echoed in the UNDRIP and the RCAP Report.[18] The TRC asserted that "Aboriginal peoples' right to self-determination [ought to be both] within, and in partnership with, a viable Canadian sovereignty."[19] More generally, the TRC commented, "the reconciliation vision that lies behind Section 35 should not be seen as a means to subjugate Aboriginal peoples to an absolutely sovereign Crown but as a means to establish the kind of relationship that should have flourished since Confederation."[20] In short, the TRC calls for a fundamental conceptual shift in Canada's perspective of its own place within Indigenous-state relations.

An important feature of self-determination is consent. In *Tsilhqot'in Nation v. British Columbia*, Chief Justice McLachlin offered a sort of limited and inverted affirmation of the desire for Indigenous consent, writing, "I add this. Governments and individuals proposing to use or exploit land, whether before or after a declaration of Aboriginal title, *can avoid a charge* of infringement or failure to adequately consult by obtaining the consent of the interested Aboriginal group."[21] Notably, the chief justice is concerned with the state's ability to avoid infringement accusations rather than to affirm the consent of Indigenous Peoples as a requirement of the Indigenous-state relationship. The hesitation is most likely related to Canada's conflation of consent and veto power, which is how Canada interpreted FPIC in the UNDRIP.[22] Consent, simply as a means for the state to avoid lengthy court proceedings, is not sufficient for Indigenous self-determination. In the wake of the SCC decision in *Ktunaxa Nation v. British Columbia*, Ktunaxa writer Troy Sebastian – with support of the Ktunaxa Tribal Council – articulated, "Denying Indigenous consent is an essential recipe for the status quo of settler society. Indigenous consent is the truth of reconciliation. Otherwise, reconciliation is just another roadside attraction."[23] While Canada, as of 2016, has now officially adopted the UNDRIP without qualification, the 2017 decision in *Ktunaxa Nation v. British Columbia* may, at least in part and for now, be evidence of the aspirational reality of UNDRIP and the limited scope of Indigenous self-determination.

Forging a New Relationship

The lack of decision-making power for Indigenous Peoples is clearly an obstacle for the protection of Indigenous religions. However, reconciliation does not simply entail the act of occupying locations of power. It requires a change in the very fabric of the institutions of power to include Indigenous knowledges and cultures. Certainly access to locations of decision-making power are important to potentially address issues of false assumptions of commensurability between cultures, but without paradigmatic shifts of the institutional parameters themselves, Indigenous Peoples will continue to be necessarily subjugated by political, legal, and public spheres authored by Euro-Canadian society.

The TRC recommends institutional change in its support for a new proclamation affirming a nation-to-nation relationship. The TRC calls the federal government to "reconcile Aboriginal and Crown constitutional and legal orders to ensure that Aboriginal peoples are full partners in Confederation, including the recognition and integration of Indigenous laws and legal traditions in negotiation and implementation processes."[24] This call echoes John Borrows's claim that all of Canada would benefit from a multi-juridical legal order that fully incorporates Indigenous legal traditions.[25] The call to action could help facilitate self-development alongside self-determination.

As noted in chapter 3, Borrows asks whether Anishinabek beliefs in a living Earth can be protected under Canada's current constitutional order. At this time, Borrows argues that protection of Anishinaabe religion is only possible if Anishinabek legal traditions function alongside the current constitutional order, which has "some distance to travel" before it can recognize a living Earth.[26] For Borrows, the Canadian constitutional order requires a metaphysical shift that finds support in the final report of the TRC.

From an Indigenous philosophical perspective, reconciliation is not anthropocentric. Blackfoot Elder Reg Crowshoe explained the conceptual shift required of reconciliation. The TRC summarizes his thoughts as follows: "reconciliation requires talking, but our conversations must be broader than Canada's conventional approaches."[27] Citing Crowshoe directly, the TRC recounts, "Reconciliation between Aboriginal and non-Aboriginal Canadians, from an Aboriginal perspective, also requires reconciliation with the natural world. If human beings resolve problems between

themselves but continue to destroy the natural world, then reconciliation remains incomplete."[28] In this respect, the new relationship between Indigenous Peoples and the Canadian state requires
a cultural shift that must include Indigenous metaphysical perspectives, knowledge, and institutions.

Conclusion

Reconciliation certainly requires recognition of the many ways in
which colonialism continues to impact Indigenous Peoples, but
the reasons that the realization of Indigenous religious freedom is
so challenging are not always explicit or obvious. Thomas King,
in his lecture "You're Not the Indian I Had in Mind," tells listeners a story that offers important insights on the identification and
assessment of colonial ideology in the twenty-first century. While
working abroad in his youth, King recalls an Australian man once
telling him that "North Americans had taken care of the [Aborig-
inal] problem in a reasonably expedient fashion."[29] King explains,
"I'm embarrassed to repeat [the man's] exact words but the gist of
it was that North Americans had shot Native men and bred Native
women until they were White."[30] King reflects, "In a perverse way,
I've always liked people like [this man]. They are, by and large,
easy to deal with. Their racism is honest and straightforward. You
don't have to go looking for it in a phrase or a gesture. And you
don't have to wonder if you're being too sensitive. Best of all, they
remind me how the past continues to inform the present."[31]

Explicit manifestations of colonial ideology premised upon the
desire to marginalize, reshape, and eradicate the diverse cultures of
Indigenous Peoples are, if anything, honest and straightforward. It
is easy to point to residential schools and a ban on Indigenous religions for what they are, attempts at cultural genocide – a sentiment
echoed by Harold Cardinal in *The Unjust Society*.[32] But Canada,
for its part, has shown, at the request and pressure of Indigenous
Peoples and international bodies, a willingness to excise some of
those explicit manifestations, markers of how the past continued to
inform the present. The final report of the TRC suggests Canada's

desire to no longer see its reflection in the man from King's narrative. However, it would be an egregious and ill-informed error to suggest that explicit forms of colonialism and cultural genocide are no longer present in Canada. From the temporary houses of Attawapiskat to the testimonials of the National Inquiry into Missing and Murdered Indigenous Women and Girls to the verdict in the murder of Colton Boushie, the continuity of explicit manifestations of colonialism is impossible to ignore. King's point, of course, is not that explicit colonialism is just a memory but that implicit forms of an ideology of superiority may be difficult to identify, though just as insidious.

In the case of Indigenous religious freedom and cosmologically significant spaces, the continuity of colonialism appears not in the construction of overt mechanisms that seek the destruction of Indigenous cultures, like residential schools, but in the spaces between the lines of Supreme Court rulings and government policy; it remains in the gestures and phrases of ministers and justices; and it remains in the questions left unasked and unanswered about the impact and existence of a dominant culture that continues to have the effect of marginalizing, forcibly reshaping, and potentially erasing Indigenous cultures. These overlapping and complex challenges, brought into focus, offer some indication as to why the realization of Indigenous religious freedom is so difficult in Canada today.

Notes

Preface

1 Vine Deloria Jr, *The Metaphysics of Modern Existence* (San Francisco: Harper and Row, 1979), 192.

2 In particular, Greg Johnson's discussion of how establishment on three levels – statutory, structural, and naturalized – impacts the religious life of Native Hawaiians generally resonates throughout this book. See Greg Johnson, "Varieties of Native Hawaiian Establishment: Recognized Voices, Routinized Charisma and Church Desecration," in *Varieties of Religious Establishment*, ed. Winnifred Fallers Sullivan and Lori G. Beaman (London: Routledge, 2013), 55–71. Also resonating with this work is Tisa Wenger's seminal book *We Have a Religion: The 1920s Pueblo Indian Dance Controversy and American Religious Freedom* (Chapel Hill: University of North Carolina Press, 2009), where she discusses the intersection of colonialism, diachronic culture, the definition of "religion," and secularism for Indigenous religious freedom in the early twentieth century (and beyond) in the United States. Also see Kristen A. Carpenter, "The Interests of 'Peoples' in the Cooperative Management of Sacred Sites," *Tulsa Law Review* 42 (2006): 37–57; Kristen A. Carpenter, "Old Ground and New Directions at Sacred Sites on the Western Landscape," *Denver University Law Review* 83 (2006): 981–1003.

3 As Greg Johnson explains, there is greater attention to consultation in the United States after the decision in Lyng v. Northwest Indian Cemetery Protective Agency, 435 US 439 (1988), but these "post-*Lyng* laws and policies that stipulate consultation are insufficiently institutionalized," making them subject to the will of changing administrations among other factors. According to Johnson, the result is that processes of consultation

may be "reduced to a shadow of their former selves ... or to nothing at all." Greg Johnson, "Reflections on the Politics of Religious Freedom, with Attention to Hawaii," in *Politics of Religious Freedom*, ed. Winnifred Fallers Sullivan, Elizabeth Shakman Hurd, Saba Mahmood, and Peter G. Danchin (Chicago: University of Chicago Press, 2015), 84. Thus, while correlations may be read, they should not be assumed to exist given the unique legal contexts of each jurisdiction.

4 Vine Deloria Jr, *For This Land: Writings on Religion in America*, ed. James Treat (New York: Routledge, 1999), 256.

5 Deloria, *For This Land*, 258.

6 Deloria, *For This Land*, 258.

7 Deloria, *For This Land*, 254–5.

8 Michael Lee Ross, *First Nations Sacred Sites in Canada's Courts* (Vancouver: UBC Press, 2005), 56–64.

9 See Catherine Bell and Val Napoleon, eds., *First Nations Cultural Heritage and Law: Case Studies, Voices, and Perspectives* (Vancouver: UBC Press, 2009).

10 See James Waldram, *The Way of the Pipe: Aboriginal Spirituality and Symbolic Healing in Canadian Prisons* (Toronto: University of Toronto Press, 1997).

11 Truth and Reconciliation Commission of Canada, "Canada's Residential Schools: Reconciliation," in *The Final Report of the Truth and Reconciliation Commission of Canada*, vol. 6 (Montreal: McGill-Queen's University Press, 2015), 4.

A Comment on Terminology

1 Dennis H. MacPherson and J. Douglas Rabb, *Indian from the Inside: Native American Philosophy and Cultural Renewal*, 2nd ed. (London: McFarland and Company, 2011), 147. Citing Dennis H. MacPherson and J. Douglas Rabb, "Transformative Philosophy and Indigenous Thought: A Comparison of Lakota and Ojibwa World Views," in *Proceedings of the 29th Algonquian Conference* (Winnipeg: University of Manitoba Press, 1999), 202–10.

2 MacPherson and Rabb, *Indian from the Inside*, 147–8.

3 Deloria, *Metaphysics of Modern Existence*; V.F. Cordova, *How It Is: The Native American Philosophy of V.F. Cordova*, ed. Kathleen Dean Moore, Kurt Peters, Ted Jojola, and Amber Lacy (Tucson: University of Arizona Press, 2007); Dale Turner, "What Is American Indian Philosophy? Toward a Critical Indigenous Philosophy," in *Philosophy in Multiple Voices*, ed. George Yancy (Lanham, MD: Rowman and Littlefield, 2007), 197–218.

4 Royal Commission on Aboriginal Peoples (RCAP), *Highlights from the Report of the Royal Commission on Aboriginal Peoples* (Ottawa: Minister of Supply and Services Canada, 1996), 26.

5 Greg Johnson and Siv Ellen Kraft, "Introduction," in *Handbook of Indigenous Religion(s)*, ed. Greg Johnson and Siv Ellen Kraft (Leiden, NL: Brill, 2017), 11.

6 Johnson and Kraft, "Introduction," 2.

7 See Linda Woodhead, "Real Religion and Fuzzy Spirituality? Taking Sides in the Sociology of Religion," in *Religions of Modernity: Relocating the Sacred to the Self and the Digital*, ed. Stef Aupers and Dick Houtman (Leiden, NL: Brill, 2010), 31–48; Brian J. Zinnbauer et al., "Religion and Spirituality: Unfuzzying the Fuzzy," *Journal for the Scientific Study of Religion* 36, no. 4 (1997): 549–64.

8 Lori G. Beaman, "Aboriginal Spirituality and the Legal Construction of Freedom of Religion," *Journal of Church and State* 44 (winter 2002): 137.

9 Joan Fleming and Robert J. Ledogar, "Resilience and Indigenous Spirituality: A Literature Review," *Pimatisiwin: A Journal of Aboriginal and Indigenous Community Health* 6, no. 2 (2008): 47. This distinction between spirituality and Indigenous spirituality also seems to be supported in international discourse, notably in the United Nations' *State of the World's Indigenous Peoples* (Department of Economic and Social Affairs, Division for Social Policy and Development, Secretariat of the Permanent Forum on Indigenous Issues. ST/ESA/328, 2009), http://www.un.org/esa/socdev/unpfii/documents/SOWIP/en/SOWIP_web.pdf; for analysis of the concepts of religion and spirituality in this UN document, among others, see Siv Ellen Kraft, "U.N.-Discourses on Indigenous Religion," in Johnson and Kraft, *Handbook of Indigenous Religion(s)*, 85–8.

10 For example, see David S. Walsh, "Spiritual, Not Religious; Dene, Not Indigenous: Tłı̨chǫ Dene Discourses of Religion and Indigeneity," in Johnson and Kraft, *Handbook of Indigenous Religion(s)*, 204–20.

11 For an in-depth study of the eight (or nine) ways in which scholars employ the term "Indigenous Religions," see Bjørn Ola Tafjord, "Towards a Typology of Academic Uses of 'Indigenous Religion(s),' or Eight (or Nine) Language Games That Scholars Play with This Phrase," in Johnson and Kraft, *Handbook of Indigenous Religion(s)*, 25–51.

12 Syndicat Northcrest v. Amselem, [2004] 2 S.C.R. 551, at para. 53. Also see Waldram, *Way of the Pipe*.

13 John Borrows, "Living Law on a Living Earth: Aboriginal Religion, Law, and the Constitution," in *Law and Religious Pluralism in Canada*, ed. Richard Moon (Vancouver: UBC Press, 2010), 171.

14 *Ktunaxa Nation v. British Columbia (Forests, Lands and Natural Resource Operations)*, [2017] S.C.C. 54, at para. 89.
15 See Courtney Bender, "The Power of Pluralist Thinking," in Sullivan et al., *Politics of Religious Freedom*, 66–77.
16 Lori G. Beaman, "Beyond Establishment," in Sullivan et al., *Politics of Religious Freedom*, 218.
17 Beaman, "Beyond Establishment," 218.
18 Beaman, "Beyond Establishment," 213; emphasis in original.
19 Michael D. McNally, "Religion as Peoplehood: Native American Religious Traditions and the Discourse of Indigenous Rights," in Johnson and Kraft, *Handbook of Indigenous Religion(s)*, 75.

Introduction

1 See J.R. Miller, *Shingwauk's Vision: A History of Canadian Native Residential Schools* (Toronto: University of Toronto Press, 1996). Missionaries had experimented with industrial schools as early as the seventeenth century with little success. Day schools were not sufficient in leading Indigenous youth away from their traditional ways. Children were able to return home and, more frustrating for missionaries, consort with immoral persons. Indigenous parents criticized conditions, and the schools often had problems of attendance. Both state officials and missionaries largely accepted off-reserve residential schools as the best course of action despite the fact that the reserve schooling was a staple of many treaties (see Miller, *Shingwauk's Vision*). There are a variety of explanations as to why the federal government adopted residential schools during this time. In his literature review on residential schools, "Native Residential Schools in Canada: A Review of Literature," *Canadian Journal of Native Studies* 18, no. 1 (1998): 49–86, Scott Trevithick explains that more specific interpretations range from the cynical (i.e., the relinquishment of responsibility and the redistribution of reserve lands) to the altruistic (misguided or otherwise) to the selfish (e.g., submission of Indigenous Peoples). Despite these specific differences, historians generally accept assimilation and civilization as the broad ideological motivations of the Canadian government.
2 Harold Cardinal, *The Unjust Society* (1969; repr., Vancouver: Douglas and McIntyre, 2009), 15.
3 Cardinal, *Unjust Society*, 145.
4 Indian Chiefs of Alberta, "Citizens Plus," *Aboriginal Policy Studies* 1, no. 2 ([1969] 2011): 189–90.

5 H.B. Hawthorn, ed., *A Survey of the Contemporary Indians of Canada: A Report on Political, Economic, Educational Needs* (Ottawa: Indian Affairs Branch, 1966–7).

6 See J.R. Miller, *Compact, Contract, Covenant: Aboriginal Treaty-Making in Canada* (Toronto: University of Toronto Press, 2009). The *Calder* decision was in 1973. (Calder et al. v. Attorney General of British Columbia, [1973] S.C.R. 313.) The James Bay and Northern Québec Agreement was completed in 1975.

7 Michael Asch, *Home and Native Land: Aboriginal Rights and the Canadian Constitution* (Toronto: Methuen, 1984).

8 See Brian Slattery, "The Generative Structure of Aboriginal Rights," in *Moving Toward Justice: Legal Traditions and Aboriginal Justice*, ed. John D. Whyte (Saskatoon, Saskatchewan: Purich, 2008), 20–48.

9 Government of Canada, *Statement of Apology – to Former Students of Indian Residential Schools*, 11 June 2008, https://www.aadnc-aandc.gc.ca/DAM/DAM-INTER-HQ/STAGING/texte-text/rqpi_apo_pdf_1322167347706_eng.pdf.

10 Roman jurists introduced a concept of absolute private ownership known as *dominium*. Four criteria needed to be satisfied in order to qualify for this type of ownership. Individuals must obtain property lawfully, and the property must be exclusive, absolute, and permanent. See Richard Pipes, *Property and Freedom* (New York: Knopf, 1999).

11 John Locke, *Two Treatises of Government* (*Second Treatise*) (1689; repr., London: Routledge, 1987), ch. 5 at para. 34.

12 Aristotle contends that conflict arises more between those who communally own land than those who own land privately. Conflict is inherent to human nature and does not simply arise from debate over "mine" and "not mine." Justice and the eradication of social conflict were ascertainable through enlightenment rather than the abolition of private property. For Aristotle, private property provides the opportunity for individuals to be more generous and, therefore, to attain a higher ethical level (see Pipes, *Property and Freedom*). The translation and rediscovery of Aristotle in correlation with academic theological studies began to shift Christian thought away from the neo-Platonic school that had informed church teachings through the thirteenth century and back to Aristotle. Thomas Aquinas responds to the question of property in his codification of church teachings, *Summa Theologica* (1265–74). In response to the first article of question 66 in the Second Part of the Second Part, he writes, "Man has a natural dominion over external things, because, by his reason and will, he is able to use them for his own profit, as they were made on his account: for the imperfect is

198 Notes to pages 9–13

always for the sake of the perfect ... Moreover, this natural dominion of man over other creatures, which is competent to man in respect of his reason wherein God's image resides, is shown forth in man's creation" (objection 3). Thomas reaffirms an Aristotelian view of property by contending that individual possessions lead to peace and justice. He adds that possessions can also benefit the community through the opportunities that arise for some to provide for others (objection 2). This understanding of property would prove to be significantly influential on later natural law theorists such as John Locke. See James Tully, *A Discourse on Property: John Locke and His Adversaries* (New York: Cambridge University Press, 1980).

13 Locke, *Second Treatise*, ch. 5 at para. 37.
14 Locke, *Second Treatise*, ch. 5 at para. 41.
15 See Barbara Arneil, *John Locke and America* (New York: Oxford University Press, 1996).
16 See Steven Newcomb, *Pagans in the Promised Land: Decoding the Doctrine of Christian Discovery* (Golden, CO: Fulcrum, 2008); Robert J. Miller, Jacinta Ruru, Larissa Behrendt, and Tracey Lindberg, *Discovering Indigenous Lands: The Doctrine of Discovery in the English Colonies* (New York: Oxford University Press, 2010).
17 Benjamin L. Berger, *Law's Religion: Religious Difference and the Claims of Constitutionalism* (Toronto: University of Toronto Press, 2015), 47.
18 James Tully, "The Struggles of Indigenous Peoples for and of Freedom," in *Political Theory and the Rights of Indigenous Peoples*, ed. Duncan Ivision, Paul Patton, and Will Sanders (Cambridge: Cambridge University Press, 2000), 36–59.
19 Tully, "Struggles of Indigenous Peoples," 37–8.
20 Tsilhqot'in Nation v. British Columbia, [2014] 2 S.C.R. 257, at para. 50. See Delgamuukw v. British Columbia, [1997] 3 S.C.R. 1010, at para. 156.
21 *Tsilhqot'in Nation*, [2014] 2 S.C.R. 257, at para. 50.
22 RCAP, *Highlights from the Report of the Royal Commission on Aboriginal Peoples*, 2; Ktunaxa Nation Executive Council, *Qat'muk Declaration* (15 November 2010), http://www.ktunaxa.org/who-we-are/qatmuk-declaration; also see Borrows, "Living Law on a Living Earth."
23 Borrows, "Living Law on a Living Earth," 181.
24 Berger, *Law's Religion*, 13.
25 Berger, *Law's Religion*, 35.
26 Berger, *Law's Religion*, 17. For more on law as culture see Paul W. Kahn, *The Cultural Study of Law: Reconstructing Legal Scholarship* (Chicago: University of Chicago Press, 1999); Lawrence Rosen, *Law as Culture: An Invitation* (Princeton, NJ: Princeton University Press, 2006).

27 Berger, *Law's Religion*, 17.
28 Elizabeth Shakman Hurd, "Believing in Religious Freedom," in Sullivan et al., *Politics of Religious Freedom*, 52.
29 Hurd, "Believing in Religious Freedom," 53.
30 Berger, *Law's Religion*, 103.
31 Matthew Adler, "Law and Incommensurability: An Introduction," *University of Pennsylvania Law Review* 146, no. 5 (1998): 1169.
32 R. v. Oakes, [1986] 1 S.C.R. 103, at paras. 68–70.
33 R. v. Sparrow, [1990] 1 S.C.R. 1075. This matter is also discussed in greater depth in chapter 5 in the context of the duty to consult and accommodate, where the state applies the ideal of the *Sparrow* test in its assessment of the degree of accommodations it will provide to Indigenous Peoples. See Dwight C. Newman, *The Duty to Consult: New Relationships with Aboriginal Peoples* (Saskatoon, Saskatchewan: Purich, 2009), 19.
34 Talal Asad, *Formations of the Secular: Christianity, Islam, Modernity* (Stanford, CA: Stanford University Press, 2003), 184.
35 Cardinal, *Unjust Society*, 10.
36 Cordova, *How It Is*, 59.
37 Cordova, *How It Is*, 60.
38 Cordova, *How It Is*, 63.
39 Cordova, *How It Is*.
40 Cordova, *How It Is*, 76.
41 Ktunaxa Nation Executive Council, *Qat'muk Declaration*, 1.
42 Cordova, *How It Is*, 64.
43 Cordova, *How It Is*, 65.
44 Cordova, *How It Is*, 75. For more information on incommensurability see MacPherson and Rabb, *Indian from the Inside*, 140–84. At this point, some readers may be concerned that the conversation around cultural incommensurability sends us into relativist factionalism, not unlike the discourse of the "clash of civilizations," popularized by Samuel Huntington in *The Clash of Civilizations and the Remaking of World Order* (New York: Simon and Schuster, 1996). Let us be clear, the challenge of cultural incommensurability refers to preconceptions in the outset and act of intercultural dialogue. In the act of starting from a place of difference, the discourse on cultural incommensurability suggests that stronger relationships can be forged. In "Overcoming Incommensurability through Intercultural Dialogue," Paul Healy advocates for "a hermeneutico-dialogical approach to the problem of intercultural communication and understanding." He asserts, "This

approach ... can give difference its due to the extent of stimulating a genuine and productive process of intercultural learning, in a manner that truly navigates between the Scylla of an ethnocentric universalism and the Charybdis of a self-sealing relativism, and thereby not only averts a destructive cultural stand-off, or clash but facilitates the emergence of a well-grounded 'fusion of horizons.'" Paul Healy, "Overcoming Incommensurability through Intercultural Dialogue," *Cosmos and History: The Journal of Natural and Social Philosophy* 9, no. 1 (2013): 266–7.

45 In Ktunaxa Nation v. British Columbia (Forests, Lands and Natural Resource Operations), [2015] B.C.C.A. 352, Qat'muk, the home of the Grizzly Bear Spirit, was compared with a Catholic high school, leading to a bizarre ruling in the BCCA (discussed in depth in chapter 3). In the BCSC decision in Cameron v. Ministry of Energy and Mines, [1998] CanLII 6834 (B.C.S.C.), the court approached the Saulteau First Nations' claim with scepticism since the sacred mountains in question were not actually "used" in any respect (discussed in detail in chapter 2).

46 Winnifred Fallers Sullivan, *The Impossibility of Religious Freedom* (Princeton, NJ: Princeton University Press, 2005), 4.

47 Sullivan, *Impossibility of Religious Freedom*, 136.

48 Sullivan, *Impossibility of Religious Freedom*, 74–5, 79.

49 Sullivan, *Impossibility of Religious Freedom*, 86.

50 Sullivan, *Impossibility of Religious Freedom*, 94.

51 Sullivan, *Impossibility of Religious Freedom*, 143–4; Sullivan makes this comment in reference to Thomas Curry, *Farewell to Christendom: The Future of Church and State in America* (Oxford: Oxford University Press, 2001).

52 *Amselem*, [2004] 2 S.C.R. 551, at para. 53.

53 Lakeside Colony of Hutterian Brethren v. Hofer, [1992] 3 S.C.R. 165; Bruker v. Marcovitz, [2007] 3 S.C.R. 607; Bentley v. Anglican Synod of the Diocese of New Westminster, [2010] B.C.C.A. 506. For a more complex assessment of these cases and the subject of the courts and authenticity, see Richard Moon, *Freedom of Conscience and Religion* (Toronto: Irwin Law, 2014), ch. 4.

54 R. v. Van der Peet, [1996] 2 S.C.R. 507, at paras. 49–50.

55 R. v. Edwards Books and Art Ltd, [1986] 2 S.C.R. 713, at para. 314.

56 What exactly constitutes "substantial burden" is a matter of debate within the United States, where several courts have offered their interpretation of the clause. See Sullivan, *Impossibility of Religious Freedom*, 10–11.

57 If "substantial burden" is met in the United States, the government may infringe a fundamental freedom under the "compelling interest" test and the "least restrictive means" standard, which resembles the *Oakes* test in Canada.

58 Legal scholars have been critical of the *Oakes* test on matters of religious freedom. In *Freedom of Conscience and Religion*, Richard Moon contends that the standards of sufficient importance and proportionality have been interpreted quite narrowly. He writes, "The Court appears willing to uphold a legal restriction if it has a legitimate objective (i.e., an objective other than the suppression of an erroneous religious practice) that would be noticeably compromised if an exception were made." He continues, the courts "have adopted in practice a very weak standard of justification under section 1 so that the right protects only a limited form of liberty" (*Freedom of Conscience and Religion*, 69). Similarly, Mary Ann Waldron writes, "It is an obvious way in which a court can use its own values and assumptions to determine a crucial part of a case without providing adequate justification for the result." Mary Ann Waldron, *Free to Believe: Rethinking Freedom of Conscience and Religion in Canada* (Toronto: University of Toronto Press, 2013), 41. In other words, critics have pointed to the subjective nature of the *Oakes* test and the tendency of the court to rule in favour of infringement. The fact that individual judges may be able to use their own personal opinions, rather than reasonable arguments, to determine the legitimacy of an infringement leaves complainants at the mercy of the good will of the court.

59 Beaman, "Aboriginal Spirituality."

60 Constitution Act, 1867, 30 & 31 Victoria, c. 3 (U.K.), s. 93; Canadian Charter of Rights and Freedoms, Part I of the Constitution Act, 1982, being Schedule B to the Canada Act 1982 (UK), 1982, c 11, s. 29 [hereafter Charter]; For more on this see Janet Epp Buckingham, *Fighting Over God: A Legal and Political History of Religious Freedom in Canada* (Montreal: McGill-Queen's University Press, 2014), and M.H. Ogilvie, *Religious Institutions and the Law in Canada*, 3rd ed. (Toronto: Irwin Law, 2010).

61 For more information on the history of the application of section 93 and subsequent related provincial legislation in Canada's courts, see Moon, *Freedom of Conscience and Religion*, ch. 5. The SCC clarified this in Adler v. Ontario, [1996] 3 S.C.R. 609. The United Nations also weighed in on this subject, rejecting Canada's commitment to the impervious nature of section 93 of the 1867 Constitution as unsupported at the end of the twentieth century. See Waldman v. Canada, HCROR, 67th Sess., Annex, Communication No 694/1996 (1996).

62 Charter, s. 2(a).
63 Charter, s. 2(a).
64 Charter, s. 1.
65 Veit Bader, *Secularism or Democracy? Associative Governance of Religious Diversity* (Amsterdam: Amsterdam University Press, 2008), 18–19.
66 Beaman, "Aboriginal Spirituality," 144.
67 Hawthorn, *Survey of the Contemporary Indians of Canada.*
68 Winnifred Fallers Sullivan and Lori G. Beaman, "Neighbo(u)rly Misreadings and Misconstruals: A Cross-border Conversation," in *Varieties of Religious Establishment*, edited by Winnifred Fallers Sullivan and Lori G. Beaman (London: Routledge, 2013), 4.
69 Note that I have used the legal category of Aboriginal Peoples here since in order to possess Aboriginal rights, a group must be federally recognized as such. More on this subject is addressed in chapter 5.
70 Slattery, "Generative Structure of Aboriginal Rights," 30.
71 The Charter does stipulate that all citizens ought to be treated equally under the law. This is confirmed in section 15(1), though section 15(2) stipulates, "Subsection (1) does not preclude any law, program or activity that has as its object the amelioration of conditions of disadvantaged individuals or groups." Whereas section 15(2) addresses the creation of new laws, section 25 extends these protections to existing Aboriginal rights. Section 25 reads, "The guarantee in this Charter of certain rights and freedoms shall not be construed so as to abrogate or derogate from any aboriginal, treaty or other rights or freedoms that pertain to the aboriginal peoples of Canada." Charter, s. 15, s. 25.
72 *Cameron*, [1998] CanLII 6834 (B.C.S.C.), at para. 165.
73 R. v. Sundown, [1999] 1 S.C.R. 393, at para. 36.
74 RCAP, *Highlights from the Report of the Royal Commission on Aboriginal Peoples*, 25.
75 Robert White-Harvey communicated this statistic in his analysis of the proportionality of land to Indigenous populations in Canada, the United States, and Australia. In Canada, Indigenous Peoples make up 3.5 per cent of the population and control less than 0.5 per cent of the provincial land mass (that is, the area where most Indigenous Peoples reside). In Australia, Indigenous Peoples make up 1.2 per cent of the population and control 10.3 per cent of the land mass. Native Americans comprise 0.8 per cent of the US population and hold 2.8 per cent of the land (excluding Alaska and Hawaii). Robert White-Harvey, "Reservation Geography and the Restoration of Native Self-Government," *Dalhousie Law Journal* 17, no. 2 (1994): 588. In the years since the publication

of White-Harvey's article, Indigenous reservations have increased substantially but only as high as 3.5 per cent of the entire land mass of Canada, as discussed in chapter 2.

76 TRC, "Canada's Residential Schools," 48.

77 Berger, *Law's Religion*, 17.

78 Taiaiake Alfred, *Peace, Power, Righteousness: An Indigenous Manifesto*, 2nd ed. (New York: Oxford University Press, 2009), 56–7.

79 Ktunaxa Nation v. British Columbia (Forests, Lands, and Natural Resource Operations), [2017] S.C.C. 54, at para. 114.

80 Iris Marion Young, *Inclusion and Democracy* (New York: Oxford University Press, 2000), 259.

1 The Depth of Religious Freedom

1 J.Z. Smith, "Religion, Religions, Religious," in *Critical Terms for Religious Studies*, ed. Mark C. Taylor (Chicago: University of Chicago Press, 1998), 269.

2 Smith, "Religion, Religions, Religious," 281.

3 Smith, "Religion, Religions, Religious," 270–1.

4 Smith, "Religion, Religions, Religious," 271.

5 Smith, "Religion, Religions, Religious," 271.

6 Smith, "Religion, Religions, Religious," 272.

7 Smith, "Religion, Religions, Religious," 276.

8 Smith, "Religion, Religions, Religious," 277.

9 Cited in Smith, "Religion, Religions, Religious," 279.

10 Smith, "Religion, Religions, Religious," 280.

11 James L. Cox, *From Primitive to Indigenous: The Academic Study of Indigenous Religions* (Aldershot, UK: Ashgate, 2007), 9.

12 Talal Asad, *Genealogies of Religion: Discipline and Reasons of Power in Christianity and Islam* (Baltimore, MD: Johns Hopkins University Press, 1993), 23.

13 Asad, *Genealogies of Religion*, 29.

14 Asad, *Genealogies of Religion*, 28.

15 Asad, *Genealogies of Religion*, 28.

16 Asad, *Genealogies of Religion*, 39.

17 Asad, *Genealogies of Religion*, 40–1.

18 Wenger, *We Have a Religion*, 13.

19 Wenger, *We Have a Religion*.

20 Asad, *Genealogies of Religion*, 42.

21 Asad, *Genealogies of Religion*, 43.

22 The ban first appears in 1894. Government of Canada, An Act to Further Amend "The Indian Act," 53 R.S.C., c. 32 (1894), s. 3. For more information, see Katherine Pettipas, *Severing the Ties that Bind: Government Repression of Indigenous Religious Ceremonies on the Prairies* (Winnipeg: University of Manitoba Press, 1994).

23 Government of Canada, An Act to Further Amend "The Indian Act," R.S.C., c. 35 (1895), s. 6.

24 For an excellent examination of the ban on the Potlatch, see Douglas Cole and Ira Chaikin, *An Iron Hand upon the People: The Law against the Potlatch on the Northwest Coast* (Vancouver: Douglas and McIntyre, 1990).

25 Government of Canada, An Act to Further Amend "The Indian Act," 53 R.S.C., c. 32 (1894), s. 11(2).

26 In the nineteenth century, the Canadian government was interested in supporting residential schools for Indigenous children. In a report on the US residential school program in 1879, Nicholas Flood Davin reported to Prime Minister Sir John A. Macdonald that Christian leaders should be in charge of schools for two reasons: the replacement of Indigenous mythology with something positive, and the fact that teachers would already contain the necessary education and virtue. Macdonald later remarked that secular education might be fine for Euro-Canadian children but that Indigenous children needed moral guidance and instruction. See Miller, *Shingwauk's Vision*.

27 Government of Canada, The Indian Act, S.C. c. 19 (1876), s. 74; Government of Canada, The Indian Act, R.S.C. c. 98 (1927), s. 143.

28 Jack and Charlie v. The Queen, [1985] 2 S.C.R. 332, at para. 7.

29 *Jack and Charlie*, [1985] 2 S.C.R. 332, at para. 8.

30 *Jack and Charlie*, [1985] 2 S.C.R. 332, at para. 9.

31 Cited in *Jack and Charlie*, [1985] 2 S.C.R. 332, at para. 18. Citing Kruger v. The Queen, [1978] 1 S.C.R. 104, 344–5.

32 *Jack and Charlie*, [1985] 2 S.C.R. 332, at para. 18.

33 *Jack and Charlie*, [1985] 2 S.C.R. 332, at para. 33.

34 *Jack and Charlie*, [1985] 2 S.C.R. 332, at para. 40.

35 Beaman, "Aboriginal Spirituality," 144.

36 John Borrows and Leonard I. Rotman, "The Sui Generis Nature of Aboriginal Rights: Does It Make a Difference?" *Alberta Law Review* 36, no. 1 (1997): 43–4.

37 *Amselem*, [2004] 2 S.C.R. 551, at para. 39.

38 *Cameron*, [1998] CanLII 6834 (B.C.S.C.), at para. 22.

39 *Cameron*, [1998] CanLII 6834 (B.C.S.C.), at para. 24.

40 *Cameron*, [1998] CanLII 6834 (B.C.S.C.), at para. 25.

41 *Cameron*, [1998] CanLII 6834 (B.C.S.C.), at para. 187.
42 *Cameron*, [1998] CanLII 6834 (B.C.S.C.), at para. 190.
43 *Cameron*, [1998] CanLII 6834 (B.C.S.C.), at para. 192.
44 *Cameron*, [1998] CanLII 6834 (B.C.S.C.), at para. 195.
45 *Cameron*, [1998] CanLII 6834 (B.C.S.C.), at para. 197.
46 Ktunaxa Nation Executive Council, *Qat'muk Declaration*, 1.
47 Ktunaxa Nation Executive Council, *Qat'muk Declaration*.
48 Ktunaxa Nation Executive Council, *Qat'muk Declaration*, 2.
49 Ktunaxa Nation Executive Council, *Qat'muk Declaration*.
50 Ktunaxa Nation v. British Columbia (Forests, Lands, and Natural Resource Operations), [2014] B.C.S.C. 2267, at para. 106.
51 *Ktunaxa Nation*, [2014] B.C.S.C. 2267, at para. 296.
52 *Ktunaxa Nation*, [2015] B.C.C.A. 352, at para. 61 (emphasis in original).
53 *Ktunaxa Nation*, [2017] S.C.C. 54, at para. 63.
54 *Ktunaxa Nation*, [2017] S.C.C. 54, at para. 70.
55 *Ktunaxa Nation*, [2017] S.C.C. 54, at para. 71.
56 *Ktunaxa Nation*, [2017] S.C.C. 54, at para. 118.
57 *Ktunaxa Nation*, [2017] S.C.C. 54, at para. 130.
58 See Waldron, *Free to Believe*; Hurd, "Believing in Religious Freedom"; Yvonne Sherwood, "On the Freedom of the Concept of Religion and Belief," in Sullivan et al., *Politics of Religious Freedom*, 29–44; Webb Keane, "What Is Religious Freedom Supposed to Free?," in Sullivan et al., *Politics of Religious Freedom*, 57–65.
59 Keane, "What Is Religious Freedom Supposed to Free?" 61–2.
60 *Ktunaxa Nation*, [2017] S.C.C. 54, at para. 131.

2 Secularization, Dispossession, and Forced Deprivatization

1 An earlier version of this chapter first appeared in Nicholas Shrubsole, "Secularization, Dispossession, and Forced Deprivatization: The Conditions of Public Religion and the Protection of First Nations' Sacred Space," *Studies in Religion/Sciences Religieuses* 45, no. 3 (2016): 335–59.
2 José Casanova, *Public Religions in the Modern World* (Chicago: University of Chicago Press, 1994).
3 David Martin, *On Secularization: Towards a Revised General Theory* (Aldershot, UK: Ashgate, 2005), 17.
4 Casanova, *Public Religions*.
5 Thomas Luckmann, *The Invisible Religion* (New York: Macmillan, 1967), 101.
6 Casanova, *Public Religions*. Most notably, Peter Berger criticizes the secularization theory on which he based his foundational work *The*

Sacred Canopy. Peter Berger, ed., *The Desecularization of the World: Resurgent Religion and World Politics* (Washington, DC: Ethics and Public Policy Center, 1999).

7 Bryan Wilson and Karel Dobbelaere continue to assert the usefulness of the paradigm. Others such as David Martin, Mark Chaves, and Steve Bruce offer revisions of the theory. In particular, proponents of secularization must address the evident discontinuities between secularization in Europe and the United States. For example, Martin addressed the historical contingencies that lead to different manifestations of secularization in different countries. Chaves deemphasizes the problematic aspects of traditional secularization theory and instead focuses more exclusively on differentiation. Bruce shifts the focus from irreligion to indifference and emphasizes the decline of pervasive world views. Karel Dobbelaere, *Secularization: An Analysis at Three Levels* (New York: Peter Lang, 2002); Bryan Wilson, "Secularization: The Inherited Model," in *The Sacred in a Secular Age: Toward Revision in the Scientific Study of Religion*, ed. Philip E. Hammond (Los Angeles: University of California Press, 1985), 9–20; David Martin, *A General Theory of Secularization* (New York: Harper and Row, 1978); Mark Chaves, "Secularization as Declining Religious Authority," *Social Forces* 72, no. 3 (1994): 749–74; Steve Bruce, *God Is Dead: Secularization in the West* (Oxford: Blackwell, 2002).

8 For example, see Rodney Stark and Roger Finke, *Acts of Faith: Explaining the Human Side of Religion* (Berkeley: University of California Press, 2000).

9 Casanova, *Public Religions*.

10 Casanova, *Public Religions*, 38.

11 Casanova, *Public Religions*, 65–6.

12 Casanova, *Public Religions*, 43.

13 This is what Casanova refers to as the "'discoursive' model of the public sphere." Casanova, *Public Religions*, 166.

14 Casanova, *Public Religions*, 166.

15 Asad, *Formations of the Secular*, 182.

16 José Casanova, "Secularization Revisited: A Reply to Talal Asad," in *Powers of the Secular Modern: Talal Asad and His Interlocutors*, ed. David Scott and Charles Hirschkind (Stanford, CA: Stanford University Press, 2006), 19.

17 Casanova, "Secularization Revisited," 29.

18 Casanova notes that not all religions must internally restructure to conform to the requirements of secularization. Religions that do not have a "high tension with the world" or ecclesiastical organizations

do not undergo this internal process. "But," as Casanova writes, "how religions ... respond to the imposition of the new global worldly regime of Western modernity becomes a very relevant question." "Secularization Revisited," 20.

19 Asad, *Formations of the Secular*, 184.

20 Casanova, "Secularization Revisited," 14.

21 Talal Asad, "Responses," in *Powers of the Secular Modern: Talal Asad and His Interlocutors*, ed. David Scott and Charles Hirschkind (Stanford, CA: Stanford University Press, 2006).

22 José Casanova, "Public Religions Revisited," in *Religion: Beyond a Concept*, ed. Hent de Vries (New York: Fordham University Press, 2008), 102.

23 Casanova, "Public Religions Revisited," 106.

24 Casanova, "Public Religions Revisited," 117.

25 For example, see Martin, *General Theory of Secularization*.

26 David Martin, "Canada in Comparative Perspective," in *Rethinking Church, State and Modernity: Canada between Europe and America*, ed. David Lyon and Margaret Van Die (Toronto: University of Toronto Press, 2000), 24.

27 David Seljak, Joanne Benham Rennick, and Nicholas Shrubsole, "Christianity and Citizenship," in *Religion and Citizenship in Canada: Issues, Challenges, and Opportunities*, ed., Paul Bramadat (report prepared for Citizenship and Immigration Canada by the Centre for Studies in Religion and Society, University of Victoria, 2011).

28 Peter Beyer, "Deprivileging Religion in a Post-Westphalian State: Shadow Establishment, Organization, Spirituality and Freedom in Canada," in *Varieties of Religious Establishment*, edited by Winnifred Fallers Sullivan and Lori G. Beaman (London: Routledge, 2013), 76.

29 Miller, *Compact, Contract, Covenant*.

30 John S. Moir and Paul Laverdure, *Christianity in Canada: Historical Essays* (Gravelbourg, Saskatchewan: Laverdure and Associates, 2002), 17.

31 Seljak, Rennick, and Shrubsole, "Christianity and Citizenship"; Miller, *Compact, Contract, Covenant*.

32 In his address following the release of *Dignitatis Humanae*, a document calling for freedom of religion, Paul VI said, "And what is it that the Church asks of you, after almost two thousand years of all manner of vicissitudes in her relation with you, the powers of earth – what is it that she asks of you today? In one of the major texts of the Council she has told you what it is. She asks of you nothing but freedom – freedom to believe and preach her faith, freedom to love God and to serve Him, freedom to live and to bring to men her message of life." John Courtney

Murray, "The Issue of Church and State at Vatican Council II," in *Religious Liberty*, ed. J. Leon Hooper (Louisville, KY: Westminster John Knox Press, 1993), 212.

33 See Martin, "Canada in Comparative Perspective."

34 Veit Bader argues that rigid secularism as a political doctrine is illiberal because it suppresses religion from the public arena. Bader contends that secularism is an unnecessary doctrine in modern states because the widespread adoption of liberal principles of equality and fundamental rights (including the right to religious freedom) has established differentiation and a foundational guarantee of religious freedom. Bader does not address the general processes of secularization and deprivatization that have been addressed in this chapter, but his arguments regarding differentiation in modern liberal states speaks to the broader argument of this section that Canada is in fact a secularized nation (see Bader, *Secularism or Democracy?*).

35 Beyer, "Deprivileging Religion in a Post-Westphalian State," 85–6.

36 With no establishment clause, the subject of religious privilege is particularly complicated in the Canadian context. See Moon, *Freedom of Conscience and Religion*.

37 R. v. Big M Drug Mart, [1985] 1 S.C.R. 295, at para. 97.

38 See Freitag v. Penetanguishene, [1999] 47 O.R. (3d) 301, O.J. No. 3524; Canadian Civil Liberties Association v. Ontario (Minister of Education), [1990] 65 D.L.R. (4th) 1, 71 O.R. (2d) 341, O.J. No. 104.

39 *Edwards Books*, [1986] 2 S.C.R. 713, at para. 54.

40 *Edwards Books*, [1986] 2 S.C.R. 713, at para. 151.

41 Beaman, "Beyond Establishment," 216–17.

42 *Amselem*, [2004] 2 S.C.R. 551, at para. 88.

43 Charter, s. 25(a).

44 *Calder*, [1973] S.C.R. 313.

45 Miller, *Compact, Contract, Covenant*.

46 Miller, *Compact, Contract, Covenant*.

47 Miller, *Compact, Contract, Covenant*, 82.

48 Miller, *Compact, Contract, Covenant*.

49 Miller, *Compact, Contract, Covenant*, 102.

50 Miller, *Compact, Contract, Covenant*, 106.

51 Miller, *Compact, Contract, Covenant*, 106.

52 Miller, *Compact, Contract, Covenant*, 164.

53 *Treaty no. 3* (1873; repr., Ottawa: Queen's Printer, 1966).

54 Treaty 5 maintained a reserve distribution of 160 acres for each family of five and included stipulations for hunting and fishing. *Treaty no. 5* (1875; repr., Ottawa: Queen's Printer, 1969).

55 Miller, *Compact, Contract, Covenant.*
56 For more information on further land claim negotiations and the
unique case of British Columbia, see Miller, *Compact, Contract, Covenant*;
Christopher McKee, *Treaty Talks in British Columbia*, 2nd ed. (Vancouver:
UBC Press, 2000).
57 Indigenous and Northern Affairs Canada, "Land Base Statistics,"
Indigenous and Northern Affairs Canada, https://www.aadnc-aandc.gc.ca/
eng/1359993855530/1359993914323, modified 24 March 2014.
58 See Alan Cairns, *Citizens Plus: Aboriginal Peoples and the Canadian State*
(Vancouver: UBC Press, 2000).
59 See Slattery, "Generative Structure of Aboriginal Rights."
60 Discussions of Aboriginal title re-emerged in the decades following
Confederation. In 1888, Canada reasserted a definitive claim regarding
its sovereignty in *St Catherine's Milling and Logging Company v. The
Queen.* The Judicial Committee of the Privy Council determined that the
Crown always held an estate in the land and that (European) occupancy
secured title. The state understood Aboriginal title to be extinguished
but Aboriginal rights to use and access to the land continued as they
had since the Royal Proclamation. St Catherine's Milling and Logging
Company v. The Queen, [1887] 13 S.C.R. 577.
61 *Sparrow*, [1990] 1 S.C.R. 1075, 1110.
62 *Sparrow*, [1990] 1 S.C.R. 1075, 1078.
63 *Sparrow*, [1990] 1 S.C.R. 1075, 1079.
64 *Mitchell v. M.N.R.*, [2001] 1 S.C.R. 911, at para. 23.
65 This is what the Ktunaxa Nation were told by Chief Justice McLachlin
in their Supreme Court decision. See *Ktunaxa Nation*, [2017] S.C.C. 54, at
para. 94.
66 *Van der Peet*, [1996] 2 S.C.R. 507, at para. 49.
67 For example, in the case of *Hupacasath First Nation v. British Columbia*,
entered into evidence was the following claim: "The Hupacasath
traditionally visited sacred sites throughout their traditional territory
for spiritual purposes, and continue to do so. The petitioners' evidence
is that their sacred sites are secret, specific to families, and must be
secluded from, and untouched by, other human beings. One particularly
important sacred site is Grassy Mountain, which is in the Removed
Lands and has never been logged" (at para. 12). Although this is not
the central argument of the Hupacasath First Nation, as a part of their
argument the court scrutinizes it along with other aspects of their claim.
Hupacasath First Nation v. British Columbia (Minister of Forests), [2005]
B.C.S.C. 1712.

68 MacMillan Bloedel Ltd v. Mullin, [1985] CanLII 154 (B.C.C.A.).
69 Canadian jurisprudence established the guidelines for an interlocutory injunction long before their application to First Nations land issues. The case cited as precedent is Wheatley v. Ellis and Hendrickson, [1944] 61 B.C.R. 55.
70 *MacMillan Bloedel*, [1985] CanLII 154 (B.C.C.A.), 21, at para. 73. For more on the 1976 Australian case cited by Seaton, see Christoph Antons, "Foster v Mountford: Cultural Confidentiality in a Changing Australia," in *Landmarks in Australian Intellectual Property Law*, ed. Andrew T. Kenyon, Megan Richardson, and Sam Ricketson (Melbourne: Cambridge University Press, 2009), 110–25.
71 *MacMillan Bloedel*, [1985] CanLII 154 (B.C.C.A.), 22.
72 Tlowitsis-Mumtagila v. MacMillan Bloedel Ltd, [1990] CanLII 1662 (B.C.C.A.).
73 *Tlowitsis-Mumtagila*, [1990] CanLII 1662 (B.C.C.A.).
74 Tlowitsis Nation v. MacMillan Bloedel, [1990] CanLII 2335 (B.C.C.A.).
75 Ross, *First Nations Sacred Sites*, 68.
76 Siska Indian Band v. British Columbia (Minister of Forests), [1999] CanLII 2736 (B.C.S.C.), at para. 12.
77 *Siska Indian Band*, [1999] CanLII 2736 (B.C.S.C.), at para. 40.
78 *Siska Indian Band*, [1999] CanLII 2736 (B.C.S.C.), at para. 42.
79 *Cameron*, [1998] CanLII 6834 (B.C.S.C.), at para. 23.
80 *Cameron*, [1998] CanLII 6834 (B.C.S.C.), at para. 35.
81 *Cameron*, [1998] CanLII 6834 (B.C.S.C.), at para. 43.
82 *Cameron*, [1998] CanLII 6834 (B.C.S.C.), at para. 63.
83 *Cameron*, [1998] CanLII 6834 (B.C.S.C.), at para. 66.
84 *Cameron*, [1998] CanLII 6834 (B.C.S.C.), at para. 100.
85 *Cameron*, [1998] CanLII 6834 (B.C.S.C.), at para. 165.
86 *Cameron*, [1998] CanLII 6834 (B.C.S.C.), at para. 206.
87 *Cameron*, [1998] CanLII 6834 (B.C.S.C.), at para. 226.
88 The Saulteau also made claims to a violation of rights stemming from Treaty 8. Although Treaty 8 only specifies hunting, fishing, and trapping rights to the land, Taylor agreed the Crown had "conducted itself in a manner consistent with the existence of the asserted spiritual or religious rights." *Cameron*, [1998] CanLII 6834 (B.C.S.C.), at para. 248.
89 The Kelly Lake Cree Nation were not involved in initial reports regarding the spiritual significance of the site for their community. Taylor was still willing to accept the fact that the Kelly Lake Cree Nation possessed spiritual beliefs intimately connected to the contested area. Taylor writes, "The area of the Twin Sisters is a territorial aspect of the exercise of religious rights and customs even though there is a dearth of evidence of actual physical exercise of the religious customs. The religious rights and customs lie in the prophesy and the intellectual stewardship with which

First Nations people view the area of the Twin Sisters." *Cameron*, [1998] CanLII 6834 (B.C.S.C.), at para. 189.
90 *Cameron*, [1998] CanLII 6834 (B.C.S.C.), at para. 161.
91 *Cameron*, [1998] CanLII 6834 (B.C.S.C.), at para. 195.
92 *Cameron*, [1998] CanLII 6834 (B.C.S.C.), at para. 251.
93 *Ktunaxa Nation*, [2017] S.C.C. 54, at para. 43.
94 *Ktunaxa Nation*, [2017] S.C.C. 54, at para. 86.
95 *Ktunaxa Nation*, [2017] S.C.C. 54, at para. 150.

3 Religions Plus? Competing Frameworks of Indigenous Religious Freedom

1 Hawthorn, *Survey of the Contemporary Indians of Canada*, 6.
2 Cited in Hawthorn, *Survey of the Contemporary Indians of Canada*, 397.
3 Indian Chiefs of Alberta, "Citizens Plus," 192.
4 Indian Chiefs of Alberta, "Citizens Plus," 193.
5 *Ktunaxa Nation*, [2014] B.C.S.C. 2267, at para. 272.
6 The Constitution Act, 1982, s. 35(1).
7 *Van der Peet*, [1996] 2 S.C.R. 507, at para. 74.
8 *Van der Peet*, [1996] 2 S.C.R. 507, at para. 44.
9 *Van der Peet*, [1996] 2 S.C.R. 507, at paras. 49–50.
10 See Haida Nation v. British Columbia (Minister of Forests), [2004] 3 S.C.R. 511.
11 Slattery, "Generative Structure of Aboriginal Rights," 30.
12 Slattery, "Generative Structure of Aboriginal Rights," 32.
13 Slattery, "Generative Structure of Aboriginal Rights," 33.
14 *Sparrow*, [1990] 1 S.C.R. 1075, at 1078.
15 *Sparrow*, [1990] 1 S.C.R. 1075.
16 Borrows, "Living Law on a Living Earth," 166.
17 R. v. Sioui, [1990] 1 S.C.R. 1025, at 1067.
18 *Sioui*, [1990] 1 S.C.R. 1025, at 1071.
19 *Sparrow*, [1990] 1 S.C.R. 1075, at 1077.
20 *Sparrow*, [1990] 1 S.C.R. 1075, at 1113.
21 Waldron, *Free to Believe*, 14.
22 Will Kymlicka, *Liberalism, Community, and Culture* (Oxford: Clarendon Press, 1989).
23 Corbiere v. Canada (Minister of Indian and Northern Affairs), [1999] 2 S.C.R. 203, at para. 13.
24 Moon, *Freedom of Conscience and Religion*, 69.
25 Trinity Western University v. British Columbia College of Teachers, [2001] 1 S.C.R. 772, at para. 36.
26 Berger, *Law's Religion*, 48.

27 Berger, *Law's Religion*, 91.
28 Smith, "Religion, Religions, Religious," 271.
29 Donald S. Lopez, Jr, "Belief," in *Critical Terms for Religious Studies*, ed. Mark C. Taylor (Chicago: University of Chicago Press, 1998), 21.
30 Lopez, "Belief," 21.
31 Lopez, "Belief," 21.
32 Lopez, "Belief," 34 (emphasis added).
33 Hurd, "Believing in Religious Freedom," 49.
34 Keane, "What Is Religious Freedom Supposed to Free?," 61.
35 See *Haida Nation*, [2004] 3 S.C.R. 511, at para. 25.
36 Borrows, "Living Law on a Living Earth," 161.
37 Borrows, "Living Law on a Living Earth," 166.
38 Borrows, "Living Law on a Living Earth," 169.
39 Borrows, "Living Law on a Living Earth," 183–5.
40 *Van der Peet*, [1996] 2 S.C.R. 507, at para. 55.
41 *Van der Peet*, [1996] 2 S.C.R. 507, at para. 56.
42 Borrows, "Living Law on a Living Earth," 179.
43 Borrows, "Living Law on a Living Earth," 181.
44 R. v. Sappier, R. v. Gray, [2006] 2 S.C.R. 686.
45 *Sappier, Gray*, [2006] 2 S.C.R. 686, at para. 38.
46 *Sappier, Gray*, [2006] 2 S.C.R. 686, at para. 49.
47 *Sundown*, [1999] 1 S.C.R. 393, at para. 36. Note that the Joseph Bighead First Nation is now called Big Island Lake First Nation.
48 *Sundown*, [1999] 1 S.C.R. 393.
49 *Amselem*, [2004] 2 S.C.R. 551, para. 53.
50 For more on the subject of group rights and liberalism, see Kymlicka, *Liberalism, Community, and Culture*.
51 Loyola High School v. Quebec (Attorney General), [2015] 1 S.C.R. 611.
52 Slattery, "Generative Structure of Aboriginal Rights," 30.
53 *Ktunaxa Nation*, [2014] B.C.S.C. 2267, at para. 233.
54 *Ktunaxa Nation*, [2014] B.C.S.C. 2267, at para. 55.
55 Ktunaxa Nation Executive Council, *Qat'muk Declaration*.
56 *Ktunaxa Nation*, [2014] B.C.S.C. 2267, schedule "F."
57 *Ktunaxa Nation*, [2017] S.C.C. 54, at para. 114.
58 Taku River Tlingit First Nation v. British Columbia (Project Assessment Director), [2004] 3 S.C.R. 550, at para 2.
59 *Mitchell v. M.N.R.*, [2001] 1 S.C.R. 911, at para. 23.
60 *Ktunaxa Nation*, [2014] B.C.S.C. 2267, at para. 241.
61 *Ktunaxa Nation*, [2014] B.C.S.C. 2267, at para. 244.
62 *Ktunaxa Nation*, [2014] B.C.S.C. 2267, at para. 275.

63 *Ktunaxa Nation*, [2014] B.C.S.C. 2267, at para. 296.
64 *Ktunaxa Nation*, [2015] B.C.C.A. 352, at para. 70.
65 *Ktunaxa Nation*, [2015] B.C.C.A. 352, at para. 73.
66 *Ktunaxa Nation*, [2015] B.C.C.A. 352, at para. 271.
67 *Ktunaxa Nation*, [2015] B.C.C.A. 352, at para. 272.
68 *Ktunaxa Nation*, [2017] S.C.C. 54, at para. 69.
69 *Ktunaxa Nation*, [2017] S.C.C. 54, at para. 100.
70 *Ktunaxa Nation*, [2017] S.C.C. 54, at para. 63.
71 *Ktunaxa Nation*, [2017] S.C.C. 54, at paras. 64–6.
72 *Ktunaxa Nation*, [2017] S.C.C. 54, at para. 80.
73 *Ktunaxa Nation*, [2017] S.C.C. 54, at paras. 64–6.
74 Nicholas Shrubsole, "The Impossibility of Indigenous Religious Freedom," *Policy Options*, 13 November 2017, http://policyoptions.irpp.org/magazines/november-2017/the-impossibility-of-indigenous-religious-freedom.

4 Dealing with Diversity Poorly and the Gustafsen Lake Standoff

1 Portions of this article first appeared in Nicholas Shrubsole, "The Sun Dance and the Gustafsen Lake Standoff: Healing through Resistance and the Danger of Dismissing Religion," *International Indigenous Policy Journal* 2, no. 4 (2011), doi: 10.18584/iipj.2011.2.4.3.
2 Tracy Leavelle, "The Perils of Pluralism: Colonization and Decolonization in American Indian Religious History," in *After Pluralism: Rethinking Religious Engagement*, ed. Courtney Bender and Pamela E. Klassen (New York: Columbia University Press, 2010), 156–77.
3 Homi Bhabha, *The Location of Culture* (New York: Routledge, 1994), 138.
4 Bhabha, *Location of Culture*, 172.
5 Bhabha, *Location of Culture*, 172.
6 Bhabha, *Location of Culture*, 2.
7 Bhabha, *Location of Culture*, 71.
8 Bhabha, *Location of Culture*.
9 Homi Bhabha, "Cultural Choice and the Revision of Freedom," in *Human Rights: Concepts, Contests, Contingencies*, ed. Austin Sarat and Thomas R. Kearns (Ann Arbor: University of Michigan Press, 2001), 46.
10 Bhabha, *Location of Culture*, 83.
11 Bhabha, *Location of Culture*.
12 Alfred, *Peace, Power, Righteousness*, 23.
13 Alfred, *Peace, Power, Righteousness*, 56–7.
14 Bhabha, *Location of Culture*, 74.

15 Bhabha, *Location of Culture*, 219.
16 Bhabha, *Location of Culture*, 227.
17 Bhabha, *Location of Culture*, 2.
18 Bhabha, *Location of Culture*, 231.
19 Cited in Daniel Francis, *The Imaginary Indian: The Image of the Indian in Canadian Culture* (Vancouver: Arsenal Pulp Press, 1992), 2–3.
20 Francis, *Imaginary Indian*, 7.
21 Francis, *Imaginary Indian*, 221.
22 Deloria, *For This Land*, 211–12.
23 Leavelle, "Perils of Pluralism."
24 See Deloria, *For This Land*.
25 Mark Ruml, "Birds Hill Park, the Dakota Eagle Sundance, and the Sweatlodge: Establishing a Sacred Site in a Provincial Park," *Religious Studies and Theology* 28, no. 2 (2009): 196.
26 This project "provides a forum for Aboriginal Elders and teachers to share their traditional teachings, stories, songs, and oral histories, focusing on the spiritual teachings and ceremonies." Mark Ruml, "The Indigenous Knowledge Documentation Project – Morrison Sessions: *Gagige Inaakonige*, the Eternal Natural Laws," *Religious Studies and Theology* 30, no. 2 (2011): 155.
27 Mark Ruml, "Indigenous Knowledge Documentation Project," 157.
28 See Cole and Chaikin, *An Iron Hand upon the People*.
29 For example, see Ross, *First Nations Sacred Sites*.
30 See Bell and Napoleon, *First Nations Cultural Heritage and Law*; Thomas Parkhill, *Weaving Ourselves into the Land: Charles Godfrey Leland, "Indians," and the Study of Native American Religions* (New York: State University of New York Press, 1997).
31 James Legrand, "Urban American Indian Identity in a US City: The Case of Chicago from the 1950s through the 1970s," in *Not Strangers in These Parts: Urban Aboriginals*, ed. David Newhouse and Evelyn Peters (Ottawa: Minister of Supplies and Services, Government of Canada, 2003); Marc V. Fonda, "Canadian Census Figures on Aboriginal Spiritual Preferences: A Revitalization Movement?," *Religious Studies and Theology* 30, no. 2 (2011): 171–87.
32 Ken Coates, "Indigenous Traditions," in *World Religions: Canadian Perspectives – Western Traditions*, ed. Doris Jakobsh (Toronto: Nelson, 2012), 223.
33 Coates, "Indigenous Traditions," 224.
34 Reginald Bibby and James Penner, *Aboriginal Millennials in National Perspective* (Lethbridge, AB: Project Canada Books, 2009).
35 Fonda, "Canadian Census Figures," 174.

36 Fonda, "Canadian Census Figures," 175, 177.

37 Naomi Alderson, "Towards a Recuperation of Souls and Bodies: Community Healing and the Complex Interplay of Faith and History," in *Healing Traditions: The Mental Health of Aboriginal Peoples in Canada*, ed. Laurence J. Kirmayer and Gail Guthrie Valaskakis (Vancouver: UBC Press, 2008), 272–88; Fonda, "Canadian Census Figures"; Adrian Tanner, "The Origins of Northern Aboriginal Social Pathologies and the Quebec Cree Healing Movement," in *Healing Traditions: The Mental Health of Aboriginal Peoples in Canada*, eds., Laurence J. Kirmayer and Gail Guthrie Valaskakis (Vancouver: UBC Press, 2008), 249–69.

38 Alderson, "Towards a Recuperation of Souls and Bodies," 276.

39 Fonda, "Canadian Census Figures," 183.

40 Fonda, "Canadian Census Figures," 183.

41 For more on the complex subject of Christianity and Indigenous Peoples see Tolly Bradford and Chelsea Horton, eds., *Mixed Blessings: Indigenous Encounters with Christianity in Canada* (Vancouver: UBC Press, 2016); James Treat, *Native and Christian: Indigenous Voices on Religious Identity in the United States and Canada* (London: Routledge, 1997).

42 Frédéric B. Laugrand and Jarich G. Oosten, *Inuit Shamanism and Christianity: Transitions and Transformations in the Twentieth Century* (Montreal: McGill-Queen's University Press, 2010).

43 Annette Francis, "Cree Community Bans FNs Spirituality," *APTN National News*, 17 January 2011, http://aptn.ca/news/2011/01/17/crees-ban -sweat-lodges-fns-spirituality-from-community.

44 Dale Stover, "Postcolonial Sun Dancing at Wakpamni Lake," *Journal of the American Academy of Religion* 69, no. 4 (2011): 823.

45 Arlene Hirschfelder and Pauline Molin, *Encyclopedia of Native American Religions* (New York: Facts on File, 2001).

46 Joseph G. Jorgenson, "Religious Solutions and Native American Struggles: Ghost Dance, Sun Dance, and Beyond" in *Religion, Rebellion, Revolution: An Inter-Disciplinary and Cross-Cultural Collection of Essays*, ed. Bruce Lincoln (New York: St Martin's Press, 1985), 112.

47 Jorgenson, "Religious Solutions and Native American Struggles," 114.

48 Hirschfelder and Molin, *Encyclopedia of Native American Religions*.

49 Paul Steinmetz, *Pipe, Bible, and Peyote among the Oglala Lakota: A Study in Religious Identity* (New York: Syracuse University, 1998), 32.

50 Steven Hume, "The Lure of the Sacred Sun Dance: What's Happened at Gustafsen Lake Is Neither Surprising Nor Unique to Anyone Who Has Been Watching the Emergence of a New, Evangelical Native Indian Religion in North America," *Vancouver Sun*, 30 August 1995, A19.

51 John W. Sayer, *Ghost Dancing the Law: The Wounded Knee Trials* (Cambridge, MA: Harvard University Press, 1997).

52 Leonard Peltier, *Prison Writings: My Life Is My Sun Dance* (New York: St Martin's Press, 1999).

53 Many Sun Dancers have not interpreted the ceremony in the same way as the AIM or, later, as those at Gustafsen Lake. For example, participants of the Dakota Eagle Sun Dance in Manitoba incorporate the ideals of the Sun Dance by helping the elderly and responding to community requests. Ruml, "Birds Hill Park." Given the adaptive nature of the ceremony, however, interpretations of the ritual that involve political action or even violence cannot be dismissed as an anomaly or rejected from the tradition altogether.

54 Splitting the Sky (1995 Gustafsen Lake Sun Dance leader), interview with author, 31 March 2011.

55 Splitting the Sky, interview. Splitting the Sky was under the impression that Richard Harris had actually been pierced on film in *A Man Called Horse*. It was several years later when he realized that Richard Harris was suited with a plastic chest piece.

56 Splitting the Sky, *The Autobiography of Splitting the Sky: From Attica to Gustafsen Lake* (Chase, BC: John Pasquale Boncore [Splitting the Sky], 2001).

57 Splitting the Sky, interview.

58 Splitting the Sky, interview.

59 Splitting the Sky, interview.

60 James Pitawanakwat, "James Pitawanakwat's Statement to the Court," in *The Gustafsen Lake Crisis: Statements from the Ts'peten Defenders* (Montreal: Solidarity, 2001).

61 Susan Lambertus, *Wartime Images, Peacetime Wounds: The Media and the Gustafsen Lake Standoff* (Toronto: University of Toronto Press, 2004); Janet Switlo, *Gustafsen Lake under Siege: Exposing the Truth Behind the Gustafsen Lake Stand-Off* (Peachland, BC: TIAC Communications, 1997). For a more comprehensive discussion of the background of the region see Nicholas Shrubsole and P. Whitney Lackenbauer, "The Gustafsen Lake Standoff," in *Blockades or Breakthroughs? Aboriginal Peoples Confront the Canadian State*, edited by Yale D. Belanger and P. Whitney Lackenbauer (Montreal: McGill-Queen's University Press, 2014).

62 Note that the Cariboo Tribal Council changed their name to the Northern Shuswap Tribal Council in 2006. See Northern Shuswap Tribal Council, "NSTC Overview," https://northernshuswaptribalcouncil.com/?page_id=34.

63 Lambertus, *Wartime Images, Peacetime Wounds*, 30.
64 An Oregon District Court, dealing with the extradition of one of the occupiers) described the plaintiffs in Clark's petition as a "Native Sovereignty Association." *United States v. James Allen Scott Pitawanakwat*, 120 F. Supp. 2d 921, No. 00-M-489-ST (14 November 2000).
65 In 2012, following the housing crisis at Attawapiskat, Ontario, and the proposal by the Conservative government to dissolve the Indian Act, elements of the grassroots, leaderless "Idle No More" movement have made similar petitions for third-party adjudication on matters pertaining to justice for Indigenous Peoples in Canada.
66 Lambertus, *Wartime Images, Peacetime Wounds*, 30.
67 Lambertus, *Wartime Images, Peacetime Wounds*, 32.
68 Cited in Splitting the Sky, *Autobiography*, 97.
69 Lambertus, *Wartime Images, Peacetime Wounds*.
70 Cited in Splitting the Sky, *Autobiography*, 104.
71 Splitting the Sky, *Autobiography*.
72 Lambertus, *Wartime Images, Peacetime Wounds*.
73 Stephen Frasher, "Is Gustafsen Lake a Sacred Site? Or More?" *100 Mile House Free Press*, 28 June 1995.
74 Switlo, *Gustafsen Lake under Siege*.
75 Lambertus, *Wartime Images, Peacetime Wounds*.
76 Constable Findley would express his frustrations during the trial for those from Gustafsen Lake but would later recant his concerns in light of the evidence of weapon caches, articulating that he was not sure if they did the right or wrong thing. Kim Pemberton, "Botched Siege Prompts a Native Mountie to Quit," *Vancouver Sun*, 11 July 1997, B4.
77 Lambertus, *Wartime Images, Peacetime Wounds*, 31.
78 Joey Thompson, "Since When Do Natives Have the Only Patent on Visions?" *Vancouver Province*, 30 August 1995, A14; Mike Roberts, "The Cast from Good, Bad, and Ugly." *Vancouver Province*, 31 August 1995, A13; "Sundance Ritual 'New to B.C.," *Vancouver Sun*, 23 August 1995, B3.
79 "Chiefs Condemn Radical Actions of 'Outsiders' at Gustafsen Lake," *100 Mile Free Press*, 23 August 1995, A3; Rudy Platiel, "Significant Differences between Native Standoffs," *Vancouver Sun*, 29 August 1995, A4.
80 Switlo, *Gustafsen Lake under Siege*.
81 "Sun Dancers Denounce Militant Action." *100 Mile Free Press*, 5 July 1995, A3.
82 Lambertus, *Wartime Images, Peacetime Wounds*, 35–6.
83 Lambertus, *Wartime Images, Peacetime Wounds*, 42.
84 Lambertus, *Wartime Images, Peacetime Wounds*.

85 Reporters and, in turn, government officials and the RCMP derived their opinions regarding the effectiveness of Ovide Mercredi from audio recordings of the meeting. Susan Lambertus argues, "Although audiotapes provide accurate quotations, other non-verbal communicative details are missing, such as body language, gestures, facial expression and eye contact. Furthermore, an awareness of the positioning and impression management that underlies such negotiations, as well as a knowledge of Native communication styles, would have provided a broader interpretive base for understanding the situation." Lambertus, *Wartime Images, Peacetime Wounds*, 60.

86 Lambertus, *Wartime Images, Peacetime Wounds*.

87 Lambertus, *Wartime Images, Peacetime Wounds*, 63.

88 Lambertus, *Wartime Images, Peacetime Wounds*.

89 Lambertus, *Wartime Images, Peacetime Wounds*.

90 Lambertus, *Wartime Images, Peacetime Wounds*.

91 "Hopes Falter for Deal with Rebels," *Vancouver Sun*, 11 September 1995, B1.

92 "Native Leaders Tightlipped After Meeting," *Victoria Times Colonist*, 11 September 1995, A1.

93 "Three Natives Shot in Firefight," *Victoria Times Colonist*, 12 September 1995, A1.

94 Lambertus, *Wartime Images, Peacetime Wounds*.

95 Susan Lambertus, in her analysis of the media and the RCMP, notes that on 1 September the RCMP were recorded stating that "smear campaigns are our speciality." In an interview with Lambertus, Sergeant Montague agreed that putting out the occupiers' criminal records could be interpreted as a smear campaign, although the term "smear campaign" does not appear in the official RCMP media plan. Lambertus, *Wartime Images, Peacetime Wounds*, 122.

96 Lambertus, *Wartime Images, Peacetime Wounds*.

97 Lambertus, *Wartime Images, Peacetime Wounds*.

98 Lambertus, *Wartime Images, Peacetime Wounds*.

99 Jeff Lee, "RCMP Told to Send in Medicine Men 3 Weeks Ago, Indian Says," *Vancouver Sun*, 19 September 1995, B2.

100 Lee, "RCMP Told to Send in Medicine Men."

101 Splitting the Sky, interview with author.

102 The Lakota tradition understands the White Buffalo Calf Woman to have brought the Lakota people their most sacred possessions and rites, including the Sun Dance ceremony.

103 Pitawanakwat, "Statement to the Court," 38.

104 See Yale D. Belanger and P. Whitney Lackenbauer, eds., *Blockades or Breakthroughs? Aboriginal Peoples Confront the Canadian State* (Montreal: McGill-Queen's University Press, 2014).

5 The Duty to Consult and Accommodate

1 Young, *Inclusion and Democracy*, 184.
2 One of the most common criticisms of deliberative politics has been the emphasis of "a universal norm of rational dialogue" to resolve disagreements in the deliberative procedure. Jürgen Habermas, *Between Facts and Norms*, trans. William Rehg (Cambridge, MA: MIT Press, 1996), 310. A set of rules and restrictions regarding dialogue may lead to the exclusion of some individuals even within the deliberative process.
3 Amy Gutmann and Dennis Thompson, *Disagreement and Democracy* (Cambridge, MA: Belknap Press of Harvard University Press, 1996), 9.
4 Young, *Inclusion and Democracy*, 32.
5 Young, *Inclusion and Democracy*, 13.
6 Habermas, *Between Facts and Norms*.
7 Dale Turner, *This Is Not a Peace Pipe* (Toronto: University of Toronto Press, 2006), 7.
8 Young, *Inclusion and Democracy*, 23.
9 Young, *Inclusion and Democracy*, 25.
10 Young, *Inclusion and Democracy*, 55.
11 Young, *Inclusion and Democracy*. In light of this criticism of deliberative democracy, Young states that "communicative democracy" may be a better term to address the shortcomings of the vast majority of deliberative democratic theories.
12 Young, *Inclusion and Democracy*, 26.
13 Young, *Inclusion and Democracy*, 72. Young also includes ideals of *greeting* and *rhetoric* in her discussion of combating internal exclusions. For purposes of concision, I only focus on narrative because it emphasizes the realities of plural publics and situation positions that are so important to the deliberative process.
14 Young, *Inclusion and Democracy*, 75.
15 Young, *Inclusion and Democracy*.
16 Habermas, *Between Facts and Norms*, 300.
17 Habermas, *Between Facts and Norms*, 322.
18 Young, *Inclusion and Democracy*, 184.
19 Young, *Inclusion and Democracy*, 32
20 Young, *Inclusion and Democracy*, 190.

21 Young, *Inclusion and Democracy*, 231. Quite simply, relational autonomy refers to the fact that "people live together." Young continues, it is "because they are together, they are all affected by and relate to the geographical and atmospheric environment, and the structural consequences of the fact that they all move in and around this region in distinct and relatively uncoordinated paths and local interactions" (222).

22 Habermas, *Between Facts and Norms*, 384 (emphasis in original).

23 Habermas, *Between Facts and Norms*, 357.

24 Habermas, *Between Facts and Norms*, 372.

25 Habermas, *Between Facts and Norms*, 379.

26 Associative democratic theorists such as Joshua Cohen and Joel Rogers have sought to address the division between civil deliberation and the state through models of associative democracy. These theories attempt to integrate civil society with the state in a less contentious way. The problem, according to Young, is the potential imbalance that can occur in the process of balancing state authority with civic deliberation. In her analysis of leading theorists on associative democracy, Young argues that analyses tend to highlight the tension rather than resolve it. Inevitably, theorists succumb to the domination of one power over the other. Although the two spheres overlap each other in a complex society, their functions are separate and must remain distinct. Joshua Cohen and Joel Rogers, "Secondary Associations and Democratic Governance," *Politics and Society* 20 (1992): 393–472; Young, *Inclusion and Democracy*.

27 Young, *Inclusion and Democracy*, 246.

28 Young, *Inclusion and Democracy*, 255.

29 Young, *Inclusion and Democracy*, 255–6. This statement holds true for Canada with the notable exception of Indigenous philosopher Taiaiake Alfred and certain grassroots organizations such as those found at Gustafsen Lake.

30 Young, *Inclusion and Democracy*, 261.

31 Young, *Inclusion and Democracy*, 263.

32 Young, *Inclusion and Democracy*, 267. Young proposes seven international regulatory bodies but admits that her list is only a few examples of the potential mediators of international politics. Her seven regulatory bodies include "(1) peace and security, (2) environment, (3) trade and finance, (4) direct investment and capital utilization, (5) communications and transportation, (6) human rights, including labour standards and welfare rights, [and] (7) citizenship and migration" (267).

33 Dwight Newman explains, "Recent discussion, however, springs from a trilogy of cases in 2004 and 2005: the Haida Nation case, the

Taku River Tlingit First Nation cases and the Mikisew Cree First
Nation case. These three cases have set Aboriginal rights in Canada,
and Aboriginal/non-Aboriginal relations, on a fundamentally
different course than they were on before. At the same time, they have
generated many questions and a great deal of uncertainty." Newman,
Duty to Consult, 7.

34 The three cases include *Haida Nation v. British Columbia*, [2004] 3 S.C.R.
511, *Taku River Tlingit First Nation v. British Columbia*, [2004] 3 S.C.R. 550,
and *Mikisew Cree First Nation v. Canada (Minister of Canadian Heritage)*,
[2005] 3 S.C.R. 388.

35 Newman, *Duty to Consult*, 16.

36 *Haida Nation*, [2004] 3 S.C.R. 511, at para. 25.

37 Newman, *Duty to Consult*, 19.

38 Habermas, *Between Facts and Norms*, 298.

39 *Haida Nation*, [2004] 3 S.C.R. 511, at para. 32.

40 In particular, Newman points to a public criticism of the lack of veto
power for Indigenous Peoples and how it may lead to government
exploitation. He cites Konrad Yakabuski, "Hydro-Québec a Slow Learner
on Native Rights," *Globe and Mail*, 12 March 2009, B2.

41 Newman, *Duty to Consult*, 64.

42 See John Borrows, *Canada's Indigenous Constitution* (Toronto: University of
Toronto Press, 2010); Turner, *This Is Not a Peace Pipe*.

43 The Taku River Tlingit took issue with the Minister of Environment,
Lands and Parks, the Minister of Energy and Mines, and the Minister
Responsible for Northern Development.

44 Taku River Tlingit First Nation et al. v. Ringstad et al., [2000] B.C.S.C.
1001, at para. 59.

45 *Taku River Tlingit First Nation et al.*, [2000] B.C.S.C. 1001, at para. 85.

46 Taku River Tlingit First Nation v. Ringstad et al., [2002] 2 C.N.L.R. 312
(B.C.C.A.), at 39.

47 *Taku River Tlingit First Nation*, [2002] 2 C.N.L.R. 312 (B.C.C.A.), at 40.

48 Taku River Tlingit First Nation, *Ha tlatgi ha kustiyi: Protecting the Taku
Tlingit Land-based Way of Life* (report submitted to the Ministry of Forests)
(Atlin, BC: Taku River Tlingit First Nation Land and Forests Department,
2000), 2, https://miningwatch.ca/sites/default/files/TRT_SUP_Route
_Options_rpt.pdf.

49 Taku River Tlingit First Nation v. Ringstad et al., [2002] B.C.C.A. 59, at
para. 174.

50 *Taku River Tlingit First Nation*, [2002] B.C.C.A. 59, at para. 194.

51 *Taku River Tlingit First Nation*, [2002] B.C.C.A. 59, at para. 100.

52 *Taku River Tlingit First Nation v. British Columbia*, [2004] 3 S.C.R. 550, at para. 2. The SCC discusses their explanation regarding the balance of societal interests at para. 42 as well.

53 In their report to the Ministry of Environment, the Taku River Tlingit clarified, it "should be obvious why the patterns of Tlingit land use, or Tlingit 'habitat' (campsites, trails, gathering areas, villages, grave sites, spiritual places, and so forth) correspond so closely with prime fish and wildlife habitat areas. The abundance and diversity of these resources are how our people survived and continue to survive today." Taku River Tlingit First Nation, *Tlatgi ha kustiyi*, 2.

54 Maria Morellato, *The Crown's Constitutional Duty to Consult and Accommodate Aboriginal and Treaty Rights* (Vancouver: National Centre for First Nations Governance, 2008); Maria Morellato, *Crown Consultation Policies and Practices across Canada* (Vancouver: National Centre for First Nations Governance, 2009).

55 Morellato, *Crown Consultation Policies and Practices*, 8.

56 Morellato, *Crown Consultation Policies and Practices*.

57 Indigenous and Northern Affairs Canada, *Aboriginal Consultation and Accommodation: Updated Guidelines for Federal Officials to Fulfill the Duty to Consult* (Ottawa: Department of Indigenous and Northern Affairs Canada, March 2011), 12, http://www.aadnc-aandc.gc.ca/DAM/DAM-INTER-HQ/STAGING/texte-text/intgui_1100100014665_eng.pdf.

58 Indigenous and Northern Affairs Canada, *Aboriginal Consultation and Accommodation*, 13.

59 Indigenous and Northern Affairs Canada, *Aboriginal Consultation and Accommodation*, 15.

60 Indigenous and Northern Affairs Canada, *Aboriginal Consultation and Accommodation*, 65.

61 Morellato, *Crown Consultation Policies and Practices*.

62 Inuit refer to this area as *Tasiujatsoak* and Innu call it *Kapukuanipant-kauashat*.

63 "Innu Admit Setting Fire at Labrador Mining Site," *Toronto Star*, 8 February 1995, B9.

64 "Innu Win Restriction on Staking," *Toronto Star*, 1 July 1995, B3.

65 Saleem H. Ali, *Mining, the Environment, and Indigenous Development Conflicts* (Tucson: University of Arizona Press, 2009), 98.

66 "Innu Object to Pace of Nickel Development," *Canadian Free Press*, 14 November 1995.

67 Daniel Ashini, "Between a Rock and a Hard Place: Aboriginal Communities and Mining," in *Conference Results: Between a Rock and a Hard Place; Aboriginal Communities and Mining* (Ottawa: MiningWatch Canada,

10–12 September 1999), 12–18, https://www.miningwatch.ca/sites/
default/files/abo_conf_booklet.pdf; Ian Bailey, "New Protests Possible to
Foil Voisey's Bay Mine," *Canadian Press News Wire*, 23 March 1996.

68 Ali, *Mining, the Environment*, 98.

69 John Hayes, "Historic Four Party Memorandum Signed," *Windspeaker* 14,
no. 11 (1997): 15.

70 *Final Panel Report for the Voisey's Bay Mine and Mill Environmental
Assessment Panel* (submitted to the LIA, Innu Nation, Minister of
Environment and Labour, Minister of the Environment, Minister of
Intergovernmental Affairs, Minister of Fisheries and Oceans, 1999),
https://www.ceaa-acee.gc.ca/default.asp?lang=En&n=0A571A1A
-1&offset=22&toc=show. The 1997 Memorandum of Understanding is
included as Appendix C in the Final Panel Report.

71 *Final Panel Report.*

72 *Final Panel Report.*

73 *Final Panel Report*, 22.

74 *Final Panel Report*, 23.

75 "Voisey's Bay Mine/Mill Project Environmental Impact Statement,"
Voisey's Bay Nickel Company, 1997, http://www.vbnc.com/eis, s. 1.4.3.

76 "Environmental Impact Statement," s. 7.4.

77 "Environmental Impact Statement," s. 16.

78 "Environmental Impact Statement."

79 Gutmann and Thompson, *Disagreement and Democracy*, 19.

80 Asad, *Formations of the Secular*, 184.

81 Asad, *Genealogies of Religion*, 17.

82 Asad, *Genealogies of Religion*, 13.

83 Asad, *Genealogies of Religion*, 12.

84 John Borrows, *Recovering Canada: The Resurgence of Indigenous Law*
(Toronto: University of Toronto Press, 2002).

85 See Turner, *This Is Not a Peace Pipe*.

86 Alfred, *Peace, Power, Righteousness*, 72.

87 See Taiaiake Alfred, *Wasáse: Indigenous Pathways of Action and Freedom*
(Toronto: University of Toronto Press, 2005); Alfred, *Peace, Power,
Righteousness*.

88 Newman, *Duty to Consult*, 39.

89 For more on the Poplar Point Ojibway First Nation case, see Ross, *First
Nations Sacred Sites*, 56–64 ; Catherine Bell et al., "First Nations Cultural
Heritage: A Selected Survey of Issues and Initiatives," in *First Nations
Cultural Heritage and Law: Case Studies, Voices, and Perspectives*, ed.
Catherine Bell and Val Napoleon (Vancouver: UBC Press, 2008), 401–4.

90 Ross, *First Nations Sacred Sites*.

91 Cordova, *How It Is*, 75 (emphasis in original).
92 *Ktunaxa Nation*, [2017] S.C.C. 54, at para. 114.

6 The Potential and Limits of International Mechanisms of Redress

1 It should be noted that beginning in the early 1970s with the approval of the Martínez Cobo Report, Indigenous Peoples were distinguished from minority communities. The reasoning, according to one of the architects of the distinction, was that in some countries, Indigenous Peoples make up the majority but still face discrimination and oppression. Augusto Willemsen Diaz, "How Indigenous Peoples' Rights Reached the UN," in *Making the Declaration Work: The United Nations Declaration on the Rights of Indigenous Peoples*, ed. Claire Charters and Rodolfo Stavenhagen (Copenhagen: International Working Group for Indigenous Rights, 2009), 22.
2 Diaz, "How Indigenous Peoples' Rights Reached the UN," 19.
3 Diaz, "How Indigenous Peoples' Rights Reached the UN," 20.
4 Diaz, "How Indigenous Peoples' Rights Reached the UN," 21.
5 Cited in Diaz, "How Indigenous Peoples' Rights Reached the UN," 23.
6 United Nations General Assembly, *Universal Declaration of Human Rights*, 10 December 1948, 217 A (III), Art. 18.
7 United Nations General Assembly, *International Covenant on Civil and Political Rights*, 16 December 1966, United Nations, Treaty Series, vol. 999, p. 171, Art. 18.
8 Natan Learner, *Religion, Secular Beliefs, and Human Rights*, 2nd rev. ed. (Leiden, NL: Martinus Nijhoff, 2012), 36.
9 Hurd, "Believing in Religious Freedom," 54.
10 José Martínez Cobo, ed., *Study of the Problem of Discrimination against Indigenous Populations* (New York: United Nations Economic and Social Council, 5 August 1983 E/CN.4/Sub.2/1983/21), ch. XIX at para. 26, http://www.un.org/esa/socdev/unpfii/documents/MCS_intro_1983 _en.pdf (hereafter Martínez Cobo Report).
11 Martínez Cobo Report, ch. XIX at para. 27.
12 Martínez Cobo Report, ch. XIX at para. 27, n9.
13 Martínez Cobo Report, ch. XIX at para. 40.
14 Martínez Cobo Report, ch. XIX at para. 51.
15 Diaz, "How Indigenous Peoples' Rights Reached the UN," 26–7.
16 United Nations General Assembly, *Declaration on the Rights of Indigenous Peoples*, resolution adopted by the General Assembly, A/RES/61/295, 2 October 2007, Art. 12 (hereafter UNDRIP).

17 UNDRIP, Art. 25.
18 Asbjørn Eide, "The Indigenous Peoples, the Working Group on Indigenous Populations, and the Adoption of the Declaration on the Rights of Indigenous Peoples," in *Making the Declaration Work: The United Nations Declaration on the Rights of Indigenous Peoples*, ed. Claire Charters and Rodolfo Stavenhagen (Copenhagen: International Working Group for Indigenous Rights, 2009), 42.
19 UNDRIP, Art. 46(1).
20 Eide, "Indigenous Peoples," 42.
21 EMRIP cited the following: Hilary Charlesworth, "Kirby Lecture in International Law: Swimming to Cambodia; Justice and Ritual in Human Rights after Conflict," *Australian Yearbook of International Law* 29 (2010): 12–13. Expert Mechanism on the Rights of Indigenous Peoples, Eighth session (20–4 July 2015), Item 8, 1, https://www.ohchr.org/Documents/Issues/IPeoples/EMRIP/Session8/A.HRC.EMRIP.2015.CRP.3.pdf.
22 Expert Mechanism on the Rights of Indigenous Peoples, *Dialogue on an Optional Protocol to the United Nations Declaration on the Rights of Indigenous Peoples* (New York: UN Headquarters, 27–9 January 2015), 7, https://undocs.org/E/C.19/2015/8.
23 Expert Mechanism on the Rights of Indigenous Peoples, *Dialogue on an optional protocol to the United Nations Declaration on the Rights of Indigenous Peoples*, 3.
24 Eide, "Indigenous Peoples," 42.
25 International Labour Organization, *Indigenous and Tribal Peoples Convention*, C169, 27 June 1989, Art. 5, Art. 7.
26 For further information on the comment on the UDHR by the UN in 1996, see Learner, *Religion, Secular Beliefs, and Human Rights*.
27 United Nations Human Rights Committee, *Sandra Lovelace v. Canada*, Communication No. R.6/24, U.N. Doc. Supp. No. 40 (A/36/40) at 166 (1981), at para. 9.9.
28 UNHRC, *Sandra Lovelace*, at para. 13.3.
29 UNHRC, *Sandra Lovelace*, at para. 17.
30 UNHRC, *Sandra Lovelace*, at para. 9.3.
31 Joanne Barker, "Gender, Sovereignty, and the Discourse of Rights in Native Women's Activism," *Meridians* 7, no. 1 (2006): 140.
32 Rodolfo Stavenhagen, *Report of the Special Rapporteur on the Situation of Human Rights and Fundamental Freedoms of Indigenous People* (Mission to Canada, E/CN.4/2005/88/Add.3, 2 December 2004).
33 Stavenhagen, *Report of the Special Rapporteur*, at para. 42.

34 Government of Canada, "Canada's Statement of Support on the United Nations Declaration on the Rights of Indigenous Peoples," 12 November 2010, http://www.aadnc-aandc.gc.ca/eng/1309374239861/1309374546142.
35 Ktunaxa Nation Executive Council, *Qat'muk Declaration*.
36 James Anaya, *Report of the Special Rapporteur on the Rights of Indigenous Peoples* (A/HRC/27/52/Add.2, 4 July 2014), http://unsr.jamesanaya.org/docs/countries/2014-report-canada-a-hrc-27-52-add-2-en.pdf, at para. 80–1.
37 Anaya, *Report of the Special Rapporteur*, at paras. 84–94.
38 Anaya, *Report of the Special Rapporteur*, at para. 96.
39 Anaya, *Report of the Special Rapporteur*, at para. 98.
40 Anaya, *Report of the Special Rapporteur*, at para. 82.
41 Anaya, *Report of the Special Rapporteur*, at para. 73.
42 Bill C-641, Second Session, Forty-first Parliament, 62–3 Elizabeth II, 2013–14.
43 Assembly of First Nations, "AFN National Chief Says Defeat of Bill on UN Declaration on the Rights of Indigenous Peoples Undermines Government's Commitment to First Nations and Canadian," *AFN*, 6 May 2015, http://www.afn.ca/index.php/en/news-media/latest-news/afn-national-chief-says-defeat-of-bill-on-un-declaration-on-the-rights.
44 Perry Bellegarde, "Joint Statement of the Assembly of First Nations; Grand Council of the Crees (Eeyou Istchee); Amnesty International; Canadian Friends Service Committee (Quakers); Chiefs of Ontario; Congress of Aboriginal Peoples; KAIROS: Canadian Ecumenical Justice Initiatives; First Nations Summit; Indigenous World Association; Native Women's Association of Canada; Samson Cree Nation; Union of British Columbia Indian Chiefs," *Permanent Forum on Indigenous Issues* (United Nations Headquarters, New York, 27 April 2015). Transcript at http://www.afn.ca/index.php/en/news-media/latest-news/permanent-forum-on-Indigenous-issues-assembly-of-first-nation.
45 Bellegarde, "Joint Statement."
46 Carolyn Bennett, "Speech for the Honourable Carolyn Bennett, Minister of Indigenous and Northern Affairs at the United Nations Permanent Forum on Indigenous Issues 16th Session," New York, 26 April 2017, https://www.canada.ca/en/indigenous-northern-affairs/news/2017/05/speaking_notes_forthehonourablecarolynbennettministerofindigenou.html.
47 *American Declaration of the Rights and Duties of Man*, O.A.S. Res. XXX, adopted by the Ninth International Conference of American States (Bogotá, Colombia, 1948), http://www.oas.org/dil/1948%20American%20Declaration%20of%20the%20Rights%20and%20Duties%20of%20Man.pdf, preamble.
48 *American Declaration of the Rights and Duties of Man*, Art. III.

49 Inter-American Court of Human Rights, "IACHR Calls on Member States to Guarantee the Right of Indigenous Peoples to Live in Their Ancestral Lands" (IACHR Press Release, 7 August 2015), http://www.oas.org/en/iachr/media_center/PReleases/2015/086.asp.

50 Recently, the IACHR offered its report on the subject of missing Indigenous women and girls in British Columbia. See Inter-American Court of Human Rights, *Missing and Murdered Indigenous Women in British Columbia, Canada*, doc. 30/14, 21 December 2014, http://www.oas.org/en/iachr/reports/pdfs/Indigenous-women-bc-canada-en.pdf.

51 Inter-American Court of Human Rights, Report No 105/09, Petition 592-07, Admissibility, Hul'qumi'num Treaty Group, Canada, 30 October 2009, https://www.cidh.oas.org/annualrep/2009eng/Canada592.07eng.htm, at para. 1.

52 IACHR, Report No 105/09, at para. 2.

53 IACHR, Report No 105/09, at para. 11.

54 IACHR, Report No 105/09, at para. 11.

55 IACHR, Report No 105/09, at para. 16.

56 IACHR, Report No 105/09, at paras. 12–13.

57 IACHR, Report No 105/09, at para. 2.

58 IACHR, Report No 105/09, at para. 21.

59 IACHR, Report No 105/09, at para. 26.

60 IACHR, Report No 105/09, at para. 3.

61 IACHR, Report No 105/09, at para. 37.

62 IACHR, Report No 105/09, at para. 41.

63 Inter-American Court of Human Rights, *Case 12.734 – Hul'qumi'num Treaty Group, Canada*, Session: 143 Period of Sessions, 28 October 2011 (audio recording), http://www.cidh.org/audiencias/143/36.mp3.

64 IACHR, *Case 12.734*.

65 For example, the Elder identified the destruction of sacred space on Salt Spring Island. For more information, see Salt Spring Island Residence for Responsible Land Use, "Walker Hook Is a Sacred Place," n.d., http://www.savewalkerhook.com/walker_hook/sacred_place.html.

66 IACHR, *Case 12.734*.

67 Berger, *Law's Religion*, 60.

68 Sheryl Lightfoot, *Global Indigenous Politics: A Subtle Revolution* (London: Routledge, 2016).

69 Kristen A. Carpenter and Angela R. Riley, "Indigenous Peoples and the Jurisgenerative Moment in Human Rights," *California Law Review* 102 (2014): 173–234.
70 TRC, "Canada's Residential Schools," 15.

Conclusion

1 TRC, "Canada's Residential Schools," 78.
2 Cited in TRC, "Canada's Residential Schools," 52.
3 TRC, "Canada's Residential Schools."
4 TRC, "Canada's Residential Schools," 118.
5 David Seljak, "Education, Multiculturalism, and Religion," in *Religion and Ethnicity in Canada*, ed. Paul Bramadat and David Seljak (Toronto: University of Toronto Press, 2009), 179.
6 TRC, "Canada's Residential Schools," 122.
7 TRC, "Canada's Residential Schools," 13.
8 TRC, "Canada's Residential Schools," 5.
9 Kathleen E. Absolon (Minogiizhigokwe), *Kaandossiwin: How We Come to Know* (Halifax, NS: Fernwood, 2011), 13.
10 Absolon (Minogiizhigokwe), *Kaandossiwin*, 12.
11 Absolon (Minogiizhigokwe), *Kaandossiwin*.
12 Absolon (Minogiizhigokwe), *Kaandossiwin*, 96, 227.
13 Berger, *Law's Religion*, 17.
14 Berger, *Law's Religion*, 195.
15 Berger, *Law's Religion*, 196.
16 J.R. Miller, *Legal Legacy: Current Native Controversies in Canada* (Toronto: McClelland and Stewart, 2004), vi.
17 TRC, "Canada's Residential Schools," 29–33.
18 TRC, "Canada's Residential Schools," 23, 28.
19 TRC, "Canada's Residential Schools," 20.
20 TRC, "Canada's Residential Schools," 49.
21 *Tsilhqot'in Nation*, [2014] 2 S.C.R. 257, at para. 97; emphasis added. Ken Coates and Dwight Newman suggest that this decision did affirm Indigenous Peoples' right to occupy a seat at the negotiating table. See Kenneth Coates and Dwight Newman, "The End Is Not Nigh: Reason over Alarmism in Analysing the *Tsilhqot'in* Decision," MacDonald-Laurier Institute, September 2014, 22.
22 Canada protested outcomes developed at the WCIP in 2014, asserting that FPIC equated to a "veto power" for Indigenous Peoples that was not supported in Canadian law. See Canada, Permanent Mission of Canada

to the United Nations, "Canada's Statement on the World Conference on Indigenous Peoples Outcome Document" (22 September 2014), http://www.canadainternational.gc.ca/prmny-mponu/canada_un-canada_onu/statements-dec-larations/other-autres/2014-09-22_WCIPD-PADD.aspx?lang=eng.

23 Troy Sebastian, "Misrepresentation and the Truth of Ktunaxa Consent: A Response from Ktunaxa Nation Council," *Quill & Quire* 84, no. 1 (January/February 2018), 13.

24 Sebastian, "Misrepresentation and the Truth," 13.

25 See Borrows, *Canada's Indigenous Constitution*; Borrows, "Living Law on a Living Earth."

26 Borrows, "Living Law on a Living Earth," 185.

27 TRC, "Canada's Residential Schools," 13.

28 TRC, "Canada's Residential Schools," 13.

29 Thomas King, *The Truth about Stories: A Native Narrative* (Toronto: House of Anansi Press, 2003), 52.

30 King, *Truth about Stories*, 52.

31 King, *Truth about Stories*, 52.

32 Cardinal, *Unjust Society*, 1.

Bibliography

Absolon, Kathleen E. (Minogiizhigokwe). *Kaandossiwin: How We Come to Know*. Halifax, NS: Fernwood, 2011.

Adler, Matthew. "Law and Incommensurability: An Introduction." *University of Pennsylvania Law Review* 146, no. 5 (1998): 1169–84.

Alderson, Naomi. "Towards a Recuperation of Souls and Bodies: Community Healing and the Complex Interplay of Faith and History." In *Healing Traditions: The Mental Health of Aboriginal Peoples in Canada*, edited by Laurence J. Kirmayer and Gail Guthrie Valaskakis, 272–88. Vancouver: UBC Press, 2008.

Alfred, Taiaiake. *Peace, Power, Righteousness: An Indigenous Manifesto*. 2nd ed. New York: Oxford University Press, 2009.

– *Wasáse: Indigenous Pathways of Action and Freedom*. Toronto: University of Toronto Press, 2005.

Ali, Saleem H. *Mining, the Environment, and Indigenous Development Conflicts*. Tucson: University of Arizona Press, 2009.

American Declaration of the Rights and Duties of Man, O.A.S. Res. XXX. Adopted by the Ninth International Conference of American States. Bogotá, Colombia, 1948. http://www.oas.org/dil/1948%20American%20Declaration%20of %20the%20Rights%20and%20Duties%20of%20Man.pdf.

Anaya, James. *Report of the Special Rapporteur on the Rights of Indigenous Peoples*. A/HRC/27/52/Add.2, 4 July 2014. http://unsr.jamesanaya.org/docs/countries/2014-report-canada-a-hrc-27-52-add-2-en.pdf.

Antons, Christoph. "Foster v Mountford: Cultural Confidentiality in a Changing Australia." In *Landmarks in Australian Intellectual Property Law*, edited by Andrew T. Kenyon, Megan Richardson, and Sam Ricketson, 110–25. Melbourne: Cambridge University Press, 2009.

Arneil, Barbara. *John Locke and America*. New York: Oxford University Press, 1996.

Asad, Talal. *Formations of the Secular: Christianity, Islam, Modernity*. Stanford, CA: Stanford University Press, 2003.

– *Genealogies of Religion: Discipline and Reasons of Power in Christianity and Islam*. Baltimore, MD: Johns Hopkins University Press, 1993.

– "Responses." In *Powers of the Secular Modern: Talal Asad and His Interlocutors*, edited by David Scott and Charles Hirschkind, 206–41. Stanford, CA: Stanford University Press, 2006.

Asch, Michael. *Home and Native Land: Aboriginal Rights and the Canadian Constitution*. Toronto: Methuen, 1984.

Ashini, Daniel. "Between a Rock and a Hard Place: Aboriginal Communities and Mining." In *Conference Results: Between a Rock and a Hard Place; Aboriginal Communities and Mining*, 12–18. Ottawa: MiningWatch Canada, 10–12 September 1999. https://www.miningwatch.ca/sites/default/files/abo_conf_booklet.pdf.

Bader, Veit. *Secularism or Democracy? Associational Governance of Religious Diversity*. Amsterdam: Amsterdam University Press, 2011.

Bailey, Ian. "New Protests Possible to Foil Voisey's Bay Mine." *Canadian Press News Wire*, 23 March 1996.

Barker, Joanne. "Gender, Sovereignty, and the Discourse of Rights in Native Women's Activism." *Meridians* 7, no. 1 (2006): 127–61.

Beaman, Lori G. "Aboriginal Spirituality and the Legal Construction of Freedom of Religion." *Journal of Church and State* 44 (winter 2002): 135–49.

– "Beyond Establishment." In Sullivan et al., *Politics of Religious Freedom*, 207–19.

Belanger, Yale D., and P. Whitney Lackenbauer, eds. *Blockades or Breakthroughs? Aboriginal Peoples Confront the Canadian State*. Montreal: McGill-Queen's University Press, 2014.

Bell, Catherine, and Val Napoleon, eds. *First Nations Cultural Heritage and Law : Case Studies, Voices, and Perspectives*. Vancouver: UBC Press, 2008.

Bell, Catherine et al. "First Nations Cultural Heritage: A Selected Survey of Issues and Initiatives." In *First Nations Cultural Heritage and Law: Case Studies, Voices, and Perspectives*, edited by Catherine Bell and Val Napoleon, 367–414. Vancouver: UBC Press, 2008.

Bellegarde, Perry. "Joint Statement of the Assembly of First Nations; Grand Council of the Crees (Eeyou Istchee); Amnesty International; Canadian Friends Service Committee (Quakers); Chiefs of Ontario; Congress of Aboriginal Peoples; KAIROS: Canadian Ecumenical Justice Initiatives; First Nations Summit; Indigenous World Association; Native Women's Association of Canada; Samson Cree Nation; Union of

British Columbia Indian Chiefs." *Permanent Forum on Indigenous Issues*, United Nations Headquarters, New York, 27 April 2015. Transcript at http://www.afn.ca/index.php/en/news-media/latest-news/permanent-forum-on-Indigenous-issues-assembly-of-first-nation.

Bender, Courtney. "The Power of Pluralist Thinking." In Sullivan et al., *Politics of Religious Freedom*, 66–77.

Bennett, Carolyn. "Speech for the Honourable Carolyn Bennett, Minister of Indigenous and Northern Affairs at the United Nations Permanent Forum on Indigenous Issues 16th Session." New York, 26 April 2017. https://www.canada.ca/en/indigenous-northern-affairs/news/2017/05/speaking_notes_forthehonourablecarolynbennettministerofindigenou.html.

Berger, Benjamin L. *Law's Religion: Religious Difference and the Claims of Constitutionalism*. Toronto: University of Toronto Press, 2015.

Berger, Peter, ed. *The Desecularization of the World: Resurgent Religion and World Politics*. Washington, DC: Ethics and Public Policy Center, 1999.

Beyer, Peter. "Deprivileging Religion in a Post-Westphalian State: Shadow Establishment, Organization, Spirituality and Freedom in Canada." In *Varieties of Religious Establishment*, edited by Winnifred Fallers Sullivan and Lori G. Beaman, 75–91. London: Routledge, 2013.

Bhabha, Homi. "Cultural Choice and the Revision of Freedom." In *Human Rights: Concepts, Contests, Contingencies*, edited by Austin Sarat and Thomas R. Kearns, 45–62. Ann Arbor: University of Michigan Press, 2001.

– *The Location of Culture*. New York: Routledge, 1994.

Bibby, Reginald, and James Penner. *Aboriginal Millennials in National Perspective*. Lethbridge, AB: Project Canada Books, 2009.

Borrows, John. *Canada's Indigenous Constitution*. Toronto: University of Toronto Press, 2010.

– "Living Law on a Living Earth: Aboriginal Religion, Law, and the Constitution." In *Law and Religious Pluralism in Canada*, edited by Richard Moon, 161–91. Vancouver: UBC Press, 2010.

– *Recovering Canada: The Resurgence of Indigenous Law*. Toronto: University of Toronto Press, 2002.

Borrows, John, and Leonard I. Rotman. "The Sui Generis Nature of Aboriginal Rights: Does It Make a Difference?" *Alberta Law Review* 36, no. 1 (1997): 9–45.

Bradford, Tolly, and Chelsea Horton, eds. *Mixed Blessings: Indigenous Encounters with Christianity in Canada*. Vancouver: UBC Press, 2016.

Bruce, Steve. *God Is Dead: Secularization in the West*. Oxford: Blackwell, 2002.

Buckingham, Janet Epp. *Fighting Over God: A Legal and Political History of Religious Freedom in Canada*. Montreal: McGill-Queen's University Press, 2014.

Cairns, Alan. *Citizens Plus: Aboriginal Peoples and the Canadian State.*
  Vancouver: UBC Press, 2000.
Canada, Government of. "Canada's Statement of Support on the United
  Nations Declaration on the Rights of Indigenous Peoples."
  12 November 2010, http://www.aadnc-aandc.gc.ca/eng/1309374239861/
  1309374546142.
– *Statement of Apology – to Former Students of Indian Residential Schools.*
  11 June 2008. https://www.aadnc-aandc.gc.ca/DAM/DAM-INTER-HQ/
  STAGING/texte-text/rqpi_apo_pdf_1322167347706_eng.pdf.
Canada, Permanent Mission of Canada to the United Nations. "Canada's
  Statement on the World Conference on Indigenous Peoples Outcome
  Document." 24 September 2014. https://www.afn.ca/2014/09/24/canadas
  -statement-on-the-world-conference-on-indigenous-peoples-outcom.
Cardinal, Harold. *The Unjust Society.* 1969. Reprint, Vancouver: Douglas and
  McIntyre, 2009.
Carpenter, Kristen A. "The Interests of 'Peoples' in the Cooperative
  Management of Sacred Sites." *Tulsa Law Review* 42 (2006): 37–57.
– "Old Ground and New Directions at Sacred Sites on the Western
  Landscape." *Denver University Law Review* 83 (2006): 981–1003.
Carpenter, Kristen A., and Angela R. Riley. "Indigenous Peoples and the
  Jurisgenerative Moment in Human Rights." *California Law Review* 102
  (2014): 173–234.
Casanova, José. *Public Religions in the Modern World.* Chicago: University of
  Chicago Press, 1994.
– "Public Religions Revisited." In *Religion: Beyond a Concept,* edited by Hent
  de Vries, 101–19. New York: Fordham University Press, 2008.
– "Secularization Revisited: A Reply to Talal Asad." In *Powers of the Secular
  Modern: Talal Asad and His Interlocutors,* edited by David Scott and
  Charles Hirschkind, 12–30. Stanford, CA: Stanford University Press,
  2006.
Charlesworth, Hilary. "Kirby Lecture in International Law: Swimming to
  Cambodia; Justice and Ritual in Human Rights after Conflict." *Australian
  Yearbook of International Law* 29 (2010): 12–13.
Chaves, Mark. "Secularization as Declining Religious Authority." *Social
  Forces* 72, no. 3 (1994): 749–74.
"Chiefs Condemn Radical Actions of 'Outsiders' at Gustafsen Lake." *100 Mile
  Free Press,* 23 August 1995.
Coates, Ken. "Indigenous Traditions." In *World Religions: Canadian
  Perspectives – Western Traditions,* edited by Doris Jakobsh, 205–37. Toronto:
  Nelson, 2012.

Coates, Kenneth, and Dwight Newman. "The End Is Not Nigh: Reason over Alarmism in Analysing the *Tsilhqot'in* Decision." MacDonald-Laurier Institute, September 2014.

Cohen, Joshua, and Joel Rogers. "Secondary Associations and Democratic Governance." *Politics and Society* 20 (1992): 393–472.

Cole, Douglas, and Ira Chaikin. *An Iron Hand upon the People: The Law against the Potlatch on the Northwest Coast.* Vancouver: Douglas and McIntyre, 1990.

Cordova, V.F. *How It Is: The Native American Philosophy of V.F. Cordova.* Edited by Kathleen Dean Moore, Kurt Peters, Ted Jojola, and Amber Lacy. Tucson: University of Arizona Press, 2007.

Cox, James L. *From Primitive to Indigenous: The Academic Study of Indigenous Religions.* Aldershot, UK: Ashgate, 2007.

Curry, Thomas. *Farewell to Christendom: The Future of Church and State in America.* Oxford: Oxford University Press, 2001.

Deloria, Vine Jr. *For This Land: Writings on Religion in America.* Edited by James Treat. New York: Routledge, 1999.

– *The Metaphysics of Modern Existence.* San Francisco: Harper and Row, 1979.

Diaz, Augusto Willemsen. "How Indigenous Peoples' Rights Reached the UN." In *Making the Declaration Work: The United Nations Declaration on the Rights of Indigenous Peoples*, edited by Claire Charters and Rodolfo Stavenhagen, 16–31. Copenhagen: International Working Group for Indigenous Rights, 2009.

Dobbelaere, Karel. *Secularization: An Analysis at Three Levels.* New York: Peter Lang, 2002.

Eide, Asbjørn. "The Indigenous Peoples, the Working Group on Indigenous Populations, and the Adoption of the Declaration on the Rights of Indigenous Peoples." In *Making the Declaration Work: The United Nations Declaration on the Rights of Indigenous Peoples*, edited by Claire Charters and Rodolfo Stavenhagen, 32–48. Copenhagen: International Working Group for Indigenous Rights, 2009.

Expert Mechanism on the Rights of Indigenous Peoples. *Dialogue on an Optional Protocol to the United Nations Declaration on the Rights of Indigenous Peoples.* New York: UN Headquarters, 27–9 January 2015. https://undocs.org/E/C.19/2015/8.

Expert Mechanism on the Rights of Indigenous Peoples. Eighth session (20–4 July 2015). Item 8. https://www.ohchr.org/Documents/Issues/IPeoples/EMRIP/Session8/A.HRC.EMRIP.2015.CRP.3.pdf.

Final Panel Report for the Voisey's Bay Mine and Mill Environmental Assessment Panel. Submitted to the LIA, Innu Nation, Minister of Environment and Labour, Minister of the Environment, Minister of Intergovernmental

Affairs, Minister of Fisheries and Oceans, 1999. https://www.ceaa-acee
.gc.ca/default.asp?lang=En&n=0A571A1A-1&offset=22&toc=show.

Fleming, Joan, and Robert J. Ledogar. "Resilience and Indigenous
Spirituality: A Literature Review." *Pimatisiwin: A Journal of Aboriginal and
Indigenous Community Health* 6, no. 2 (2008): 47–64.

Fonda, Marc V. "Are They Like Us, Yet? Some Thoughts on Why Religious
Freedom Remains Elusive for Aboriginals in North America." *International
Indigenous Policy Journal* 2, no. 4 (2011). http://ir.lib.uwo.ca/iipj/vol2/iss4/4.

– "Canadian Census Figures on Aboriginal Spiritual Preferences: A
Revitalization Movement?" *Religious Studies and Theology* 30, no. 2 (2011):
171–87.

Francis, Annette. "Cree Community Bans FNs Spirituality." *APTN
National News*, 17 January 2011. http://aptn.ca/news/2011/01/17/
crees-ban-sweat-lodges-fns-spirituality-from-community.

Francis, Daniel. *The Imaginary Indian: The Image of the Indian in Canadian
Culture*. Vancouver: Arsenal Pulp Press, 1992.

Frasher, Stephen. "Is Gustafsen Lake a Sacred Site? Or More?" *100 Mile
House Free Press*, 28 June 1995.

Gutmann, Amy, and Dennis Thompson. *Disagreement and Democracy*.
Cambridge, MA: Belknap Press of Harvard University Press, 1996.

Habermas, Jürgen. *Between Facts and Norms*. Translated by William Rehg.
Cambridge, MA: MIT Press, 1996.

Hawthorn, H.B., ed. *A Survey of the Contemporary Indians of Canada: A Report on
Political, Economic, Educational Needs*. Ottawa: Indian Affairs Branch, 1966–7.

Hayes, John. "Historic Four Party Memorandum Signed." *Windspeaker* 14,
no. 11 (1997): 15.

Healy, Paul. "Overcoming Incommensurability through Intercultural
Dialogue." *Cosmos and History: The Journal of Natural and Social Philosophy*
9, no. 1 (2013): 264–81.

Hirschfelder, Arlene, and Pauline Molin. *Encyclopedia of Native American
Religions*. New York: Facts on File, 2001.

"Hopes Falter for Deal with Rebels." *Vancouver Sun*, 11 September 1995.

Hume, Steven. "The Lure of the Sacred Sun Dance: What's Happened at
Gustafsen Lake Is Neither Surprising Nor Unique to Anyone Who Has
Been Watching the Emergence of a New, Evangelical Native Indian
Religion in North America." *Vancouver Sun*, 30 August 1995.

Hurd, Elizabeth Shakman. "Believing in Religious Freedom." In Sullivan
et al., *Politics of Religious Freedom*, 45–56.

Indian Chiefs of Alberta. "Citizens Plus." *Aboriginal Policy Studies* 1, no. 2
([1969] 2011): 188–281.

Indigenous and Northern Affairs Canada. *Aboriginal Consultation and Accommodation: Updated Guidelines for Federal Officials to Fulfill the Duty to Consult.* Ottawa: Department of Indigenous and Northern Affairs Canada, March 2011. http://www.aadnc-aandc.gc.ca/DAM/DAM -INTER-HQ/STAGING/texte-text/intgui_1100100014665_eng.pdf.
– "Land Base Statistics." *Indigenous and Northern Affairs Canada.* https:// www.aadnc-aandc.gc.ca/eng/1359993855530/1359993914323, modified 24 March 2014.
"Innu Admit Setting Fire at Labrador Mining Site." *Toronto Star,* 8 February 1995.
"Innu Object to Pace of Nickel Development." *Canadian Free Press,* 14 November 1995.
"Innu Win Restriction on Staking." *Toronto Star,* 1 July 1995.
Inter-American Court of Human Rights. *Case 12.734 – Hul'qumi'num Treaty Group, Canada.* Session: 143 Period of Sessions, 28 October 2011 (audio recording). http://www.cidh.org/audiencias/143/36.mp3.
– "IACHR Calls on Member States to Guarantee the Right of Indigenous Peoples to Live in Their Ancestral Lands." IACHR Press Release, 7 August 2015. http://www.oas.org/en/iachr/media_center/PReleases/2015/ 086.asp.
– *Missing and Murdered Indigenous Women in British Columbia, Canada.* Doc. 30/14, 21 December 2014. http://www.oas.org/en/iachr/reports/ pdfs/Indigenous-women-bc-canada-en.pdf.
– Report No 105/09, Petition 592-07, Admissibility, Hul'qumi'num Treaty Group, Canada. 30 October 2009. https://www.cidh.oas.org/annualrep/ 2009eng/Canada592.07eng.htm.
International Labour Organization. *Indigenous and Tribal Peoples Convention.* C169, 27 June 1989.
Johnson, Greg. "Reflections on the Politics of Religious Freedom, with Attention to Hawaii." In Sullivan et al., *Politics of Religious Freedom,* 78–88.
– "Varieties of Native Hawaiian Establishment: Recognized Voices, Routinized Charisma and Church Desecration." In *Varieties of Religious Establishment,* edited by Winnifred Fallers Sullivan and Lori G. Beaman, 55–71. London: Routledge, 2013.
Johnson, Greg, and Siv Ellen Kraft, eds. *Handbook of Indigenous Religion(s).* Leiden, NL: Brill, 2017.
Johnson, Greg, and Siv Ellen Kraft. "Introduction." In Johnson and Kraft, *Handbook of Indigenous Religion(s),* 1–24.
Jorgenson, Joseph G. "Religious Solutions and Native American Struggles: Ghost Dance, Sun Dance, and Beyond." In *Religion, Rebellion, Revolution:*

An Inter-Disciplinary and Cross-Cultural Collection of Essays, edited by
  Bruce Lincoln, 97–128. New York: St Martin's Press, 1985.
Kahn, Paul W. *The Cultural Study of Law: Reconstructing Legal Scholarship.*
  Chicago: University of Chicago Press, 1999.
Keane, Webb. "What Is Religious Freedom Supposed to Free?" In Sullivan
  et al., *Politics of Religious Freedom*, 57–65.
King, Thomas. *The Truth about Stories: A Native Narrative.* Toronto: House of
  Anansi Press, 2003.
Kraft, Siv Ellen. "U.N.-Discourses on Indigenous Religion." In Johnson and
  Kraft, *Handbook of Indigenous Religion(s)*, 80–91.
Ktunaxa Nation Executive Council. *Qat'muk Declaration.* 15 November 2010.
  http://www.ktunaxa.org/who-we-are/qatmuk-declaration.
Kymlicka, Will. *Liberalism, Community, and Culture.* Oxford: Clarendon Press,
  1989.
Lambertus, Susan. *Wartime Images, Peacetime Wounds: The Media and the
  Gustafsen Lake Standoff.* Toronto: University of Toronto Press, 2004.
Laugrand, Frédéric B., and Jarich G. Oosten. *Inuit Shamanism and Christianity:
  Transitions and Transformations in the Twentieth Century.* Montreal: McGill-
  Queen's University Press, 2010.
Learner, Natan. *Religion, Secular Beliefs, and Human Rights.* 2nd rev. ed.
  Leiden, NL: Martinus Nijhoff, 2012.
Leavelle, Tracy. "The Perils of Pluralism: Colonization and Decolonization
  in American Indian Religious History." In *After Pluralism: Rethinking
  Religious Engagement*, edited by Courtney Bender and Pamela E. Klassen,
  156–77. New York: Columbia University Press, 2010.
Lee, Jeff. "RCMP Told to Send in Medicine Men 3 Weeks Ago, Indian Says."
  Vancouver Sun, 19 September 1995.
Legrand, James. "Urban American Indian Identity in a US City: The Case of
  Chicago from the 1950s through the 1970s." In *Not Strangers in These Parts:
  Urban Aboriginals*, edited by David Newhouse and Evelyn Peters, 267–80.
  Ottawa: Minister of Supplies and Services, Government of Canada, 2003.
Lightfoot, Sheryl. *Global Indigenous Politics: A Subtle Revolution.* London:
  Routledge, 2016.
Locke, John. *Two Treaties on Civil Government.* 1689. Reprint, London: Routledge,
  1987.
Lopez, Donald S. Jr. "Belief." In *Critical Terms for Religious Studies*, edited by
  Mark C. Taylor, 21–35. Chicago: University of Chicago Press, 1998.
Luckmann, Thomas. *The Invisible Religion.* New York: Macmillan, 1967.
MacPherson, Dennis H., and J. Douglas Rabb. *Indian from the Inside: Native
  American Philosophy and Cultural Renewal.* 2nd ed. London: McFarland and
  Company, 2011.

– "Transformative Philosophy and Indigenous Thought: A Comparison of Lakota and Ojibwa World Views." In *Proceedings of the 29th Algonquian Conference*, 202–10. Winnipeg: University of Manitoba Press, 1999.

Martin, David. "Canada in Comparative Perspective." In *Rethinking Church, State and Modernity: Canada between Europe and America*, edited by David Lyon and Margaret Van Die, 23–33. Toronto: University of Toronto Press, 2000.

– *A General Theory of Secularization*. New York: Harper and Row, 1978.

– *On Secularization: Towards a Revised General Theory*. Aldershot, UK: Ashgate, 2005.

Martínez Cobo, José, ed. *Study of the Problem of Discrimination against Indigenous Populations*. New York: United Nations Economic and Social Council, E/CN.4/Sub.2/1983/21, 5 August 1983.

Mazur, Eric M. *The Americanization of Religious Minorities: Confronting the Constitutional Order*. Baltimore, MD: Johns Hopkins University Press, 1999.

McKee, Christopher. *Treaty Talks in British Columbia*. 2nd ed. Vancouver: UBC Press, 2000.

McNally, Michael D. "Religion as Peoplehood: Native American Religious Traditions and the Discourse of Indigenous Rights." In Johnson and Kraft, *Handbook of Indigenous Religion(s)*, 52–79.

Michaelsen, Robert S. "Is the Miner's Canary Silent? Implications of the Supreme Court's Denial of American Indian Free Exercise of Religion Claims." *Journal of Law and Religion* 6, no. 1 (1988): 97–114.

Miller, J.R. *Compact, Contract, Covenant: Aboriginal Treaty-Making in Canada*. Toronto: University of Toronto Press, 2009.

– *Legal Legacy: Current Native Controversies in Canada*. Toronto: McClelland and Stewart, 2004.

– *Shingwauk's Vision: A History of Canadian Native Residential Schools*. Toronto: University of Toronto Press, 1996.

Miller, Robert J., Jacinta Ruru, Larissa Behrendt, and Tracey Lindberg. *Discovering Indigenous Lands: The Doctrine of Discovery in the English Colonies*. New York: Oxford University Press, 2010.

Moir, John S., and Paul Laverdure. *Christianity in Canada: Historical Essays*. Gravelbourg, Saskatchewan: Laverdure and Associates, 2002.

Moon, Richard. *Freedom of Conscience and Religion*. Toronto: Irwin Law, 2014.

Morellato, Maria. *Crown Consultation Policies and Practices across Canada*. Vancouver: National Centre for First Nations Governance, 2009.

– *The Crown's Constitutional Duty to Consult and Accommodate Aboriginal and Treaty Rights*. Vancouver: National Centre for First Nations Governance, 2008.

Murray, John Courtney. "The Issue of Church and State at Vatican Council II." In *Religious Liberty*, edited by J. Leon Hooper, 199–228. Louisville, KY: Westminster John Knox Press, 1993.

"Native Leaders Tightlipped after Meeting." *Victoria Times Colonist*, 11 September 1995.

Newcomb, Steven. *Pagans in the Promised Land: Decoding the Doctrine of Christian Discovery*. Golden, CO: Fulcrum, 2008.

Newman, Dwight C. *Community and Collective Rights: A Theoretical Framework for Rights Held by Groups*. Oxford: Hart, 2011.

– *The Duty to Consult: New Relationships with Aboriginal Peoples*. Saskatoon, Saskatchewan: Purich, 2009.

Ogilvie, M.H. *Religious Institutions and the Law in Canada*. 3rd ed. Toronto: Irwin Law, 2010.

Parkhill, Thomas. *Weaving Ourselves into the Land: Charles Godfrey Leland, "Indians," and the Study of Native American Religions*. New York: State University of New York Press, 1997.

Peltier, Leonard. *Prison Writings: My Life Is My Sun Dance*. New York: St Martin's Press, 1999.

Pemberton, Kim. "Botched Siege Prompts a Native Mountie to Quit." *Vancouver Sun*, 11 July 1997.

Pettipas, Katherine. *Severing the Ties That Bind: Government Repression of Indigenous Religious Ceremonies on the Prairies*. Winnipeg: University of Manitoba Press, 1994.

Pipes, Richard. *Property and Freedom*. New York: Knopf, 1999.

Pitawanakwat, James. "James Pitawanakwat's Statement to the Court." In *The Gustafsen Lake Crisis: Statements from the Ts'peten Defenders*. Montreal: Solidarity, 2001.

Platiel, Rudy. "Significant Differences between Native Standoffs." *Vancouver Sun*, 29 August 1995.

Roberts, Mike. "The Cast from Good, Bad, and Ugly." *Vancouver Province*, 31 August 1995.

Rosen, Lawrence. *Law as Culture: An Invitation*. Princeton, NJ: Princeton University Press, 2006.

Ross, Michael Lee. *First Nations Sacred Sites in Canada's Courts*. Vancouver: UBC Press, 2005.

Royal Commission on Aboriginal Peoples. *Highlights of the Report of the Royal Commission on Aboriginal Peoples*. Ottawa: Minister of Supply and Services Canada, 1996.

Ruml, Mark. "Birds Hill Park, the Dakota Eagle Sundance, and the Sweatlodge: Establishing a Sacred Site in a Provincial Park." *Religious Studies and Theology* 28, no. 2 (2009): 189–206.

– "The Indigenous Knowledge Documentation Project – Morrison Sessions: *Gagige Inaakonige*, the Eternal Natural Laws." *Religious Studies and Theology* 30, no. 2 (2011): 155–69.

Salt Spring Island Residence for Responsible Land Use. "Walker Hook Is a
    Sacred Place." n.d. http://www.savewalkerhook.com/walker_hook/
    sacred_place.html.
Sayer, John W. *Ghost Dancing the Law: The Wounded Knee Trials*. Cambridge,
    MA: Harvard University Press, 1997.
Sebastian, Troy. "Misrepresentation and the Truth of Ktunaxa Consent:
    A Response from Ktunaxa Nation Council." *Quill & Quire* 84, no. 1
    (January/February 2018): 12–13.
Seljak, David. "Education, Multiculturalism, and Religion." In *Religion and
    Ethnicity in Canada*, edited by Paul Bramadat and David Seljak, 178–200.
    Toronto: University of Toronto Press, 2009.
Seljak, David, Joanne Benham Rennick, and Nicholas Shrubsole.
    "Christianity and Citizenship." In *Religion and Citizenship in Canada:
    Issues, Challenges, and Opportunities*, edited by Paul Bramadat, 14–54.
    Report prepared for Citizenship and Immigration Canada by the Centre
    for Studies in Religion and Society, University of Victoria, 2011.
Sherwood, Yvonne. "On the Freedom of the Concept of Religion and Belief."
    In Sullivan et al., *Politics of Religious Freedom*, 29–44.
Shrubsole, Nicholas. "The Impossibility of Indigenous Religious Freedom."
    Policy Options, 13 November 2017. http://policyoptions.irpp.org/
    magazines/november-2017/the-impossibility-of-indigenous-religious
    -freedom.
Shrubsole, Nicholas, and P. Whitney Lackenbauer. "The Gustafsen Lake
    Standoff." In *Blockades or Breakthroughs? Aboriginal Peoples Confront the
    Canadian State*, edited by Yale D. Belanger and P. Whitney Lackenbauer,
    314–55. Montreal: McGill-Queen's University Press, 2014.
Slattery, Brian. "The Generative Structure of Aboriginal Rights." In *Moving
    toward Justice: Legal Traditions and Aboriginal Justice*, edited by John D. Whyte,
    20–48. Saskatoon, Saskatchewan: Purich, 2008.
Smith, J.Z. "Religion, Religions, Religious." In *Critical Terms for Religious
    Studies*, edited by Mark C. Taylor, 269–84. Chicago: University of Chicago
    Press, 1998.
Splitting the Sky. *The Autobiography of Splitting the Sky: From Attica to
    Gustafsen Lake*. Chase, BC: John Pasquale Boncore (Splitting the Sky), 2001.
Stark, Rodney, and Roger Finke. *Acts of Faith: Explaining the Human Side of
    Religion*. Berkeley: University of California Press, 2000.
Stavenhagen, Rodolfo. *Report of the Special Rapporteur on the Situation of
    Human Rights and Fundamental Freedoms of Indigenous People*. Mission to
    Canada, E/CN.4/2005/88/Add.3, 2 December 2004.
Steinmetz, Paul. *Pipe, Bible, and Peyote among the Oglala Lakota: A Study in
    Religious Identity*. New York: Syracuse University, 1998.

Stover, Dale. "Postcolonial Sun Dancing at Wakpamni Lake." *Journal of the American Academy of Religion* 69, no. 4 (2011): 817–36.

Sullivan, Winnifred Fallers. *The Impossibility of Religious Freedom.* Princeton, NJ: Princeton University Press, 2005.

– "Religion, Land, Rights." In *Varieties of Religious Establishment*, edited by Winnifred Fallers Sullivan and Lori G. Beaman, 93–106. London: Routledge, 2013.

Sullivan, Winnifred Fallers, and Lori G. Beaman. "Neighbo(u)rly Misreadings and Misconstruals: A Cross-border Conversation." In *Varieties of Religious Establishment*, edited by Winnifred Fallers Sullivan and Lori G. Beaman, 1–11. London: Routledge, 2013.

Sullivan, Winnifred Fallers, and Lori G. Beaman, eds. *Varieties of Religious Establishment.* London: Routledge, 2013.

Sullivan, Winnifred Fallers, Elizabeth Shakman Hurd, Saba Mahmood, and Peter G. Danchin, eds. *Politics of Religious Freedom.* Chicago: University of Chicago Press, 2015.

"Sun Dancers Denounce Militant Action." *100 Mile Free Press*, 5 July 1995.

"Sundance Ritual 'New to B.C.'" *Vancouver Sun*, 23 August 1995.

Switlo, Janet. *Gustafsen Lake under Siege: Exposing the Truth behind the Gustafsen Lake Stand-Off.* Peachland, BC: TIAC Communications, 1997.

Tafjord, Bjørn Ola. "Towards a Typology of Academic Uses of 'Indigenous Religion(s),' or, Eight (or Nine) Language Games That Scholars Play with This Phrase." In Johnson and Kraft, *Handbook of Indigenous Religion(s)*, 25–51.

Taku River Tlingit First Nation. *Ha tlatgi ha kustiyi: Protecting the Taku Tlingit Land-Based Way of Life.* Report submitted to the Ministry of Forests. Atlin, BC: Taku River Tlingit First Nation Land and Forests Department, 2000. https://miningwatch.ca/sites/default/files/TRT_SUP_Route_Options _rpt.pdf.

Tanner, Adrian. "The Origins of Northern Aboriginal Social Pathologies and the Quebec Cree Healing Movement." In *Healing Traditions: The Mental Health of Aboriginal Peoples in Canada*, edited by Laurence J. Kirmayer and Gail Guthrie Valaskakis, 249–69. Vancouver: UBC Press, 2008.

Thomas, Constantine. *The Peyote Road: Religious Freedom and the Native American Church.* Norman: University of Oklahoma Press, 2010.

Thompson, Joey. "Since When Do Natives Have the Only Patent on Visions?" *Vancouver Province*, 30 August 1995.

"Three Natives Shot in Firefight." *Victoria Times Colonist*, 12 September 1995.

Treat, James. *Native and Christian: Indigenous Voices on Religious Identity in the United States and Canada.* London: Routledge, 1997.

Trevithick, Scott. "Native Residential Schools in Canada: A Review of Literature." *Canadian Journal of Native Studies* 18, no. 1 (1998): 49–86.

Truth and Reconciliation Commission of Canada. "Canada's Residential Schools: Reconciliation." In *The Final Report of the Truth and Reconciliation Commission of Canada*, vol. 6. Montreal: McGill-Queen's University Press, 2015.

Tully, James. *A Discourse on Property: John Locke and His Adversaries*. New York: Cambridge University Press, 1980.

– "The Struggles of Indigenous Peoples for and of Freedom." In *Political Theory and the Rights of Indigenous Peoples*, edited by Duncan Ivision, Paul Patton, and Will Sanders, 36–59. Cambridge: Cambridge University Press, 2000.

Turner, Dale. *This Is Not a Peace Pipe*. Toronto: University of Toronto Press, 2006.

– "What Is American Indian Philosophy? Toward a Critical Indigenous Philosophy." In *Philosophy in Multiple Voices*, edited by George Yancy, 197–218. Lanham, MD: Rowman and Littlefield, 2007.

United Nations. *State of the World's Indigenous Peoples*. Department of Economic and Social Affairs, Division for Social Policy and Development, Secretariat of the Permanent Forum on Indigenous Issues. ST/ESA/328, 2009. http://www.un.org/esa/socdev/unpfii/documents/SOWIP/en/SOWIP_web.pdf.

United Nations General Assembly. *Declaration on the Rights of Indigenous Peoples*. Resolution adopted by the General Assembly, A/RES/61/295, 2 October 2007.

– *International Covenant on Civil and Political Rights*. 16 December 1966. United Nations, Treaty Series, vol. 999, p. 171.

– *Universal Declaration of Human Rights*. 10 December 1948, 217 A (III).

"Voisey's Bay Mine/Mill Project Environmental Impact Statement." Voisey's Bay Nickel Company, 1997. http://www.vbnc.com/eis.

Waldram, James. *The Way of the Pipe: Aboriginal Spirituality and Symbolic Healing in Canadian Prisons*. Toronto: University of Toronto Press, 1997.

Waldron, Mary Ann. *Free to Believe: Rethinking Freedom of Conscience and Religion in Canada*. Toronto: University of Toronto Press, 2013.

Walsh, David S. "Spiritual, Not Religious; Dene, Not Indigenous: Tłįchǫ Dene Discourses of Religion and Indigeneity." In Johnson and Kraft, *Handbook of Indigenous Religion(s)*, 204–20.

Wenger, Tisa. *We Have a Religion: The 1920s Pueblo Indian Dance Controversy and American Religious Freedom*. Chapel Hill: University of North Carolina Press, 2009.

White-Harvey, Robert. "Reservation Geography and the Restoration of Native Self-Government." *Dalhousie Law Journal* 17, no. 2 (1994): 587–611.

Wilson, Bryan. "Secularization: The Inherited Model." In *The Sacred in a Secular Age: Toward Revision in the Scientific Study of Religion*, edited by Philip E. Hammond, 9–20. Los Angeles: University of California Press, 1985.

Woodhead, Linda. "Real Religion and Fuzzy Spirituality? Taking Sides in the Sociology of Religion." In *Religions of Modernity: Relocating the Sacred to the Self and the Digital*, edited by Stef Aupers and Dick Houtman, 31–48. Leiden, NL: Brill, 2010.

Yakabuski, Konrad. "Hydro-Québec a Slow Learner on Native Rights." *Globe and Mail*, 12 March 2009.

Young, Iris Marion. *Inclusion and Democracy*. New York: Oxford University Press, 2000.

Zinnbauer, Brian J., Kenneth I. Pargament, Brenda Cole, Mark S. Rye, Eric M. Butter, Timothy G. Belavich, Kathleen M. Hipp, Allie B. Scott, and Jill L. Kadar. "Religion and Spirituality: Unfuzzying the Fuzzy." *Journal for the Scientific Study of Religion* 36, no. 4 (1997): 549–64.

Index

Printed and bound by CPI Group (UK) Ltd, Croydon, CR0 4YY

13/04/2025

14656518-0001